THE INNS OF STONY STRATFORD

A FULL HISTORY

BRYAN DUNLEAVY
KEN DANIELS
ANDREW POWELL

THE INNS OF STONY STRATORD

Published by Magic Flute Publications 2014

ISBN 978-1-909054-08-0

Magic Flute Publications is an imprint of
Magic Flute Artworks Limited
231 Swanwick Lane
Southampton SO31 7GT
www.magicfluteartworks.com

A catalogue description of this book is available from the British Library

Contents

Preface

We embarked on this project almost two years ago when Ken wondered if it would be possible to plan a "virtual pub crawl" based on the historic inns of Stony Stratford. Bryan thought that would be possible, with a little resarch. That "little research" became a larger proposition on deeper digging; hence the expansion of time.

We started with Sir Frank Markham's useful compilation published almost 70 years ago and have been able to develop his work using sources which may not have been known to him at the time. We have approached residents of houses which were once inns, and they have been unfailingly kind and helpful to the project. They have also contributed information and their own insights. Andy joined the project in 2014 to contribute his photographic expertise.

There are still gaps in our knowledge. Some inns are merely names in a deed at a particular date; nothing was known of them prior to that, and nothing since. Others have had a lengthy history but have changed their names. Some inn names have been duplicated at different times for different establishments, and sometimes this has been a source of confusion. We have tried to sort out, or at least explain, contradictions. We have also tried to be comprehensive by including every known use of an inn name. For completeness, we have also included pubs in Calverton, Old Stratford, Wolverton and the Bradwells.

The book falls into three parts: Part One is a narrative history of Stony Stratford's origins and the development of the inn trade; Part Two is an alphabetical compendium of all known establishments, with brief details of each; Part Three contains some appendices which discuss and explain some of the issues raised in the narrative.

We have been fortunate in being able to tap into the enthusiasm and good will of many people who have been able to contribute their knowledge, anwer questions, make suggestions and offer advice.

Bryan Dunleavy, Ken Daniels, Andy Powell - January 2015

Acknowledgements

A project such as this does not come to fruition without the shared knowledge and help of a lot of people, many of whom have contributed their wisdom in passing. First then, a general thank you to everyone.

May we in particular thank Mason and Gladys Edwards, Tony and Nazira Ismail-Kaye, Darren Marshall and Alan and Gwen Yates for inviting us into their homes, which were formerly inns, and contributing much useful information. We also thank Giovanni Nicastro for an extensive tour of his premises, formerly the Bell Inn. Thank you too to the landlords of the Bull, (Dave Ludden), the Duke of Wellington (Geoff and Maureen Moloney), the White Horse (Tim Standring) and the Kardamon Lounge (Akbar Ali) for permission to explore their premises.

David Odell has been especially helpful in identifying the site of the former Britannia Brewery and the access door from Odell's Yard.

Helen Aylott has brought a good deal of information about the former Talbot to light.

David Leslie, a former resident of the Case is Altered, contributed some useful information about the building.

Dennis Mynard, the former Milton Keynes archaeologist, put a lot of energy into identifying the source of an 18th century drawing, purportedly of Stony Stratford.

Mike Brown, a veteran researcher into pub history, and the author of ABC: A Brewer's Compendium has generously shared his notes on Stony Stratford and led us to new discoveries.

We would also like to acknowledge the work of Colin Barby in rescuscitating many old photographs of Stony Stratford from a century ago.

It has also been very useful to check from time to time against the knowledge of people like Robert Ayers, Ian Spires, Chris Gleadall, Peter Levitt and Chris Barrett.

And finally, a thank you to Daphne Harvey, who kindly read the final manuscript, proofed it, and suggested amendments.

Part One:
A history

Chapter One
Inns, Taverns and Alehouses

The inn must be almost as old as travel itself, and places for rest, food and refreshment, are at the core of all societies where movement is necessary. Travel is a difficult and expensive enterprise and only in recent times has it become a swift and comfortable experience. Prior to the 19th century journeys were not an undertaking for the faint of heart or even for the physically weak. Miles had to be walked or ridden on horseback and at the end of an arduous day with few miles actually covered the traveller needed a place for rest and sustenance. Inns no doubt began their trade in an informal way, much like the modern B&B, but as the commercial possibilities became obvious to those with houses in certain locations, they grew into organised hostelries.

The Old English word Inn follows a similar journey. Originally it meant a dwelling house, but with the growth of a trade in providing lodging for travellers the word tended to become exclusive to its commercial purpose. The word survived as such for many centuries until it fell out of favour in the 19th century for the grander-sounding hotel. For most of the period covered by this book, *inn* had the same specialised meaning that we would now apply to *hotel*. It was a place where one could could lodge overnight, or longer if need be, and be provided with refreshment. Taverns, deriving their name from the much older Latin word, *taberna*, came to have a specialised meaning in the middle ages. Like inns, they may have provided accommodation, but their particular function was to retail wine. At periods in the middle ages the retailing of wine was reserved to only a few houses, and taverns once held an air of exclusiveness. The last distinctive group under discussion here was the alehouse. Places such as these existed only to provide alcoholic refreshment. Rarely did they provide accommodation.

As regulation of the sale of alcohol became more stringent in the 18th and 19th centuries, most particularly in the 19th century, some of the older terms dropped away, and apart from the group known as hotels, the term Public House (pub for short) came to describe houses that sold wine, beer and spirits for consumption on the premises. The "victuallers" of the 18th century became "licensed victuallers", although in recent decades this term has fallen from favour, even though there is still a Licensed Victuallers Association. In the twentieth century publicans were often called the *landlord* although this was one status they did not have; they were mostly tenants or managers. the landlord was usually the brewery.

These are some of the special terms we will use in this book; however, the term *inn* will be used in a general sense to describe all of the establishments named in these pages. It is the oldest English word and for much of the period covered by this book had the longest currency.

Alcohol became a staple of the inn trade. Although the inn's prime function is to offer shelter and sustenance to the traveller, it has, for "time out of mind", as some of our ancestors might have remarked, been associated with the supply of alcoholic beverages.

From the time it was first invented, alcohol has retained and even increased its popularity. The inns and taverns and public houses of Stony Stratford, although their names and numbers have changed in accordance with market fashion, are never empty. The range of alcoholic beverages has tended to increase over the years and the humble alehouse or beer shop, if they achieved any longevity, aspired to offer a greater range of drinks to their customers.

During the Roman occupation wine appears to have been the beverage of choice. It was imported in quantities and consumed with vigour. Thousands of amphorae, or fragments of them, have been discovered by archaeologists in abundance across the country. Whether poorer people could afford this luxury is open to some question but we can at least conclude that this was popular in Roman Britain.

The supply of wine came to an abrupt end with the departure of the Romans in 400AD. The grape does not grow well in these northern climes and the native Britons had to resort to traditional means of fermentation. Mead was a native British alcoholic beverage which could be made readily without time-consuming and expensive viticulture. It was made from the washings of a bee's honeycomb after the honey had been extracted. The honeycomb was crushed, water and spices were added and the concoction was boiled and fermented. The wax rose to the top of the vat and it was skimmed off and used for beeswax. The remaining liquid was strained through a cloth and boiled again. Mead is not much used now, but its use did prevail amongst country folk until the 19th century.

It is said that ale (öl) was introduced to England by the Vikings, but that is probably arguable. Ale making can be traced to the Sumerian civilization in Mesopotamia, who had the good grace to leave us a poem dedicated to their goddess of ale-making, Ninkasi, some 4,000 years ago, which would lead us to believe that the process was understood at a much earlier date. Certainly this knowledge would have spread to western Europe long before the Saxons landed on the eastern shore of this island. Ale can be made with simple equipment and the process itself is not complicated. Up to the time of brewery domination in recent centuries, it was a process that could be easily undertaken on the premises of most inns. However, the scarcity of wine in the 6th century probably helped to establish ale as the popular choice amongst the Angles and Saxons and the native Britons.

In fact the range of stimulating beverages was always limited until our own era. Beverages like tea and coffee were to be a discovery that would have to wait 1000 years in England and distilled spirits were something that would have to wait for the more advanced technology of the middle ages.

Ale was a central feature in Norse mythology. There are surviving descriptions from the tales of the Norse Gods, about physically large characters who delighted in eating plenty of meat and washing it down with long draughts of ale. The spirits of the dead who had fallen in battle feasted every day in Valhalla, a huge banqueting hall, where the former warriors ate prodigiously and never drank water. The supply of ale was limitless. These gods, whose names only survive in the names of our weekdays, have otherwise vanished from history, but the appetite for drinking ale seems undimmed by time.

The first inns in Stony Stratford were probably rudimentary establishments. Some might be ordinary houses taking in a traveller or two for the night, a medieval B&B. Some were almost certainly larger, two storey buildings with several rooms together with outbuildings, such as stables for horses, a dairy, and the essential brewhouse. The strip lots at Stony Stratford supporting these early hostelries were between a half and one acre and had plenty of pasture for the grazing of animals. There are no survivors of these early buildings but we can reasonably suppose that they were cruck-built, that is, with a timber frame which provided for ground floor hall with a sleeping loft above. The roofs of the time had a steep rake and were thatched, with an overhang to protect the crude walls from water damage.

Most buildings in the Wolverton area were constructed around wooden frames. Stone was available from local quarries but wood was in reasonably plentiful supply and was, of course, more workable. Bricks were available but it appears not to have occurred to people before the 16th century that they could be used on their own for construction. Typically they were used for niggin, that is replacing the wattle and plaster between the wooden frames, usually laid diagonally in a herringbone arrangement. Although brick had been known for thousands of years it was not commonly adopted in Britain until the Tudor period.

This drawing from the Luttrell Psalter depicts a 14th century inn. We could take it as representative of Stony Stratford inns of the period. The bush or ale-stake was a sapling marking out the house as an inn or ale house.

We would be entirely right to picture Stony Stratford High Street in the 13th to 16th centuries as a collection of low, timber-framed buildings, probably no more than two storeys. The *Rose and Crown* and the *Cross Keys*, which are buildings that survive from the late medieval period might have been the typical profile, possibly among the larger buildings of the time. The imposing Georgian facades of the *Cock*, the *Bull* and the *Swan* come from 18th century rebuilding.

We can also assume steady improvement in accommodation. Early medieval buildings would be luxurious indeed if guests had a separate chamber but it is probable that wall partitions were added as time progressed. Even so, privacy would only be possible for the richest and most prestigious guests. The ordinary traveller would be expected to share a bed with several other people. The mattress would be a straw filled pallet, by no means hygienic, and quite possibly home to the eggs of fleas only too anxious to find a new host.

Timber framed inns do survive from the late 15th and early 16th century in parts of the country, but are only superficially ancient in their appearance. Additions and improvements over the centuries such as a new roof or third storey transformed these medieval buildings.

The common layout had the main house fronting the road with outbuildings - stables, brewhouse, buttery, and outhouses built around a central courtyard area, The entrance through the middle was probably typical. Bear in mind that until the invention of sprung carriages in the 17th century most carriages were low to the ground and would not need a high entrance to access the courtyard. The passage to the *Cross Keys* may illustrate the lower height required for unsprung carts and carriages. The higher entranceways at the *Cock* and the *Bull* are of 18th century origin.

Stony Stratford is somewhat unusual in that it developed several inns, each under different management, and certainly by the 16th century the product of private enterprise. In most small towns there were only two institutions with the resources to develop inns: the church and the Lord of the Manor. Monasteries and priories were often favourite places to stay in the 11th and 12th centuries. They had grown up with the custom of accommodating travellers and they also had the facilities. Some monasteries grew large and prosperous from the income generated by travellers. Bradwell Priory, which was Wolverton's monastic house, never seemed to develop in this way. Although slightly off the beaten track, this would not necessarily have deterred the medieval traveller in the absence other facilities; yet this was not to be its destiny and this must be entirely set down to the development of sufficient accommodation at Stony Stratford.

The other potential hostelry was the manor house itself or a guest house built by the lord for the purpose. In many villages you will discover a public house called The _____ Arms, usually named after the local land-owning family. This tradition began when the lord of the manor first accommodated wayfarers in his own quarters and then built a separate house for the purpose. The sign hanging outside, with the coat of arms of the lord, would signify its purpose. And it is interesting that no such establishment was ever recorded in Stony Stratford.[1] There was never, as far as we know, a Wolverton Arms or Longueville Arms or a Bolbec Arms, or Basset Arms or de Vere Arms on either side of the street. Every house of its type appears to be independent of the lordship. That in itself tells us a great deal about the unique character of Stony Stratford's development.

Not long after the foundation of Stony Stratford the new settlement grew in size and property, and the only reasons for this growth were the new occasional markets and trade from travellers. The latter must have been the major factor in the economic growth of the new town so one can suggest that inns became the lynchpin of the economy. In 1290, for example, when Queen Eleanor's funeral cortege left Lincoln on its way to London, most of the stopping places were monastic foundations. For example, the party stayed at Delapré Abbey outside Northampton, and the following day made its way to Stony Stratford. After an overnight stay the party moved to Woburn Abbey and from there to Dunstable and St Albans, where there were also abbeys. Stony Stratford was a most unusual stopping point, but the stay by this huge royal party does tell us that there was a sufficient number of inns of adequate quality to entertain the royals.

The churches in Stony Stratford were not necessarily aloof from this trade bonanza. Both St Giles and St Mary Magdalen appear to have been established early in the 13th century as Chapels-of-Ease for travellers. Both were under the jurisdiction of their parent houses on the Wolverton and Calverton sides. Over time both chapels accumulated sufficient resources from the donations of travellers, and by the close of the century, could afford to build new churches. They

1 The White Swan was renamed the Stratford Arms in the late 20th century. This was a contrived name with no provenance.

6

may also have set up their own hostelries or inns, although there is little evidence to support this other than records of an inn named The Bell on the Calverton side and a similarly named place on the Wolverton side. *The Bell Inn* was a favoured name for a church hostelry. Markham makes a similar argument for the *Cross Keys*, which he suggests was once called *St Peter's Keys*. It is a name which has ecclesiastical associations. He further speculated that it may have been used as an ecclesiastical house for the refreshment of priests, but that may be questioned. An exclusive hostelry for travelling clerics would have been difficult to sustain for a community the size of Stony Stratford, and it is evident from medieval sources (Chaucer's Canterbury Tales, for example) that itinerant ecclesiastics mingled with the common herd. In any case the site of the *White Horse*, which may have been known as *The Key* in the early 16th century, would be more convenient for clergy who might be associated with St. Giles.

This drawing from a 14th century manuscript show a humble ale-house at the roadside. The ale-stake above the doorway was a cheap but universally recognised sign, often signifying that ale had been freshly brewed.

In the Middle Ages, as now, there were different kinds of drinking establishments catering for differing needs of the population. To reiterate what we said at the beginning of this chapter we may distinguish between three types. The Inns were hostelries, designed to feed and shelter travellers and stable their horses or oxen. In the case of drovers a fenced field or pen might be offered for the geese or sheep or cattle. They would be the largest buildings of their type in any community and would generally charge a high price for their services. They probably tended towards the exorbitant and overcharging must have become a source of constant complaint by the middle of the 14th century. In 1350 King Edward III signed a statute to limit charges by inns.

The tavern, which took its name from the Roman *taberna*, was generally found in towns. They may have had some of the features of inns, but in the main they served a resident population. They were distinct from ale houses in that they sold wine and because they relied on imported goods under the direct control of the Crown, and were tightly regulated. The 17th century antiquarian, Sir Henry Spelman, noted that only three taverns were permitted in London during the reign of Edward III, "one in Chepe, one in Walbrook, and the other in Lombard Street."[2] Taverns as such may not have been found in Stony Stratford during the early medieval period, but after the formation of the Vintner's Guild in 1473 at least one may have been permitted. The data collected from 1577 shows two, putting the town on a level with a number of larger English towns in this respect. We find John Vawse on the east side designated as a "vintner and inn holder" and Michael Hipwell on the west side as a "taverner and Innholder". I take this to mean that both were innkeepers with a special licence to sell wine. One of the houses owned by Michael Hipwell was deliberately named the *Swan with Two Necks*, to signify to all that he was a member of the prestigious Vintners Guild.

At the bottom end was the humble ale house. Ale was (and is) a cheap drink to make. The ingredients are inexpensive and ready to hand, the fermentation process is quick, and the equipment is simple. Taxes alone ensure that the price is high. Thus people of very modest means could set up an ale house, and so they did, until more tightly-regulated times made this more difficult. This ease of entry came to an end in 1872 when all houses serving alcohol were placed under tight licensing control.

Alehouses grew up in towns and alongside roads, sometimes in quite remote spots. Their distinguishing feature was the ale stake or ale pole, which was essentially a bushy sapling stuck in the wall over the house entrance. These places had no name. The ale pole was sufficient to identify what they were. In consequence some alehouses acquired the local name of the *Bush* or in tandem with a later inn sign,

---

2 Ian Spencer Hornsey. A History of Beer and Brewing. The Royal Society of Chemistry, 2003.. p. 294.

The *Bull and Bush*. These names, where they survive, are among the oldest pub names.

They were not always respectable. A man who had need of ale but wished also to protect his reputation might find a way of slipping through the back door. Shakespeare offers some glimpses into the ale houses of his time and some of the characters who might frequent them. Malvolio's complaint about the late night roistering of Sir Toby Belch and his friends in Twelfth Night sums up the general opinion of alehouses:

"Do you make an alehouse of my Lady's house?"[3]

John Stow, an Elizabethan writer who published a book called The Survey of London, offered this description:

" One Wotton, a Gentleman born, and sometime a Merchant of good Credit, but falling by Time into Decay . . . kept an Alehouse at Smart's — very near Billingsgate. . . . And in the same house he procured all the Cutpurses about the City to repair to his House. There was a School-house set up, to learn young Boys to cut Purses: two Devices were hung up, the one was a Pocket, the other was a Purse. The Pocket had in it certain Counters, and was hung about with Hawk's bells, and over the top did hang a little Sacring Bell. The Purse had silver in it. And he that could take out a Counter without any Noise was allowed to be a public Foyster. And he that could take a piece of silver out of the Purse without Noise of any of the Bells was adjudged a judicial Nypper, according to their Terms of Art. A Foyster was a Pickpocket, a Nypper was a Pickpurse or Cutpurse."[4]

It seems that the model for Fagin had been around for 300 years before Dickens created his character.

Alehouses were very numerous and difficult to control. In the general assessment of 1577 the country had 14,202 alehouses, 1631 inns and 329 taverns. Inns and taverns were held under some legislative control but alehouses were often free to set up and disappear at will.

Stony Stratford grew from almost nothing in the late 12th century to a town that was important enough to be literally 'on the map' by the 14th century. Its economy was built on markets, fairs and provision for

3 William Shakespeare. Twelfth Night. Act II, scene iii.
4 John Stow. A Survey of London. London: Whittaker, 1842.

travellers and it is this latter part of its history that this book relates. Much of this history is undocumented but it is possible to construct a fair picture of the town's development through the inn trade. The next chapter describes the origin of the town.

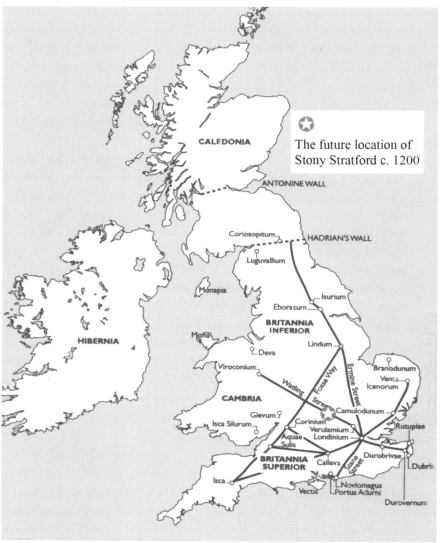

The future location of Stony Stratford c. 1200

The Romans engineered a system of streets during their occupation of Britannia. One of them followed a line from London to Wroxeter. In Anglo-Saxon times this road acquired the name Watling Street. It was a principal highway until very recent times and the medieval town of Stony Stratford was well-placed to do roadside business.

Chapter Two

Beginnings

The Watling Street

If ever the question, "What did the Romans do for us?" is put to the residents of Stony Stratford, the answer is simple and straightforward. They built the road. The way from London to Wroxeter, on its present line was made soon after the Roman occupation and is now almost 2000 years old. For almost that whole length of time armies and civilians have perennially moved up and down the highway. Without it there would have been no opportunity for an inn trade nor any scope for the development of the town we came to call Stony Stratford. As we shall discover, there were many factors in the eventual development of the town and the thriving inn trade but the road is a starting point.

It is one of those random acts of decision-making that has a long-term impact on history. Had the Romans been less addicted to constructing roads that followed straight lines we might just as easily be talking about Passenham today. Passenham was always the older settlement, and could have been chosen because of its easy river crossing. The Romans didn't do detours, so their road forged straight ahead, addressing whatever obstacle was in the way, in this instance taking them across the River Great Ouse at a wide crossing.

The road was built for military purposes. The Romans took their military conquests seriously and believed in long-term occupation, establishing a full government for the land they called Britannia. To keep the native population under control the Roman garrison needed to be able to move swiftly across the country. Roads were the answer, and we might observe from the fact that the Romans remained for 400 years that these communications links were very effective. Not all of these ancient highways survive; many fell into disuse over the centuries. This famous road, which in Saxon times became known as Watling Street, retained its function and line until the post war period, when the huge increase in motorised traffic necessitated the building of town by-passes and newer, more important roads.

Along the course of these roads the Romans established small military outposts to provide for the victualling of men and horses.

These were known as *mansiones* and the keepers *mancipes*. They were official outposts whose sole purpose was to support military movement. We do not know if they were ever used to sustain the travelling public but the likelihood is, given concerns about security, that they were for the exclusive use of the Roman garrison. The next question, whether or not a local settlement grew up around the *Mansio*, is more difficult to answer.

Stony Stratford and Old Stratford are at a river's crossing point and when historians came to consider such matters, many intuitively assumed that this would be an obvious spot for a Roman station. Many eagerly adopted this view and up to the 19th century the conventional opinion, even recorded on maps, was that Lactodoro had to be Stony Stratford, or at the very least Old Stratford. However, 20th century research has firmly identified the site of Lactodoro[5] with Towcester and no-one to date has found any substantial evidence of Roman occupation in either Stony or Old Stratford. The one journey along this road that was recorded, the march of the Emperor Antoninus to the south at some point in the second century AD (the actual date is uncertain), records him marching from Bannavanto (Whilton Lodge) to Magiovinto (Dropshort- south of Fenny Stratford), a distance of 28 miles, without stopping overnight at Lactodoro (Towcester). This is scanty evidence, but without any archaeological support, the idea of a Roman settlement or camp on either side of the river must remain unanswered. We must conclude from this that they were prepared to negotiate the river crossing of the Ouse and march on to either Magiovinto or Lactodoro. There may have been a provisional resting place on either side of the River Ouse, but we must conclude that it was not significant during the Roman occupation and it is unlikely that any *tabernae* (taverns) were to be found here. It can also be noted that there were many river crossings along this road where the Romans did not trouble to build a settlement or camp. One might further observe that the Ouse crossing is at a mid point between Magiovinto and Lactodoro, a total distance of 16 miles. A party with

---

5 The name was Latinised in the 18th century to Lactodorum, although it is a Celtic word. A.L.F. Rivet and Colin Smith. The Place-Names of Roman Britain. Batsford, 1979. discuss this issue in Chapter 2 and have adopted the naming convention we use in this book.

laden wagons, travelling at, say, two miles an hour, could comfortably reach the Ouse from either place in the morning, cross the river, and reach an overnight stop in the afternoon.

Nevertheless they built the road and the road endured. Throughout the early middle ages it must have been well-enough used to form a boundary between all the manors on either side of the street. Calverton and Wolverton are good examples of this. Each are bounded by the River Ouse on the north and a line signified by Two Mile Ash in the south with the Watling Street as a division between them.

That there was probably no organised Roman settlement at or near the Ouse crossing gives us no reason to discount the possibility that some enterprising soul did not establish some kind of hostelry there in the early middle ages. There must have been travellers, and travellers needed shelter and sustenance. A house near to the river on either side may have been established to cash in on the trade. Evidence from other ancient roads across the empire tell us that *tabernae* were set up at points along these roads where there was sufficient traffic for money to be made. These *tabernae* are the ancestors of the medieval inn. Whatever may have existed has been covered by centuries of development so this thought will remain speculation only.

We should also note that there were two ancient cross country roads in the district. These were ridgeways, high roads that generally took a line above the valley. Early travellers or drovers preferred to take the high road, which were generally drier and more passable in poor weather conditions and provided better lookout for potential trouble. The road to the north followed a line above the valley from Buckingham to Old Stratford and from there traced the contour above Haversham westwards. The southern route made its crossing at Gib Lane and took a westward line to Green Lane, part of which still survives in Wolverton.

It will be noticed that neither of these crossroads goes anywhere near the present site of Stony Stratford and intuitively one would expect to find any early traces of a mansio or taberna at either the Gib Lane crossing or the Old Stratford crossroads. No evidence has been discovered, which is not to say that no such place existed.

The Road at Domesday

The first 1000 years of the history of inns in and around Stony Stratford is therefore a complete blank. We must fast forward to the great enterprise of William I, the Domesday survey of 1086, for some facts. The record provides details about Wolverton and Calverton but is silent on Stony Stratford. What can we infer from this? Were there any roadside inns at the time of the survey? One might reasonably expect some provision. Those who moved goods up and down the road might expect to average 2 miles an hour which may have meant that 12 to 16 miles was a day's journey. Travellers on foot and on horseback could do better but even so would need places of refreshment and overnight stay along the road. Were there such places in Calverton and Wolverton along the roadside? We may speculate.

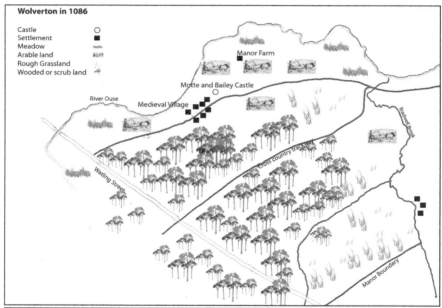

Wolverton in 1086

Castle ○
Settlement ■
Meadow
Arable land
Rough Grassland
Wooded or scrub land

Manor Farm

Motte and Bailey Castle

River Ouse

Medieval Village

Watling Street

Cross country track way

Broadwell Brook

Manor Boundary

The area was scarcely populated in 1086 when the Domesday survey was undertaken. The manor of Wolverton supported under 200 people and Calverton about 150. It is possible that there was a roadside inn here during this period but a concentration is unlikely.

Some writers have offered the opinion that towns like Stony Stratford were not mentioned because the Domesday commissioners were interested only in the land and the major tenancies. Burgesses, where they existed, counted for less. Professor Francis Hyde argued cogently that the relatively high assessments of Wolverton and Calverton in the Domesday book, compared to equivalent sized manors along the Great Ouse, may have been due to commercial activity along the Watling Street.[6] There is some merit to this argument.

The Norman Conquest did actually change everything. The Wolverton manor at 1066 was divided between three thanes. Sometime after that it was one of the possessions of Manno le Breton, one of William's supporters and one of some 200 magnates in the new realm. Meanwhile Hugh of Bolbec, in some ways a more important man than Manno, held Calverton; however Manno decided to make Wolverton the caput or head of his barony and thereafter Wolverton, with almost double the wealth of Calverton, held more importance.[7]

It is very difficult to construct a history for inns at Stony Stratford before the 12th century. While we have concluded that it was a sensible place to stop because of the river crossing, it must be noted that although river crossings can become a focus for communities this is not invariably the case. Other factors have to come into play.

The cross country ridgeways, as discussed above, did not come anywhere near the later site of Stony Stratford and it is a curiosity that neither place formed the crux of a town settlement. What compelling reason could there be for east-west travellers to go a mile out of their way in search of accommodation?

The answer may lie in security. What transformed Wolverton in particular after 1066, was that a baron chose to establish himself at Wolverton. This meant, whether he was in personal attendance or not, he maintained a few household knights to provide a continuous military presence in Wolverton. We know that at least two knights were maintained on the manor and this led to the creation of a number of men skilled in the use of arms. This must have been a deterrent to highwaymen and footpads who might otherwise prey on travellers. The eventual site of Stony Stratford was in plain view of the castle at Wolverton. The road crossing at Gib Lane was out of sight and Old Stratford was beyond the baron's control. This must have been a factor in its choice for roadside settlement.

---

6 F.E.Hyde and S.F. Markham. A History of Stony Stratford, 1946, p.11.
7 Bryan Dunleavy. Manno's Manor: A History of Wolverton to 1838. 2012.

The Birth of Stony Stratford

In the late 12th century the fog that surrounds Stony Stratford begins to lift. There are definite land transactions during the time of Hamon, the third Baron of Wolverton. They are undated, but the barony of Hamon prevailed between 1155 and his death in 1184 so theoretically they could have been made at any time during this 29-year period; however, given the speedy growth of Stony Stratford at the end of the century, the dates would probably be closer to 1184 than 1155. Three strips of land, each at one acre, were granted abutting the Watling Street. We don't know their precise location but from the subsequent development of the town we might reasonably suppose that the town found its beginnings on land opposite St Giles church. The site of the Cock Hotel may well have been one of the earliest, a point we shall return to later. In the final years of the 12th century Stony Stratford is mentioned in royal charters. This is without doubt the birth of medieval Stony Stratford.[8]

Another influence that contributed to the importance of the new settlement in the 11th, 12th and 13th centuries was the increased popularity of pilgrimages. The fervent desire to achieve salvation was a dominant theme of medieval Christianity and a pilgrimage to a holy shrine became an important method of gaining absolution for accumulated sins. The rich could achieve this through good works, such as building churches or priories and going on expensive pilgrimages to Jerusalem. The merchant classes, could make smaller bequests or travel on pilgrimages closer to home. These opportunities expanded and one such related to a woman who became known as "The Lady of Walsingham." She was the lady of the manor of Walsingham Parva in Norfolk. Her name was Richeldis. In 1061 her devoted life of prayer and good works brought her a vision, in which she was taken by Mary and shown the house in Nazareth where the angel Gabriel had announced the birth of Jesus. Mary then urged Richeldis to build a replica of this house at Walsingham. Accordingly the house was built and Walsingham acquired a reputation as England's Nazareth.

As the news spread across the country Walsingham became a focal point for pilgrimage and travellers from the west tended to take a

8 R.H. Britnell. The Origins of Stony Stratford. Records of Bucks. Vol. XX Part 3, 1977.

route that would bring them close to Stony Stratford. A century after Richeldis a benefactor built a priory at Walsingham and the fame of the shrine grew. This coinicided with the beginnings of Stony Stratford.

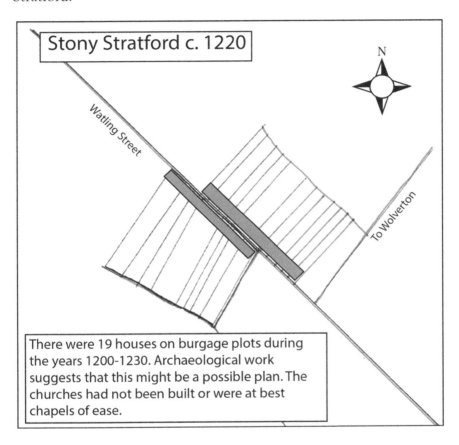

Stony Stratford c. 1220

Watling Street

To Wolverton

N

There were 19 houses on burgage plots during the years 1200-1230. Archaeological work suggests that this might be a possible plan. The churches had not been built or were at best chapels of ease.

The other significant event was the breakaway of some Oxford scholars and their foundation of a new university at Cambridge in 1202. Any journey between the two centres of learning would take them close to Stony Stratford.

The confluence of these factors led to the creation and growth of Stony Stratford. Certainly by the end of the 12th century when a lord on the Calverton side was aggressively seeking a market charter, Stony Stratford was already a place.

Early medieval England had managed well enough without urban development. Centres like London, Winchester, York and Norwich were few in number and unusual in this period. The majority of the country found its livelihood and social organization in the manor, a defined territory of land which contained the agricultural village under the control of a lord. Circumstances changed towards the end of the 12th century after Henry II's long reign had brought peace and prosperity to the country. In these conditions trade increased and new market settlements started to emerge. Many places which later became large towns and cities owed their origin to this period of English history. Improvement in trade brought traffic along the Watling Street, and it was obviously not too long before someone saw the commercial possibilities.

One such was a man called Gilbert Bassett who was married to Egelina, daughter of Reginald de Courtenay, probably before 1194. Neither had an obvious connection to Stony Stratford until we discover that Egelina had first been married to Walter de Bolbec, Baron of Whitchurch. One of Walter's manors was Calverton and it is probable that part of the manor, approximately that part from the Calverton Road north to the river, had been given to Egelina in dower. Walter died in 1190 and as a widow with property Egelina would have been of great interest. Gilbert was the successful suitor.

The couple understood the economic potential of this neck of land and in the late 12th century there was money to be made through the establishment of a market. Because of the money involved, markets were restricted, and were only possible through a king's charter. This the couple sought, and first managed to get a charter under Richard's seal on 30th April 1194. It was granted at Portsmouth on one of the rare occasions that Richard I was in the country.

The lucrative potential of this market is underscored by the Bassett's anxiety about their charter, which must have cost them a good deal of money. The charter of 1194 was authenticated by the king's seal, but this seal had fallen into Austrian hands when Richard had been captured on his return from the Crusade. A new seal had since been made, but the Bassetts, fearing that their first charter might be open to legal challenge, took the precaution of seeking a second charter under the new seal. This was granted on 20th January 1199. And again, after John had succeeded to the throne, the couple acquired a third charter under John's seal on 21st March 1200. John, always on the lookout for additional revenue, was only too agreeable. The timing of the charters was no accident. Richard I's reign was very expensive, beginning with his Crusade, continuing with his costly ransom and concluding at his untimely death with a huge military campaign in France. His brother John inherited an almost bankrupt treasury and was assiduous in finding ways to replenish it. An easy solution presented itself with the sale of rights to fairs and borough rights. In 1200, for example, an annual payment of £200 to King John gave Southampton the right to self-government and the right to keep any surplus revenue. On a medieval scale this can be compared to the UK government's sell-off of public utilities in the 1980s.

The date of 1194 offers an "official" date for Stony Stratford as an entity. Commercial settlement had preceded that date but now there was a critical mass of activity that made its recognition inevitable.

In the 13th century the new town grew quickly. By 1230 there were at least 19 plots in one acre or half acre strips abutting both sides of the street, coalescing into a recognisable town settlement. By the end of that century the number had increased to 29. Each plot would have buildings on it and some of these would be inns and alehouses. The churches of St Mary Magdalen and St Giles can trace their foundation to these years, probably beginning as Chapels-of-ease for travellers, but as the town expanded they increasingly served the local population. By the end of the 13th century both were fully fledged church buildings.

This new growth must have resulted in new wealth for Wolverton and Calverton. Travellers needed to be accommodated and victualled, horses required stabling and feeding. Some families could now support themselves in specialist trades and this period must have opened up opportunities for blacksmiths, wheelwrights, ostlers, brewers, and innkeepers.

Stony Stratford did not acquire borough status. The separate ownership of land on both sides of the street may have posed barriers to such an arrangement. (Wolverton controlled one side and Calverton the other.) There were two lords and two parishes and it is still evident today that the east and west side grew differently. The Wolverton side grew along the street in strips abutting the road and extending quite a distance to the east. The Calverton side grew in a similar fashion, but then expanded building to the Market Square, which was possibly the land first designated by Gilbert and Egelina Basset for their market. Similar field areas were later established, such as Horse Fair and Cow Fair (now Silver Street) and eventually buildings grew on all sides of these greens. There may have been a similar market area on the Wolverton side. If there was one such, it may have been in the field surrounding St Mary Magdalen church.

The foundation of Stony Stratford came from a need to serve the travelling public. The intersection of a main road and a cross country road must also have helped to make it attractive and the establishment of markets was a certain way to enhance commercial appeal. But for this the Wolverton and Calverton manors may have continued their timeless agricultural practices. Not all farming settlements straddling the Watling Street formed towns, and unique features came into play to create this town.

Once a 15th century Winchester inn, this house, formerly the Blue Boar, has been extensively restored. However the main lines of the structure have been retained and it is a good example of what may have been encountered in Stony Stratford. Many Stony Stratford buildings once had overhanging jetties like this but they were mostly cleaned up and re-faced in the 18th century.

Chapter Three

Medieval Inns in Stony Stratford

In 1283, a few miles down the road at Dunstable, the Prior of Dunstable supervised the installation of a large mechanical clock. It was designed to signal the regular divisions of the day for those in holy orders. The word clock derives from the French word *cloche*, which means bell. This elaborate timepiece had an audible signal. This new invention was introduced at a time when most people had little need for a clock as the rhythms of the day were determined by the rising and the setting of the sun. Work started at daybreak and finished with the ending of daylight. Evening activities were regulated by candlelight. The regular division of the day into hours and minutes was probably of little general concern and would not matter to the inhabitants of Stony Stratford until regular stage coaches became a feature of Stony's life.

The mechanical clock was symbolic of a new age. Mechanical devices were being applied to make work and warfare easier and more successful. The clock was perhaps the most sophisticated of these, and two centuries later Leonardo da Vinci was to fill his notebooks with drawings of devices that could revolutionise human affairs.

As this early clock sounded the midnight bell on the last day of 1299 the population of England had swelled to 5 million from perhaps a million and a half at the end of the 11th century. England in the first half of the 14th century was a crowded island by the standards of the age. In the middle of the 14th century this steady growth suffered a dramatic setback. The bubonic plague that spread through Western Europe after 1348 wiped out as much as 40% of the population. This meant that after 1349 England's population fell back to 3 million. It was not to recover until the 18th century.

Its social and economic impact was to free the bond between the agricultural worker and his lord. These ties had already been loosening but the extreme labour shortage after 1349 meant that landlords could no longer depend on feudal ties (land for service) and had to pay wages in order to get their crops sown and harvested. This enhanced the economic life of the newish towns such as Stony Stratford. The introduction of more money into the economy meant that a villein working on the manor at Furtho could give that up and go to work, for pay, as an ostler in Stony Stratford. Or better still, find plentiful work as a farrier.

There is evident growth in Stony Stratford during this century. Two churches had been built at the close of the 13th century and the population were clearly able to support these two foundations. The record of "Grilkes Herber" in 1317 suggests to us that the town may have extended to its northern limit, at least on the west side.

By accident, one record from the 14th century does survive.[9]

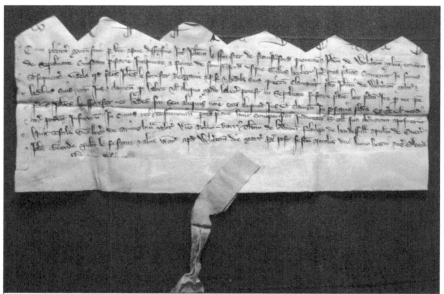

The 14th century deed which records "Grilkes Herber" is in the Bodleian library at Oxford. The serrated cut at the top of the deed signifies that there were once two or more parts. The transaction was copied onto the same sheet of parchment and the parts were cut like this so that they could be matched up if need be. This was a device to eliminate forgery.

It is in Latin. The deed relates to the transfer of rights to the fish ponds between the Stony Stratford bridge and "Grilkes Herber" from John le Forester to Sir John de Wolverton. It is dated in the tenth year of the reign of Edward II, which makes it 1317. The fish ponds were on the west side of the High Street and Sir John was keen to get some control of land on that side. "Grilkes Herber" is named in the deed to help locate that land in question, and it is not part of the

9 Ms. Radcliffe dep, deed 258.

22

sale. However either the de Wolvertons or the Longuevilles must have acquired Grilkes Herber because it does appear in the *Particular of the Manor* of Wolverton in 1713 under the name of "Gregg's Arbour."[10]

So from this casual reference we can infer that there was an inn near to the river, probably on the very north edge of the town. The word herber probably derives in this case from the French word to mean an inn - now auberge. "Grilke" is probably Grik or Gryk (Greek) and about this time there is a Thomas le Gryk who appears as a witness to documents dated 1296 and 1304.

There is a consensus that this inn was most likely on the site of that strip of land between the river and the beginning of Stony Stratford. It has been suggested that it was where the house that used to be the *Barley Mow* now stands. Some partial excavation has revealed some medieval foundations although it has to be said that a full excavation has not been undertaken. In 1713 "Gregg's Arbour" was leased to William Perry, the miller, with rights to moor boats. There is no indication that this included any buildings, so if there still was an inn here, it must have been separated from the land at some point. We

This view from the causeway shows the 18th Century Barley Mow. The stretch of meadow in the foreground was known as "Gregg's Arbour in the 18th century. It is possible that "Grilkes Herber" was near here in the 14th century.

10 Ms. Radcliffe dep. deed, c.18.

should also take into account that when the Barley Mow was sold in 1807 it was sold by the manor of Calverton, then in the possession of the Marquess of Salisbury. If it never left the manor then any building on Grilkes Herber may have been closer to the riverbank. In the 13th or 14th century the "herber" was probably an outgrowth of a toll bar that would have been placed here to charge merchants coming to sell at the Stony Stratford markets.

This house was on the very edge of the town and the most likely explanation for its location arose from a toll bar beside the bridge. The relative prominence of the le Gryk family in this period, judging from their inclusion in deeds, may suggest that they were of sufficient status for the lord to allow them to operate the toll bar.

There is not sufficient evidence to say that there has been an inn continuously on or near this site since the middle ages, and given that it is part of the flood plain of the Ouse, was not a desirable place for building. Today, and since the 18th century, the furthest reach of Stony Stratford is the house at 185 High Street that used to be the *Barley Mow*, formerly the *Angel*.

In the meantime there must have been several establishments at the heart of the town. We do not know what or where they were or how they were named, but from later evidence it is probable that there were hostelries on the sites of the *Bull*, the *Cock*, the *Swan*, probably something adjacent to St Mary Magdalene and on the site now occupied by Feagan's. On the west side, the site now occupied by the *White Horse*, next to St. Giles, seems to be an obvious location and the sites formerly occupied by the *Talbot* and the *Cross Keys* are plausible medieval foundations. In between there would be a quantity of alehouses. It is not immediately obvious why the east side was more popular than the west side. Perhaps there was better access to pasture and meadow on the Wolverton side of the street. Or, since the west side properties are prone to flooding and the water table is often high, the east side of the street offered some immunity from those dangers.

Given the location of the *Cock Hotel* at the very heart of Stony Stratford it is not too outlandish to claim this as the earliest of the known medieval inns. The plot of land was probably one of the three that was granted by Baron Hamon at some time in the years around 1180. The southernmost of these three is also the site of the *Bull*, but we have some difficulty here because there is no documentary evidence for its use as an inn before the 17th century. The earliest known record dates to 1619 where there is a reference to the *Bulls Head* and a record from 1710 which speaks of the *Bull* being established 80 years earlier. Either way it looks like an early 17th century foundation under that name. There may have been, and probably was, another establishment on the same land under a different name from an earlier date. We do not know. What is clear from the 18th century documents is that the land had always been leased by the lord of the manor. None of the inns on the eastern side owned their own land, with the single exception of the *Cock*. In the case of the *Cock*, we can only conclude, in the absence of a single written record, that the land was granted outright at some date before the 13th century when records survive. The land on which The *Cock* site was granted to someone, possibly one of the baron's household retainers in the latter part of the 12th century.

The Cock Hotel as it appeared 100 years ago. Its outward appearance has not changed today. This hotel was rebuilt with the present frontage after a fire in 1742, but there were several forerunners of this building. While we have no absolute proof, it is highly likely that this was one of the first sites developed in Stony Stratford.

Now whether or not it started out as an inn is an open question. Its place on the road would certainly have caused passing travellers to knock at the door and enquire about accommodation and so it may have become quickly apparent to the owners that opening a hostelry was a good idea. It should be noted that this plot was at the most one acre at a time when 30 acres was considered a viable unit for a prosperous peasant family. One acre would scarcely have been of much use unless it was used to generate inn trade. It seems probable then that improving trade in England at that period led the first owners to establish an inn on that site. If so, then this place marks the starting point of Stony Stratford. All subsequent development, on both sides, radiated from this point.

But there is a long period, until 1520 in fact, before we find any solid documentary evidence that there was an inn under the name of the *Cock* in Stony Stratford.[11] It is therefore only possible to develop a plausible scenario from other evidence. Nothing is conclusive.

The Gough map, so named after the man who owned it when it was revealed in the 18th century has been dated to the latter part of the reign of Edward III. It is in essence a road map, showing by straight lines the connecting roads between important places. Of interest to us is the identification of Stony Stratford. The road is a straight line from London, through St Albans and Dunstable to Stony Stratford, where it branches to Northampton and Buckingham. Woburn Chapel is also marked on the map, off the road, but indicated as a place to stay. We don't know the purpose of the map, but if it was used as a guide for medieval travellers, then we can assume from this that Stony Stratford was of some importance.

We know that the restless King John stayed there for two or three nights in 1215, very early in the new life of the infant town. It would hardly become a stopover unless the town could provide for a royal entourage, which apart from feeding and accommodating a large body of people would have to stable and provide pasture for the horses. Even in those early days of Stony Stratford's life it was considered suitable to accommodate a king and his retinue, as was confirmed

11 George Lipscomb, History and Antiquities of Bucks, vol IV, p. 367. He adds this footnote: Mr. Serjeant Pigot willed, in 1519, that the Town of Stoney Stratford should have his Inn there, called The Cock, towards the sustentation and reparation of the Bridges. Now the actual will makes no mention of this but there may have been a deed of some sort. Lipscomb is probably relying on hearsay evidence, which does not mean that it is not true.

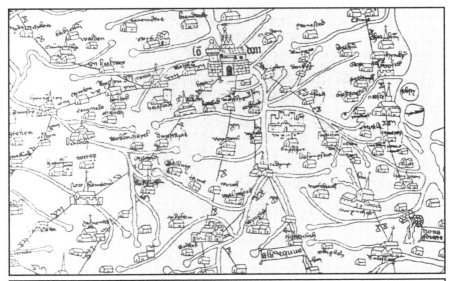

This map, probably drawn between 1360 and 1370, clearly marks Stony Stratford and it must have been a well-known stopping place at this date. It is called the Gough map after its 18th century owner. Note that East is always at the top of medieval maps, rather than north which is today's convention.

later in the century when the funeral cortege of Queen Eleanor stopped overnight in Stony Stratford.

The legal deeds preserved from the middle of the 13th century by the Wolverton Manor were only interested in transactions where there was, in effect, a sale. There are no deeds to records leases or rentals. Rentals were probably recorded elsewhere in a ledger of sorts but the property always remained in the hands of the lord of the manor. Since these latter were accounting records rather than legal documents they most likely became out-of-date and of no value and were thus disposed of. Land that had been granted prior to the 13th century, and the *Cock* (as noted above) might fit into this category, never appears in the deeds of the Lord of the manor. That transaction was over and done with and any further transfers of the property (which there must have been) were the responsibility of the succeeding owners (old and new) of the property. They may have had deeds but they were obviously less scrupulous about keeping them over the centuries and are now lost to us.

So by the time we get to the 18th century where we do have detailed records of leases, only inns on land which was never sold are described. Thus, for example, we have much more detail about the *Bull* in 1710 than the *Cock*.

This 15th century drawing from Caxton's printed book of the Canterbury Tales, shows the pilgrims gathered round the table for a meal. Much of the inn experience was communal. Private dining, private rooms, even a private bed, was an uncommon if unknown experience in medieval times.

Medieval Stony Stratford developed as narrow strips of land, side by side, fronting the Watling Street on both sides. The evidence for these strips survives today, although at that time they probably stretched back some distance. These "burgage plots" as they were known were either one or half an acre. As remarked earlier the typical Wolverton villein would hold a virgate (30 acres) or half a virgate to support his family so by the standards of the day an acre would have been quite inadequate. We must therefore deduce that those who chose to live in Stony Stratford were reliant on travellers for a large part of their livelihood. These would include farriers, wheelwrights, chaplains, carters, leather workers and innkeepers. The innkeepers employed domestic servants, ostlers and stable boys. The land behind the inn was used for pasture and probably growing some food. Busier inns leased pasture lands in the nearby meadows.

The interior of the former Cross Keys at 97 High Street shows some posts and door jambs surviving from the 15th century.

We can only speculate from later evidence about the number and location of inns and it is only in 1577 that a surviving register provides us with a definite number of licence holders. Natural hostelries could be found next to the church as the church took an early lead in providing for travellers. Thus sites adjacent to St Giles and St Mary Magdalene are likely. The *Swan* is almost certainly an old inn as was the *Cock* and possibly the *Bull*. The *Lion* and the *Horseshoe*, on the land latterly occupied by Feagan's are likely medieval foundations. On the west side the former Talbot was a medieval foundation, as appears from some internal timbers. It is earlier than the *Cross Keys*, which from outward appearance looks much older.

The *George* and the *Rose and Crown* were probably 16th century foundations at the earliest. This may be a controversial view.[12] The south end of Stony Stratford was late in development. The Wolverton

---

12 See my discussion of the *Rose and Crown* on page 41.

Road, as it was later known, was a 16th century construction; the earlier medieval road followed a line starting further to the north.

Stony Stratford enjoyed some prosperity during its first century and by the end of the 13th century the new town boasted two fine churches. The original chapels brought in substantial donations from grateful travellers wishing to guarantee their continuing safety along the road. The town's merchants must also have prospered and by 1290 there was enough money to build not one but two churches. Professor Hyde estimated that from three houses in 1180 the town had grown to 29 houses at the beginning of the 14th century. This number of properties was not affected by the Black Death as there were 30 houses at the beginning of the 15th century.[13] Although given the savage culling of the population a generation earlier, this is no reliable indicator of population. The figures can only be taken as indicative of growth and cannot be used as a population estimate. Houses with land attached would take no account of poorly constructed hovels which were accommodation for the poor. Nevertheless the figure do show that Stony Stratford grew quickly and then stabilised. Business was driven by travellers on the road and once that market had been established it had no reason to grow until roads improved in the 18th century.

The population of England remained static after the Black Death and so it must have been with Stony Stratford and it seems reasonable to infer from the number of inns, taverns and alehouse that were recorded in 1577 that this was close to the situation in the 14th century.

13 F.E. Hyde. The Growth of a Town, Part II. Town lanning Review, Vol. XX No 3. October 1949. pp. 187-201.

Chapter Four

Kings and Inns and Stony Stratford

Despite little evidence for actual inns in Stony Stratford during the medieval period we do have records of medieval kings using the town as a stopover, and we may take this as sure evidence of sufficient accommodation for a royal party. Kings did not travel light; in fact until the later medieval and early Tudor period, when government became more centralised, everything was done on the hoof. King John famously lost some of his treasury while attempting to skirt the Wash in 1217. This could only happen because it was necessary to carry money to pay for goods and services en route.

King John

King John was the first king to keep detailed records of his administration. He was also highly mobile, travelling throughout his dominions to dispense justice and try to maintain control.

It is possible to map John's movements over the whole of his reign from the various places he stopped and had to conduct court business; For this reason a charter survives that was issued and witnessed at Stony Stratford. This charter considers the appeal of one Godfrey Blundus of Northampton for some rights that were his due on the death of Roger Harengus and is dated 22nd February 1215. John stayed at Stony Stratford from 19 February 1215 to 5 March 1215.

The details of this charter have little meaning for us, but John's choice of Stony Stratford tells us that there was a sufficient number of inns to accommodate the Royal retinue. This date, quite early in the life of the town, must surely indicate that it had grown quickly. The exact numbers staying on this occasion are not known but the best guess, based on other records for similar courtly progresses, would be several hundred. Thomas Beckett, at the time Henry II's Chancellor, journeyed on an embassy to Paris in 1158 with him 200 mounted horsemen, eight wagons and 250 men on foot. In that decentralised age kings and great noblemen carried all the paraphernalia of court life and administration with them. Hollywood images of kings sitting on gilded thrones in great halls serving judgement belong to a later era, not this period.

Richard I, although he was rarely in the country and probably knew nothing of Stony Stratford, signed a charter in Portsmouth in 1194, allowing a market to be held there. This is the first royal recognition and may mark the birth of the place.

Below, Edward IV and Elizabeth Woodville, who met, fell in love, and secretly married at Grafton, while Edward was staying in Stony Stratford in 1464

A contemporary portrait of King John

Prior to taking over Stony Stratford in that week in February they had stayed at John's manor of Brill, a favourite royal lodging, where presumably accommodation and food were kept in readiness. It is a testament to Stony Stratford's readiness for a royal party that a king would consider staying there.

The growth of Stony Stratford in the first 15 years of John's reign must have appeared remarkable to contemporaries. Even though there were, as far as we can tell, only 19 plots occupied on both sides of the street at that time, the new population probably equalled the number already living on the Wolverton manor. There might easily have been the same number of inns as were discovered in the 16th century - four on the east side and four or five on the west side. 200 people, even if the number was a low estimate, is a lot to cater for and those people came with baggage and horses. Few would get beds to sleep on overnight but they would all, at least, be accommodated indoors. There was also the massive undertaking of providing food for the royal party and fodder and stabling for the horses, storage for the carts and wagons and lock-up facilities for the baggage.

Edward I and Queen Eleanor

Later in the century, when the body of Queen Eleanor was being transported from Lincoln to London in 1290, Stony Stratford faced another big challenge, and was apparently up to it. The previous night the cortege had stayed at Delapre Abbey in Northampton and the following night stayed at Woburn Abbey. Abbeys were favourite places to stay because they had the accommodation and facilities to cope with large numbers.

Edward ordered that a cross should be erected at each overnight stop. They were originally wooden, but after a few years each was replaced by a stone cross. The Stony Stratford Cross, which was

The Eleanor Cross at Hardingstone, one of the few surviving monuments. The Stony Stratford cross may have been less imposing.

probably on the High Street at the entrance to the town remained there for a few hundred years until it was vandalised by soldiers during the civil war. The base of the cross remained for some time after and was then removed. Nobody knows when this happened.

The site of the cross is believed to be at the north end of the town where there is a slight widening of the road. It may not mark the exact point where the body of Eleanor rested but was simply sited at a convenient point at the side of the road on the edge of town. Houses may have been later built around the cross.

It is highly probable that medieval kings travelled through Stony Stratford on a number of occasions, given their itinerant lifestyle. Unfortunately, at this distance in time we can only work from actual surviving records. As noted above King John issued a charter at Stony Stratford on 22nd February 1215 so we know he was there. His son Henry III may have passed through Stony Stratford several times during his long reign, but there is no record. Edward I must have travelled up and down this road on many occasions to reach the north west of England and North Wales, but the only recorded time was after the death of his wife, Eleanor of Castile.

Edward IV and the Woodvilles

Up to the 15th century references to kings and Stony Stratford have only the briefest mentions in official documents. In the reign of the Yorkist king, Edward IV, we can discover a full blown story which was a sensation in its day.

On April 30th 1464 King Edward IV and his party stopped overnight at Stony Stratford. We don't know which Inn the king himself stayed at but it is likely that the king's entourage was a large one and they probably used up all the inn space at Stony Stratford between them. So far nothing remarkable, but the following day Edward quietly slipped away and rode out to Grafton where the Woodville or Wydville family had a manor house. His objective was the beautiful widow Elizabeth de Grey (formerly Woodville) and apparently that day they were secretly married. The King returned to Stony Stratford and said he had been hunting, that he was tired and went to sleep. The following day he returned to Grafton, and for three successive days and each night he and Elizabeth came together for a secret assignation.

This is about the only fact we have. It has been said that he first encountered her at the "Queens Oak" in Whittlewood forest while hunting. It is also said that she had resolved to approach the king over the forfeited estates of her previous husband. There may be a grain of truth here but many questions went unanswered at the time and historians have never fully resolved the sequence of events or motives. Had the king encountered Elizabeth Woodville while hunting it would have happened in a very public environment with the likelihood of other observers and reporters on the meeting. There were apparently none, and the marriage itself was kept secret for 6 months. It is of course possible, given Edward's established womanizing reputation, that his courtiers paid no especial attention to his apparent fling with the de Grey widow.

Writers of the period, such as Dominic Mancini, who was an Italian envoy or perhaps a spy, made this comment:

> he was licentious in the extreme. He pursued with no discrimination the married and the unmarried, the noble and the lowly; however, he took none by force.[14]

Kings led very public lives and were rarely out of sight of anybody. Any dalliance with Elizabeth de Grey would have been noticed. However, if it were thought of as no more than a casual affair ,nobody would have paid much mind to what was going on. The announcement on October 4th that he was married was a sensational revelation.

The details of this story come from a contemporary chronicler, Robert Fabyan.

It was a marriage that astonished his contemporaries and historians

14 Dominic Mancini, The Ursurpation of Richard III. Oxford 1969. p. 67.

have generally been at a loss to explain Edward's choice other than sheer impetuousness. It is not even clear when Edward first met Elizabeth Woodville and became enamoured of her. He did spend three days in Stony Stratford in 1461 when he pardoned Lord Rivers and this has been suggested as a time for a first meeting, but if so one wonders why it took three years for Edward's passion to incubate.

The point is that Edward could have, should have made a marriage which was more dynastically important. In fact, even after the secret marriage negotiations continued for a French marriage, and a Burgundian marriage was still contemplated. Edward must have been conscious that his marriage would cause dismay, to put it at its mildest, amongst the English nobility, because he kept his secret until October when the French marriage plans had reached a point of decision.

And what of Elizabeth Woodville? She was a beautiful woman and at the time of her marriage to Edward a 27 year-old widow with two young sons. Her first husband was Sir John Grey of Groby who had been killed at the Battle of St Albans in 1461 fighting on the Lancastrian side. As a widow she was relatively impoverished which might in part explain why men were not lining up to marry her. The usual tale that is told of the whirlwind pursuit by Edward is that she virtuously resisted his advances and the only way of breaking down her resistance was to propose marriage. This may be so, although we simply have no way of knowing.

Elizabeth Woodville brought with her a set of difficult problems for the monarch, partly through her own rather icy personality and partly through the preferment of her very large family. Elizabeth, although beautiful, lacked warmth and generosity of spirit. She bore grudges for a very long time and worked tirelessly and often unscrupulously to enrich her own family. And that family was very large. She had 11 brothers and sisters, as well as two sons from her first marriage, and waged a constant campaign to see that they married into money or were given honours that brought in great wealth. A certain amount of self help in this area was to be expected and tolerated, but the Woodvilles were, in the opinion of some contemporaries, greedy, and resentment gradually increased to the point where the Yorkist regime was fatally undermined. It was as much the prospect of Elizabeth Woodville and her family running the monarchy that shifted significant support to

Richard of Gloucester after the early death of his brother Edward IV. It can be argued that were it not for the Woodvilles sudden rise to power, the Yorkist dynasty may well have continued and the Tudor name would not have come into our history.

Edward IV was the eldest son of Richard, Duke of York, who was actually the first to style himself with the surname Plantagenet. While historians have conventionally labelled the dynasty that began with Henry II in 1154 as "Plantagenet", the name was not actually used before the last two kings of that long line. The choice of the name was political. Richard of York claimed descent from Edward III's second surviving son Lionel, Duke of Clarence, and was able to advance a superior claim to the throne than his cousin Henry VI, who descended from the third son, known as John of Gaunt.[15] None of this would have mattered much if Henry VI had been competent, and had put the talents of Richard of York (who was undoubtedly very able) to good use. In the end it came to war and Richard was killed at the Battle of Wakefield on December 30th 1460.

Edward succeeded to his titles on that day and carried on with the cause. He had better luck than his father and after the very bloody battle of Towton on March 29th 1461 emerged triumphant. He was quickly proclaimed king by Parliament after the deposition of Henry and was crowned on June 28th 1461. He was just 19 years old.

The throne was not yet secure but Edward had some things going for him: he was a tall and commanding figure, he had proved himself on the field of battle, he was personally charming, and he established a reputation as a good administrator. Over the next decade he introduced measures to transform the country's finances from a parlous deficit to a healthy surplus. He modernised government by introducing able and educated officials into the various offices of state and he introduced policies that enabled and encouraged foreign trade. The merchant adventurers, who spearheaded the growth of English trade in the succeeding centuries, owe their origin to Edward IV.

Edward IV did not have a particularly stable reign either. He was

---

15 By the middle of the 15th century many of the English aristocracy were related to one another and a large number could claim royal lineage. This is too complex to explain in this narrative but genealogical charts published in most histories of the period may help to unravel the relationships..

deposed in October 1470 and regained the throne six months later. He probably had Henry VI quietly murdered and also had his brother George executed in 1478 for plotting against him. It has to be said that his youngest brother Richard was always loyal to his eldest brother.

Richard III and Stony Stratford

Upon Edward IV's death on April 9th 1483 at the relatively early age of 41 Richard acted swiftly and ruthlessly. The twelve year old Edward was at Ludlow and Richard was at Middleham in Yorkshire. Both parties were heading for London. When Richard reached Northampton, the young king's party was already in Stony Stratford. Messages were exchanged between Richard and Earl Rivers, the young king's Woodville uncle and at Richard's suggestion they agreed to meet at Northampton. Rivers and Richard met in Northampton on April 26th although by this time young Edward and his uncle had moved

This painting shows some of the principal players involved in the drama at Stony Stratford in 1483: Edward IV and his Queen Elizabeth sit on the throne. Standing beside them on the right of the picture is Prince Edward, later the uncrowned Edward V. Kneeling to present a book is Elizabeth's brother Anthony, Earl Rivers, who was executed at Pontefract on the orders of Richard III.

on to Stony Stratford. The following day Richard arrested Earl Rivers and other members of his retinue and despatched them to Pontefract Castle. He then went to Stony Stratford and picked up the young king and accompanied him to London where he was placed in the tower with his younger brother "for their own safety". Richard then methodically proceeded against the Woodville camp by launching an undoubtedly false accusation that they were plotting against the crown. The Woodville clan had enough enemies for Richard to find sympathetic ears. Richard was appointed Protector of the crown and over the next two months continued with his campaign to discredit the Woodvilles and advance his own claims to the crown.

Richard organised a judicial deposition of Edward V. Parliament voted for his deposition on the grounds that he was the illegitimate son of Edward IV - the secret marriage of Edward and Elizabeth was declared non-existent. The projected coronation of Edward V became instead a coronation of Richard III. He was crowned on July 6th 1483 at Westminster Abbey.

Edward V and his younger brother Richard were held in the tower and never emerged. It is estimated that they were murdered either on June 22nd or June 26th 1483.

Richard III lost his life and his throne at the battle of Bosworth in 1485. He was replaced by Henry Tudor whose claim to the throne was more tenuous than any of the other claimants. He was in fact descended from one of John of Gaunt's bastard sons by Katherine Swynford. However, as Henry VII, he secured the state and his own dynasty prevailed throughout the 16th century.

Richard III was portrayed as a monster by black Tudor propaganda. He was said to be deformed - a hunchback, although there is no contemporary evidence that even hints at this. However it suited Henry Tudor, by no means secure in his own claim to the throne to blacken the name and reputation of the man he had replaced. Further fuel was added to this fanciful fire by Shakespeare's chilling portrayal of Richard III. Now that the bones of Richard III have been exhumed it does appear that there was substance to the idea of Richard Crookback; however, he was not the severely humped, foot dragging caricature of Laurence Olvier's portrayal. His slight deformity did not prevent him from being a good athlete and skilful warrior.

A portrait of Richard III.

Partly because the Tudor propaganda was so extreme various modern historians have tried to rehabilitate Richard III., and some have been tempted to swing the pendulum of opinion too far in his favour. Although he almost certainly eliminated his two young nephews his behaviour may have been no worse than many other Plantagenet and Tudor kings. This does not excuse the deed, of course.

Richard's reign was short because discontent centred around Henry Tudor and because Richard precipitously engaged with the small Tudor force at Bosworth. Had Richard waited for reinforcements from the north our history may well have been different.

These events at Stony Stratford have placed the town at the centre of one of English history's pivotal moments and there is no reason why the town should not enjoy this fame. Understandably, subsequent generations have tried to identify a physical location for the arrest of Edward V. It is claimed that he stayed at the *Rose and Crown*. There is no written evidence for this - only hearsay.

Henry VIII and Grafton

In the 16th century Stony Stratford began to fade from Royal history. Government became more centralised during the reigns of the Yorkist kings and Henry VII and there was less reason to enact government business on the hoof. In any case nearby Grafton Manor, which came into royal hands through Henry's grandmother, had been developed to accommodate a royal retinue. After the death of her husband Edward IV in 1483, Elizabeth became dowager queen. Her eldest daughter, also Elizabeth, married Henry VII and her second son Henry succeeded to the throne in 1509. Elizabeth Woodville spent her last days at St Saviour's Abbey in Bermondsey, where she died in 1492.

Henry VIII used Grafton occasionally and there are some reports relating to Stony Stratford. Stony Stratford was the venue when he drafted two letters to the Pope, Clement VII, on 20th September 1525.[16] In 1531 the household accounts show that he paid the bills of the two Hungarian Ambassadors for their stay at Stony Stratford when they visited him at Grafton.[17] Unfortunately the inn where they stayed was not recorded. The bill amounted to 16s 6d. The value appears small to us today, but in 1531 this sum was about 15% of the average annual family income. We might expect the ambassadors to take the best accommodation. They most likely travelled with their own small retinue, and while this may not tell us much about the cost of an average stay at an inn, it may tell us that the inn trade in Stony Stratford was in robust health.

In July 1537 there was an outbreak of the plague across the country and a cautionary letter from Sir Francis Bryan to Thomas Cromwell points out the difficulty for the king in travelling to Grafton.

> I cannot see what way the King can come to Grafton. I hear they die at Reading, and am sure they do at Thame and also within a mile of Mr. Williams' house at Buckingham. The King might come from Esthampstead to Bishops Owburne, thence to Berkhampstead, 12 miles, thence to Eston, my lady Bray's, 7 miles, for neither my Lord nor my Lady is at home. Then to Whaddon, 7 miles, and thence to Grafton, 7 miles.[18]

This shows the slowness of royal travel in those times. At best, carts laden with all the appurtenances necessary for royal progress would move at a maximum speed of two miles an hour on roads that were scarcely more than tracks. Stony Stratford he reports is "as yet clear" of the plague but he advises that none of the king's servant from the town come to Grafton.

In the same letter he reports on a riot in Stony Stratford that started as a quarrel between a shoemaker and the town's organ player. Others got involved and the upshot was that six shoemakers were sitting in gaol at Little Brickhill to await the king's pleasure. How

---

16 Letters and Papers. Henry VIII, ii (1), 1628, 1649.
17 Letters and Papers. Henry VIII, v, p. 756.
18 Letters & Papers Henry VIII, xii (2) 275.

these troublesome shoemakers were judged is unknown.

One may also make mention here that Margaret, Queen of Scotland, a sister of Henry and progenitor of the Stuart line of English kings, stayed in Stony Stratford in 1516 where on April 27th she wrote a letter to her brother:

> "I am in right good head, and as joyous of my said journey toward you as any woman may be in coming to her brother."[19]

Once more there is no mention of the inn where she stayed.

After this period monarchs were less likely to stay at inns. They had their own accommodation such as Grafton, and the dissolution of the monasteries had led to a spate of building large country houses which could easily entertain royal parties.

Dating the Rose and Crown

This plaque on the wall of 28 High Street marks the arrest of the king-designate, Edward V, on April 27th 1483. He was taken from Stony Stratford to the Tower of London. He never emerged and is believed to have been murdered with his younger brother. His uncle Richard was crowned in his stead as Richard III and ruled for two years before being killed at the Battle of Boswoth..

It is a curiosity of Stony Stratford's history that an inn that has almost no history at all has become a prominent attraction today. On the street wall of Number 28 High Street is a plaque telling us that the young prince Edward, then the uncrowned King Edward V, was arrested here by his uncle Richard on his way to London to succeed his father as king. This may have happened at the Rose and Crown but there is unfortunately not a scrap of evidence to support this notion. Professor Hyde correctly noted the evidence we do have and is careful to repeat the words of Browne Willis who believed there was an older tradition associating the prince with the Swan in the centre of the town.[20]

What we do know is that Richard Duke of Gloucester and Henry

19 Letters and Papers. Henry VIII, ii (1), 1829.
20 Add.MS. 5839, f. 194

Duke of Buckingham enticed Edward's uncle Lord Rivers to a meeting in Northampton while leaving his nephew in Stony Stratford. Gloucester and Buckingham used the opportunity to arrest Rivers and send him under armed guard to Pontefract castle. He was later executed. Buckingham and Gloucester then rode to Stony Stratford early the next morning, placed armed guards at all entrances to the inn where they were staying and placed the young Edward "under their protection". They then rode back to Northampton for breakfast and subsequently took Edward to London and that is the end of Stony Stratford's role in the story.

The former Rose and Crown as it appears today.

The Rose and Crown becomes notable due to the surviving will of Michael Hipwell. He was a successful innkeeper in the town and in his lengthy will of 1609 it is clear that he was a man of some substance, owning a number of properties, including the *George*, the *Rose and Crown* and the *Swan with Two Necks*. In his will he names the *Swan with Two Necks* and the *Rose and Crown* specifically, but not the *George*. Later documents are able to identify the three houses that constituted the *George* as the inn. The *George* was on record in 1619, so it might be reasonable to infer that it was an inn at an earlier date. In a list of inn holders compiled in 1577, thirty years before Michael Hipwell's death, he is recorded as a "taverner and inn holder" on the west side, presumably only owning the *Swan with Two Necks*. At that date he does not appear to have any inns on the east side.

In 1936 a late Elizabethan fireplace and the remnant of a mural painting were uncovered at the former Rose and Crown. This line drawing and reconstruction was made by Francis W. Reader, a specialist in Tudor wall paintings.

Somewhere between 1577 and 1609, during the course of his working lifetime, he acquired the *Rose and Crown*.

Michael Hipwell's will was remarkable for its public benefaction. Hipwell wanted to found a school there and it was his bequest that after 99 years a school should be founded on the property and a schoolmaster be funded from the proceeds of the investment. The schoolhouse was to be established in a newly built barn at the back of the *Rose and Crown*. It is not clear how long the *Rose and Crown* continued as an inn, but certainly by the middle of the 18th century the buildings were modernised and converted into two houses.

What we know of the building itself is that the structure is now largely 18th century with some late Tudor framework inside. The stone fireplace in the dining room is late 16th century.

Some excitement arose in 1936 when some mural painting over the fireplace was uncovered during some repair work. When reconstructed this turned out to be a painting of the royal coat of arms, probably painted at the end of Elizabeth's reign. Those who believe that the prince stayed there in 1483 saw this as supporting evidence.

The name *Rose and Crown* should indicate something but it is unlikely that it had this name in 1483, assuming that it was an inn at this date. The rose as a royal symbol began with Edward III who used a golden rose. His son, John Duke of Lancaster used a red rose and in the next century Richard, Duke of York adopted a white rose, a badge of the Mortimers. Richard's mother was Anne Mortimer and through her he inherited the lands and the title of the Earl of March. During the 15th century civil war they became badges for the opposing sides. Henry VII amalgamated the two into the Tudor rose and added a crown above it. The *Rose and Crown* as a potential inn name cannot date earlier than this. A number of English inns named the *Crown* were known to have added the rose, that is the English rose, after the accession of a Scottish king in 1603 to assert their "Englishness". That said, this is possibly the strongest tip that the inn might have had royal associations. Equally it could tell you that Michael Hipwell was a strong monarchist.

Browne Willis, the 18th century MP and local historian was of the view that the *Swan* was the inn where the prince's party stayed. This may have been hearsay but Browne Willis was 200 years closer to the event. One can also construct a supportive argument for this. The Swan was considered to be one of the premier inns in Stony Stratford at the time with possibly only the *Cock* to rival it. One has to ask why the royal party, which was a large one, would travel further up the street to a smaller inn on the site of the *Rose and Crown*. Browne Willis did have the advantage in 1736 of knowing the old Swan which may still have had medieval foundations at that date.

The fire of 1742 changed everything. An accidental fire started by a chambermaid at the *Bull* in May 1742 initiated a conflagration that completely wiped out everything to the north. A large number of houses were destroyed as well as the *Bull*, the *Cock*, the *Swan*, the *Red Lyon* and the *Horseshoe*. All of the buildings which now front the High Street are after that date. The parts of medieval and 16th century

Stony Stratford that do survive are to be found to the south of the Bull and on the Calverton side of the street.

The sum of the evidence is that we have a building at Number 28 which has 16th century elements in its structure. We have a name for it in Michael Hipwell's will of 1609, which would certainly lead us to make royal associations. A mural painting discovered in the 20th century displaying the royal coat of arms tends to reinforce this speculation. We have records of the events of 1483.

Is this enough to make categorical assertions about the events of 1483 occurring at the former *Rose and Crown*? I would have to say not. In the 15th century the south was still the "country" end of the town and was little developed. Guild buildings were erected on the site of the later alms houses in 1476 so it is reasonable to infer that some building may have been at the *Rose and Crown* site in the late 15th century. It may well have been a new inn, and this may have recommended itself to the prince who may have elected to stay there while others of his party made do with older accommodation. The absence of evidence does not make the suggestion implausible, but we need to be on our guard against making definite statements which cannot at present be proved. Some dendrochronogical evidence from the timbers might help to date the building and help us to be more certain.

But for Michael Hipwell's will we would have no knowledge at all of any inn under the name *Rose and Crown*. He certainly did not have a property there in 1577 when he was recorded as an inn holder and taverner on the west side, but we know that he did in 1609. It is therefore not known whether it carried this name prior to his ownership. How long it lasted as an inn or even under this name is not known because there is no further mention of it as an inn. With Michael Hipwell's will to guide us we might fairly assume that it persisted in its trade for a further 99 years, until 1708. We do know that his charity survived and that it limped through to the 19th century fulfilling its purpose. What happened to the inn is unclear. The name never appears in any record so we can assume one of two outcomes: either it closed as an inn and the house was used for other purposes, or it continued as an inn but under a changed name. There are many candidates in the 18th century for such a name.

For the moment there can be no firm conclusions about this one way or the other. The *Rose and Crown* could have been constructed in the late 15th century, in which case it could have been a newly built property in 1483, or, on the basis of known archaeological evidence we can assert that the building was early Tudor. And if so, it does not remove the possibility that the Tudor construction replaced an earlier building. Hearsay evidence and inference currently places the site at the former *Rose and Crown*, Browne Willis's 18th century note about the *Swan* being the place where Edward V stayed is equally unsupported. Until some concrete evidence emerges, if it ever does, we may as well stay with the active legend.

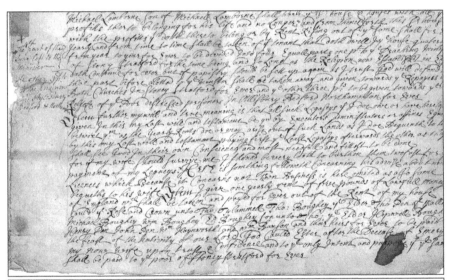

An extract from Michael Hipwell's first will of 1603 supplies the first documented mention of the Rose and Crown. Here he bequeaths the annual rent of £5 to his executors to be distributed amongst the poor of Stony Stratford. In his last will of 1609 he improved on this with the intention of funding a school.

Very little of Medieval Stony Stratford is in evidence today.

The building above was known in the 18th century as the Cross Keys, and has a typical central entrance to a yard. It is a much-modifed late medieval building.

Below, the George, which has been in continuous use as an inn or restaurant since the early 17th century.

Chapter Five

Stony Stratford in Tudor and Stuart Times

The 16th Century

John Leland, the Tudor traveller, visited Wolverton in 1540 and recorded a brief note about Sir John Longueville's house. He may have travelled through Stony Stratford but he did not pause to comment. Had he done so he might have left us with a few clues about late medieval Stony Stratford. Celia Feinnes, a most unusual and adventurous woman, who rode through Stony Stratford on horseback in 1697, is almost equally unhelpful:

> Thence to Stony Stratford, so Cross ye river Aven again 12 mile, and Enter Buckinghamshire. At Stony Stratford wch is a little place built of stone they make a great deale of bonelace and so they do all here about, its the manuffactory of this part of ye Country, they sit and worke all along ye streete as thick as Can be.

She was heading for Great Horwood, where she stayed in the great house there, and so was uninterested in inns, noticing only the women who sat outside the house working on their lace.

Almost all of the town was either destroyed by the spate of eighteenth century fires or rebuilt and remodelled at various times during the later centuries. The former *Rose and Crown* building retains some 16th century elements, as does the former *Talbot*, which, in common with the *Cross Keys*, has 15th century timbers in the structure. The St Mary Magdalene tower was rebuilt in the 18th century and St Giles was much enlarged in the 18th century. To gain any concept of 16th century Stony Stratford inns we are almost entirely reliant on documentary sources.

We are somewhat fortunate in that we can at least gauge the scope of innholding in the 16th century. A licensing act of 1522 led to records of licensees. Few survive, and we have a list of innholders and alehouse keepers for Buckinghamshire and Stony Stratford for the single year 1577. Somewhat disappointingly the list does not include the names of the inn signs. However we do have some numbers.

On the east (Wolverton) side of the High Street were four inn holders and seven alehouse keepers. The inns were most likely the

Cock, the forerunner of the *Bull*, the *Swan* and the *Horseshoe*. It would be fair to assume that John Vawse, as a Vintner and Innholder, had one of the premier inns on the east side like the Cock or the Swan.

On the Calverton side there were five inn holders. Michael Hipwell, of later fame because of his generous charitable bequest, was probably at the *Swan with Two Necks* in 1577. From his will of 1609 we learn that he had acquired the *Rose and Crown* on the other side of the street and also owned three houses opposite which are later identified with the *George*. This building is late 16th century at the earliest and probably early 17th century.

The medieval centre of the town was closer to St Mary Magdalene, but in the last years of the reign of Queen Elizabeth building started to push north and 100 years later the High Street from the *Angel* to St Giles churchyard was densely packed. Similar developments were taking place on the Square; the south side had probably been developed by the middle of the 17th century with extensive gardens reaching into Cofferidge Close. The *Old Barley Mow*, when offered for sale in 1820, had two acres of land behind it. It is probable that the adjoining houses had equally large gardens too.

Apart from the *Swan with Two Necks*, whose location is not known, there are not many obvious places for inns in 1577 on the west side. The site of the *White Horse*, possibly using the name *The Key* might be one.

In 1522 William Turville and John Wyke sold a burgage plot, together with its buildings and land to Peter Percevall of Newport Pagnell. What is of interest here is that the land is described as a strip from the Watling Street to the Square "between the burgage of the late Richard Barton and the inn called le the key."[21] We could therefore place the inn called *The Key* on the approximate location of the present *White Horse*.

Two other 16th century sites may be the former *Talbot* and the *Cross Keys*. The house once known as the *Rising Sun* in the 18th century is another possible location for a 16th century inn. It might then have been known as the *Lyon*, although the evidence for this assertion is sketchy.

The redevelopment of Stony Stratford has been so complete and

---

21 Ms. Radcliffe dep. Deed 295.

the archaeological evidence to date so thin that we come away with little idea of what really existed. I do not think that there would have been inns on the Square at this early date, although that possibility cannot be discounted. Scattered somewhere between these inns were no fewer than eleven alehouses.

The *Fleur de Lys* (written Fleur de Luce) occurs in a deed dated 1526 where a man called William Taylor sold a tenement called the "Fleur de Luce" to William Payton. It may not have been an inn in 1526, but the name would suggest former usage as an inn.[22]

We are also made aware of a house called The *Red Lion*, an early use of that name which did not become truly common until after the accession of James I. This name turns up in a dispute over the will of William Edy who owned the Malletts estate on the east side and the contention was recorded in the Court of Requests in the twenty-first year of the reign of Henry VII, that is in 1529-30.[23] The details need not concern us here and are in any case obscure but the information that comes to us is that there was an inn called the *Red Lion*. As with all these documents the exact location is never detailed and is left to the knowledge and understanding of the protagonists. Some historians have associated this *Red Lion* with the house that was next door to the Horseshoe, sometimes called the *Red Lion* and later known as the Lyon. This *Red Lion* however appears in the 17th and 18th centuries as the property of the manor, leased by Sir Edward Longueville to John Warr, in 1635 and leased to others by the Radcliffe Trust in the 18th century. If so then it is arguable that this land never left the manor and was not part of the Edy estate. The site of the 16th century *Red Lion* must therefore have been elsewhere.

"Red Lyon Leyes" are described in the early Radcliffe Trust manorial documents from 1713. They are obviously in the ownership of the manor but this collection of meadows under this name might suggest that they were once leased to the 16th century Red Lyon, and when the meadow was enclosed it was given this name because at that point the land was customarily used by the *Red Lyon*. The 18th century Red Lyon was leasing a quite different set of fields for meadow and pasture but the survival of the old name may point to an earlier *Red Lion*.

---

22 Ms. Radcliffe dep. deed. Bodleian 1526.
23 Ct. of Req. bdl. 2 no.186; Feet of Fines Bucks. Mich . 21 Hen VIII.

The prospectus also notes that the Red Lyon Leyes " may be built on with advantage," which suggests that the field was either touching the High Street or had easy access to it, otherwise it would have had no appeal for building purposes. That said, this intellgence does not help us to locate it.

17th Century

Several new inn or alehouse names emerge in the 17th century as we discover odd documents in various archives. The *George* has already been mentioned but it would also appear that the Market Square was being developed at this time with inns on the south side and west side, backing onto fields for pasture. The *White Hart* appears in 1625 according to one source and the *Kings Head* in 1640. The alehouse known as the *Crooked Billet* makes its first appearance in 1684.

The *Bull* (at least under this name) dates from this period. The account book of Sir Gyles Mompesson records a fine against Michael Boughen for £5 on 16th July 1619. This is the earliest reference, although it was named in this record as the *Bull's Head*.

Documents that refer specifically to the *Bull* begin to appear in the late 17th century. These have been noted in the Hyde-Markham book on the History of Stony Stratford in the appendix. From that time the *Bull* is fairly well documented but because of its destruction by fire in 1742 there is no way of identifying an earlier building until some archaeological work is undertaken on the foundations.

In a prospectus which was prepared in 1710 for the sale of the Wolverton Manor there is this entry:

> The Bull Inn has been lett for as much this 80 years, no land about the Town of Stoney Stratford but what letts for forty-fifty shillings an Acre, when any to lett; several are Courting for it their being not Ground anough to supply the Occasions of ye Towns people.[24]

This 80-year estimate allows us a start date of 1630, although from the fine information we can place it at least a decade earlier.

Sir Gyles Mompesson has left an interesting record although one founded entirely upon his corrupt and frankly criminal practices. He was born in Wiltshire circa 1583 to a prominent family and became

24 Nottinghamshire Archives. DD 4P 55/15-17.

MP for Great Bedwyn in 1614.

Soon after he was able to persuade the prominent and influential Duke of Buckingham to create the position of Commissioner for Inns. Up to that point the licensing of inns was in the hands of Justices of the Peace. By 1617 he was in a position to levy fines against inns which were not fully compliant with the law. Moreover he had the power to set the fines himself. The fines went to the treasury but he was able to keep 20% of the money collected for himself.

He then set about pursuing his new position with great zeal and it has to be said in an entirely unethical manner. It was an easy matter to close an inn or tavern for some minor disturbance of the peace, however the landlord could reopen the following day on payment of a fine. This was in fact an extortion racket. He used various underhand tricks, such as sending anonymous agents to inns to request bed and board overnight. The following morning, having caught the innkeeper red-handed for some minor infringement, they announced themselves and assessed a punitive fine.

This particular reign of financial terror was relatively brief and within a few years Mompesson had become one of the most hated men in England. He was summoned before Parliament for trial but fled the country. He was tried in his absence and subjected to a massive fine of £10,000, the loss of his knighthood and life imprisonment. To demonstrate their further contempt for the man, Parliament also ordered that he ride a horse facing backwards through the streets of London. In the end, he escaped serious punishment. When Charles I came to the throne he showed some leniency towards Mompesson and it seems that he lived at his home in Wiltshire out of sight and out of mind until his death in 1663, near to his eightieth birthday.

The prosecution at his trial estimated that 3,320 inns and taverns had been prosecuted and fined by Mompesoon in his period as commissioner. The benefit to us today from this sorry tale of corruption was that the Mompesson account books have left us some names and evidence for 17th century inns in Stony Stratford.

The *Peacoke* (William Taylor), the *Green Dragon* (Thomas Whitnell), the *Golden Lion* (William Huddson), the *White Lion* (Edward Michell) as well as established houses like the *Cocke* (Thomas Greene), the *George* (Frances Eve), the *Horse Shooe* (Nicholas Smith) all came under his oppression. The fines were not light either. £5, which was the standard fine, was a poor man's annual income. The Mompesson accounts only record fines (much of which went into his own pocket) so other inns and alehouses which escaped punishment were not mentioned in these accounts.[25]

It is interesting that Oliver Ratcliffe in his book published in 1900 throws out the name of the *Peacock* as an old inn name, which he had picked up from hearsay only. This record from 1619 supports his mention although the *Peacock* is never heard of again and is not recorded at all in the 18th century.

The Longueville papers reveal some more names, although in most cases it is difficult to identify a location.

A house called the *Bell* crops up on the east side in 1625 in a lease to Thomas Rawbone.[26] He was a butcher in Stony Stratford who died in 1637 leaving a substantial estate. Since the inn was a lease it was not mentioned in his will and either the lease was taken up by one of his heirs or passed on to someone else. Rawbone in any case probably employed an under tenant to manage the inn. It is never heard of again, at least on the Wolverton side.

In 1629 a lease was granted to Lettice Ashby, and we learn from this same document that it had been leased to George Walton in 1613. This was for the house known as the *Angel*, which again was at an unknown location.[27]

Again on the east side, in an unknown location, Sir Edward Longueville granted a lease to William Sheapard for the *Rowbuck* Inn in 1642. Twelve years later he leased the *Crown* to James Barnes. This is not the *Crown* on the Market Square and again the location is unknown.

Robert Edge was granted a lease in 1678 for the *Blue Anchor*.[28] The lease came with "all that messuage, or tenement, with the appurtenances situate on the east side" and "a pyghtle of pasture", meaning a small field. We don't know its location, but through name

---

25 Centre for Buckinghamshire Studies. Photocopy (note: photocopy may be incomplete) of two account books of Sir Giles Mompesson [see D.N.B.], royal commissioner for licensing of innkeepers in England. D=X648/1.
26 Ms. Radcliffe dep. deed, 359.
27 Ms. Radcliffe dep. deed, 363.
28 Ms. Radcliffe dep. deed, 319.

association only, it might be considered a forerunner of the 18th century inn the *Drum and Anchor*, which eventually became the *Coach and Horses*. There was a piece of land behind this site which was once known as The Pyghtle.

We also discover the *Black Boy* in 1625 through a conveyance by Michael Boughey to one John Parsons of Passenham.[29]

This row of three houses on the Square date from the same period. On the left, the former White Hart, in the middle, The Crown, which is still in business, and on the corner, The Barley Mow, which closed in 1820.

The Square

We don't have any concrete evidence for any inns or alehouses on the Square before the 17th century. This is not to say there were none. After all, the presence of a periodic market might tempt an entrepreneur to open up an alehouse at least, but the balance of available evidence indicates that filling in the south west side of the High Street and the encroachment on the bounds of Cofferidge Close only started at the beginning of the 17th century.[30] From this we might deduce that the Market place was a field that was occasionally used

29 Ms. Radcliffe dep. deed, 302.
30 Hyde & Markham. A History of Stony Stratford. 1948. Markham relates an account of this development on pages 80-84.

55

for market purposes and its definition as a square, surrounded on all sides by houses, originated in this period.

Stony Stratford's High Street was long enough to accommodate a number of inns on this prime space. The road was more likely to be better maintained and travellers were more likely to take a bed or refreshment along the main road rather than deviate into a side street or a square that might be unpaved and muddy during the winter months.

In the 18th century we have some good evidence for inns and alehouses on the Square and, in many cases their precise locations. Properties on the south and west side offered some advantages. They could have a spacious frontage and almost an acre of land behind them for outbuildings, stables and pasture but they were never designed to compete with the larger inns on the High street who were comparatively large scale employers.

The *Crown* has the longest record of all. It makes its first documented appearance in 1666, although it may have been built 15 years earlier, and is continuously recorded in later centuries. It remains in business at its present address, 9 Market Square.

Next door on the corner at Number 10 was the *Barley Mow*. We know it as the *Barley Mow* from 1753 until its final closure in 1810. It is probable that its history originates in the 17th century.

The *King's Head* at 11 Market Square, on the west side adjoining Silver Street, and at some time known as "Pig Market" was also a 17th century foundation. The Victoria County History offers a date of 1640. It is mentioned in the Overseer's papers in 1678 and in the Parish register in 1798. It was continuously licensed from 1753 until its final closure in 1914. The *King's Head* does not crop up in other parts of Stony Stratford so there is no ambiguity about determining its location.

In addition we know about the alehouse known as the *Crooked Billet*. This first appears in Calverton's manorial records in 1684 and appears to have operated continuously until the property was sold in 1821. According to Markham the house was regarded as disreputable. There is no physical evidence for its existence today. It was part of a row of buildings on the south side of Church Street which were demolished in the 1940s. It may have been known as the *Sun and*

Moon at an earlier date, 1660, because a house at this location was known in this period from 1660-1672.

Another part of the Square that was cleared was the north side, backing onto Church Street. On the left was a covered market, and somewhere among the complex of buildings behind it was the Crooked Billet.
The original watercolour was painted by J.C. Hassell for the engraving that was reproduced in his 1819 book on the Grand Junction canal.

There was also an inn with the sign of the *Plough* at Number 2 Market Square in the 18th century. It may have had its origins in the 17th century. This inn had a yard which backed onto the yard of the George. The Plough was licensed to Edward Salter from 1753 to 1764 but it must have been in business earlier as either this Edward Salter, or his father, finds mention in Stony Stratford documents in 1710. In 1765 this building was acquired by Thomas Honeybone who changed the name to the *White Lion*.

At number 5 or 6 was an alehouse known as the *Green Dragon*. This appears on record from 1753 to 1755 and disappears after this date. It is highly likely that it was operating before 1753 although it is impossible to date earlier with accuracy. There is a record of 1619 of a fine made against the *Green Dragon*, although it may not have been this *Green Dragon*.

The *White Hart* at Number 8 has sometimes been thought of as a 17th century inn, Indeed there are references to a *White Hart* in 1625

This postcard from 100 years ago shows the Square before it was redeveloped. On the right hand side you can see a fragment of the former White Hart and next to it Number 7, home to the brewer William Tomkins in the 19th century. From here everything to the east has been demolished. One of the two cottages next to Number 7 was the former Green Dragon and in the distance, towards the High Street you can see the former Plough/White Lion.

in the Victoria County History, although that date is unreferenced. There is a record of a *White Hart* in 1670 in the Overseer's accounts. A third reference occurs in 1758 in the licensing register but this *White Hart* only continues until 1773. It does not reappear until 1820 when it is definitely at number 8, The Square. These intervals make it difficult to assume any continuity. It is possible that the building was used as an inn throughout the period but that, like so many others, it changed its name. Or, the earlier *White Harts* may have been found somewhere else in Stony Stratford. Towards the end of the 19th century the *White Hart* on the Square became a Working Men's Club and subsequently Council Offices after the club moved to the London Road.

The building still stands impressively on the Square although on the basis of this evidence we have to question the continuity of the *White Hart*, and leave the question of the location of earlier *White Harts* open. We only know with certainty that the *White Hart* was on the Square from 1820 until 1890, and in the middle of that period it was associated with the Tomkins brewery next door at number 7. Markham's comment that it "sold the best beer in Stony Stratford" may derive from that association.

The grant of the rights to a market in 1194 to Gilbert and Egelina Basset was, as discussed earlier, the foundation of Stony Stratford. The day allowed was Sunday. Fairs were occasional, usually on feast days. Thus from medieval times the market place was always in use. In later centuries, we have evidence from place names that some of the activities of the market or fairs changed location. There was Pig Market at the western edge of the Square, Cow Fair along Silver Street and Horse Fair, still commemorated by Horse Fair Green. As a business or market area the Market Square, or Market Place as it was then called, was a natural draw for refreshment houses and their trade would probably have come from local farmers and business people coming into the town to do business.

Civil War Period

Inns and alehouses must have done a brisk trade in some years of the 17th century Civil War. The war did not come to Stony Stratford in terms of pitched battles but it came through Stony Stratford as troop movement on several occasions and there were skirmishes nearby. The dividing line of the Watling Street actually divided local sympathies. The Longuevilles of Wolverton took the Royalist side while the Bennets of Calverton were Parliamentary supporters. The town had strategic value for both sides due to its position on the arterial road.

In 1643 a sizeable force of the royalist army was gathering in North Bucks:

> 'We have advertisement that there are 4,000 or 5,000 horse and foot drawn together at Buckingham, Stony Stratford and those parts, and that they have 12 pieces of ordinance; they expect the earl of Manchester with a greater strength to join with them."[31]

This was a large force descending on Stony Stratford. It is thought that the men camped in Sir Thomas Longueville's fields at Wolverton, but it would not be surprising if any of the men did not stray to fill the alehouses of Stony Stratford.

In June of that year these troops were driven out by the Earl of Essex who marched from Aylesbury with this objective, but once Essex returned south the Royalist troops filtered back to the area.

---

31 Letter from Sir Edward Nicholas to the Earl of Forth. March 21 1643.

In October the Parliamentary forces took and held Newport Pagnell and there were sorties from there to launch attacks on the forces at Stony Stratford. The Royalists held position over the winter but in the Spring of 1644 lost their command of the Watling Street and the river crossing and the town was filled with Roundhead troops for a change.

By June 1645 Stony Stratford's part in military activities was over as this was the date of the decisive Battle of Naseby. Sir Thomas Fairfax stopped at Stony Stratford on June 3rd while troops were mustering. On June 14th the army of Fairfax and Cromwell emerged victorious from the battle.

A by-product of this troop movement, according to legend, was that some of the Parliamentary troops took it upon themselves to destroy the Eleanor Cross that had stood in Stony Stratford's High street for almost 350 years. Presumably this was seen as a monument to royalty and therefore offensive in the eyes of some Parliamentary soldiers.

Having said this, there are no contemporary records that I am aware of that mention the destruction of the monument or the disposition of the rubble. It was hardly an official act. Although it may have been sanctioned by officers, it was not an event to be recorded. So it is hearsay evidence that we must go on. We can be sure of two facts: it was built and it was subsequently destroyed, so completely in fact that the original location can only be guessed at.

We might however assume that drinking in one alehouse or another played its part in inciting the men to their destructive act.

When Browne Willis visited the town in 1735 he recorded speaking to one William Hartley, then 80 years of age, who recalled seeing the base standing. He also thought that it was built closer to the site of the Horseshoe Inn, later St Paul's school. However a street plan of 1806 marked its former location at a point further north where the road widens.[32]

Armies place huge demands on communities when they descend upon them. In many respects they are like locusts and consume everything in sight. Here again we find indirect evidence of Stony Stratford's level of organisation in that it was able to host so many people. The Eleanor Cross, from its erection to its destruction, marks a period where Stony Stratford showed its ability to host large numbers.

---

32 Add. MS. 5839, f. 194.

The Old Barley Mow on the Market Square, together with the King's Head in the background, probably opened for business during or shortly after the 17th century Civil War. It was in this century that the inn trade extended off the High Street. Both properties at one time had extensive yards and provision for pasture.

The photograph below left shows the former Fighting Cocks and the former Bell Inn on the west side of the Square. they may originate in the 17th century and were definitely active in the 18th century. The Fighting Cocks most likely had a third storey added in the 19th century.

The photograph lower right shows the rough hewn rafters inside the former Bell Inn at 16 Market Square.

Ride a Cock Horse

Ride a cock-horse to Banbury Cross,
To see a fine lady upon a white horse;
Rings on her fingers and bells on her toes,
And she shall have music wherever she goes..[1]

This is an 18th century version of a common rhyme. The meaning of "cock-horse" is not known with certainty and some have advanced the thought that it might refer to a horse from the *Cock Inn* at Stony Stratford. There was a road from Stony Stratford to Banbury and coaches and waggons travelled this route regularly in the 18th and 19th centuries. It is also believed that the rhyme had in mind the famous lady traveller, Celia Fiennes, mentioned at the beginning of this chapter.

---

1 I. Opie and P. Opie, The Oxford Dictionary of Nursery Rhymes (Oxford: Oxford University Press, 1951, 2nd edn., 1997), pp. 65-7

Chapter Six

The Highway and the 18th Century

Roads, Inns and the Coaching Trade

When the 18th Century opened, the people of England, although they did not know it at the time, were on the brink of a long period of rising prosperity. The religious strife which had dominated and undermined the previous century had reached a peace of sorts and the role of monarchy was brought into some balance with the powers of Parliament. There was now time to focus attention on more mundane matters, not least of which was the appalling condition of the roads, which were, in many parts of the country, barely passable. Given the position of Stony Stratford on the Watling Street this was a matter of great importance.

As good a description as any of the parlous state of the roads was this account by an attendant of Prince George of Denmark, husband of Queen Anne, who travelled in 1702 from Windsor to Petworth to meet King Charles III of Spain, then on a state visit to England. The journey of 50 miles took 14 hours, less than walking pace, and is here described by one of his attendants.

"We set out at six in the morning by torchlight to go to Petworth and did not get out of our coaches (save only when we were overturned or stuck fast in the mire) till we arrived at our journey's end. 'Twas hard service for the Prince to sit fourteen hours in a coach that day without eating anything and passing through the worst ways I ever saw in my life. We were thrown but once indeed in going, but our coach, which was the leading one, and his Highness's body coach would have suffered very much if the nimble boors of Sussex had not frequently poised it or supported it with their shoulders from Godalming almost to Petworth; and the nearer we approached the Duke of Somerset's house the more inaccessible it seemed to be. The last nine miles of the way cost us six hours to conquer them; and indeed we had never done it if our good master had not, several times, lent us a pair of horses out of his own coaching whereby we were able to trace out the road for him."[33]

We can take this as typical. After an Act of Parliament in 1657 had established the office of Postmaster General and a Royal Mail service, the average speed of travel was no better than 3 miles an hour, and often less. At first there was not, and could not be, a mail coach; the roads could not support such a method of delivery. Instead, a post boy, either riding a laden horse or leading a pack horse, trudged up and down the highways to deliver the mail packets. When a post office was established at Little Brickhill in 1687, this marked a full 12 hours journey time from London. Another three hours were required to reach Stony Stratford.

The old society, dominated by agriculture, had hardly witnessed much development since the invention of the horse-drawn plough, but would undergo a dramatic transformation in the 19th and 20th centuries. In 1700, there was only a glimmer of the light of change on the horizon, enough for some people to pay attention. The demand for raw materials and manufactured goods was on the rise and the old seaways and riverways were no longer adequate for satisfactory delivery. Mercantile and industrial interests were developing in parallel and the men leading these activities required improved communication which could only come through an improved road system.

Medieval England had made do with the old Roman military roads and old ridgeways for cross country travel. Over the years new trackways had developed, some for through traffic and some for local farm traffic. The Thomas Jeffreys map of 1770 shows the pre-railway road system, probably much as it would have been found in 1700, except for a marked improvement in the quality of the road surface. On the map you can see all grades of roads in the Parish, from farm tracks, to cross-country roads and to the Watling Street as a principal highway.

It was the introduction of Turnpike Acts in the 18th century that made possible huge improvements to road travel. Up to that time the responsibility had been laid upon the parish, which may have been effective enough for a local road running through the parish, where there was obvious self interest in maintenance, but it was much harder to get cooperation for an arterial road like the Watling Street, where

33 The London Magazine, No. IX, Dec. 1828, p. 585.

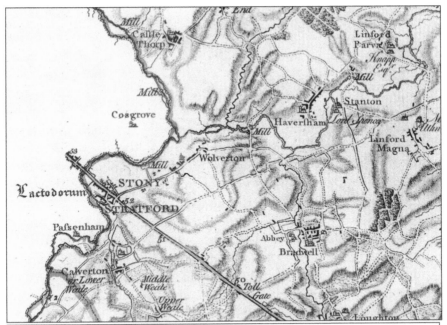

A map from the 1760s by Thomas Jeffreys shows the Watling Street as something more than a track and a toll gate at Two Mile Ash.

small parishes, not unreasonably, could see no advantage in keeping up the road for travellers passing through. Governments tried various coercive measures, with mixed results, but it was not until a "user pay" system, permitted by Turnpike Acts, allowed the collection of tolls to pay for the upkeep of roads that a systematic road maintenance scheme came into being.

The very first of these acts involved Stony Stratford. An act of 1707 formed a Turnpike trust for the section of road between Fornhill (near Hockliffe) and Stony Stratford (a distance of about 15 miles) and was steered through Parliament by Sir John Wittewronge, who owned the manor of Stantonbury. Wittewronge also held estates near Harpenden and had a vested interest in good communication between his two mansions but it says something for the vision of these men in that they were able to understand the importance of a good arterial road. In an age when travel might be measured in days the saving of half a day was considerable. Once the act had been passed, the commissioners, who included men like Browne Willis, the MP from Whaddon Hall, were able to borrow money at 4 per cent annual interest and rebuild and maintain the road to a standard. A scale of charges was set at each toll bar and the income raised was used to pay off the loan and invest further into the maintenance of the roads. We can look back with some surprise that the scheme was successful. There would have been much temptation for the less scrupulous to pocket the proceeds and neglect the roads, but it seems that across the country, various worthy gentlemen took their responsibilities seriously. Through thousands of acts of Parliament in the succeeding years, the road system was brought up to a good standard. Stony Stratford benefited. As the 18th century progressed the engineering of roads improved, so that they became more stable with better drainage.

Toll rates were set to broadly reflect road usage. A coach drawn by four horses was charged 1 shilling, whereas a chaise drawn by a single horse paid only 6d. A horse and rider would only pay 1d. and a pack horse was charged only half that. There were some curious exceptions: a wagon would be charged 1 shilling except if it was laden with grain when the toll was only 6d. Smaller carts only paid 8d. As a rule, animals, which were expected to do less damage to the road, were charged much less. You could move a score of oxen for 6d and the same number of pigs for 3d. Twenty sheep or lambs were assessed at 1 penny.

Toll gates were erected at each end of the Wolverton manor - at the Stony Stratford bridge and at Two Mile Ash. Travellers would encounter another gate at Loughton and then at Fenny Stratford, so any journey that was not locally limited could become expensive.

Nevertheless, the user-pay system worked and eventually built a decent road system throughout the country. The Wolverton to Newport road was turnpiked with a toll gate close to Debb's Barn. Once this bar was set up all commercial movement between Wolverton and Stony Stratford (and there must have been a great deal) was subject to toll. Journeys from Wolverton to Cosgrove by road had to pay two tolls so there was a great incentive to use the track to Wolverton Mill and make the crossing there, toll free of course, which put a great strain on the track and the wooden bridge.

Other mechanical improvements followed the establishment of good road surfaces. Carriages could now be designed with lighter and narrower wheels which could travel at much greater speeds. Wider wheels, which had once been necessary to straddle the ruts in the road could now be discarded.

The other technological improvement was the invention of sprung carriages. Earlier systems, at first developed in Hungary, suspended the carriage on an underframe over the axles with chains. This helped to absorb the shocks of riding on bumpy roads. Over time these chains were replaced with leather, and by the late 17th century these leather straps were held by C shaped springs made from laminated iron. Steel springs a century later made this ride even more comfortable. The twin developments of improved roads and lighter, more comfortable carriages, combined to improve road travel.

By the mid 18th century it was possible to travel from London to Manchester in 4½ days, at an average speed of 5 miles per hour. This gave added importance to Stony Stratford which was now conveniently a day from London and a day from Birmingham. The inns must have enjoyed their heyday in this period and they grew in size and number and the town prospered. Even though there were disastrous fires, particularly the one of 1742, the Inns quickly recovered their trade and the splendidly rebuilt facades of the *Cock*, the *Bull* and the *Three Swans* remain as evidence of their 18th century prosperity.

As the century progressed average speeds doubled and the road system became highly organised. Time was of the essence and "stages" were established along the road so that each coach could be supplied with a team of fresh horses. The journey could continue after a break of only minutes to the next stage. In some respects the ostlers in each innyard were organised like a Formula 1 crew at a pit stop. The horses, once refreshed, let out to pasture, fed and stabled, could then be teamed up on a returning coach.

The road system became even more sophisticated with the development of posting houses. These posting houses were originally established to carry the Royal Mail so that the post boy could pick up a new mount at each house and make reasonable speed to the next house. By the end of the century the system of coaching inns with teams of fresh horses every twenty or so miles meant that average speeds of almost twelve miles per hour became standard on the principal routes.

Before too long it occurred to travellers and innkeepers alike that the same system could be utilised by ordinary travellers. So travellers would in effect rent a horse for each stage of the journey.

Which brings us once again to the premier industry, apart from agriculture, of Wolverton, Calverton and Stony Stratford, the coaching trade. Now that improved roads had placed Stony Stratford at a mere day's journey from London, it assumed a greater importance. The inns which established themselves on both sides of the road can now occupy our attention.

Inns on the Wolverton Side

The major inns developed on the east side, closer to the centre of the town. By the 18th century (and probably earlier) there were five large inns - *The Cock, The Bull, The Three Swans, The Red Lyon* and *The Horseshoe*. Smaller inns, like the *Queen's Head, Drum and Anchor* and the *White Horse*[34] also thrived on the east side bringing the total offering to eight for the 18th century traveller. The *Cock* and the *Bull* are still in business today. The *Three Swans* survives as an 18th century building at Numbers 92-94 High Street. The *Red Lyon* and the *Horseshoe* occupied the land on which St Paul's School was built in the late 19th century, although neither remained in business at the end of the eighteenth century.

The *Cock* may be the oldest and there is some circumstantial and some actual evidence to support this view as was discussed in an earlier chapter. It is interesting to note that throughout the centuries The *Cock* Inn does not get into financial difficulties, which would suggest that outright ownership of the land meant that they never had to find money for rent, or even, at one time, taxes.

The other four inns leased their land from the manor. We do not know when these leases began and we can only deduce dates from records from the late 15th century. The *Swan* was a place of record in 1526 because it was next door to a property owned by Bradwell Priory. This would suggest an earlier establishment.

As the *Bull* rented land from the Radcliffe Trust we can get a clearer idea of the scale of the enterprise from the recorded rents it was paying, first to Sir Edward Longueville and then to the Radcliffe Trust. This document shows us that The Bull was renting about 50

34 This inn, which flourished until 1780, is not the present White Horse on the West Side of the High Street.

acres from the Trust, and while nowhere near as big as the larger farms on the manor, which varied from 200 to 300 acres, appears to be a sizeable land holding and suggests a scale of food production that would be needed to satisfy their guests. The fields, parts of West Rylands and East Rylands and The Leys were all to be found between Stony Stratford and the later Wolverton House. In addition The *Bull* had a close (that is an enclosed field) of four acres at the back of the Inn. For all this the leaseholder paid the Trust £94 per annum. It was a large sum, but only occupied 1/3 to 1/2 of the land occupied by the three main farmers, Richard Wodell, James Brittain and William Swannell, who were paying £270, £210 and £225 respectively. Good agricultural land could generate a large income and was always in those days worth more than buildings. It is a measure of the demand for good pasture for horses and the ability of the inn trade to pay that these premium rates could be charged. In the 1713 Particular of the Manor a Mr. Sanders has the *Bull* and its related fields, although in the following year his name is crossed out and that of William Ayres written in. In the third survey of this set, about three or four years later, Ayres has a lease with 11 years to come, so he may have been given a 15 year lease.

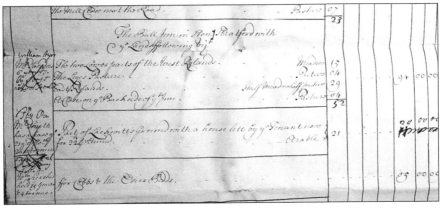

Details of the Bull lease, 1710

The *Horseshoe Inn* had a lease of 74 acres in total in 1713, which gives some idea of the scale of this enterprise. In that year it was held by Matt Eyres and his mother for 40 years, with another 20 to come. The similarity between the names might suggest that William Ayres was from the same family. The *Horseshoe* was known as a wagon inn and tended to specialise in accommodation for wagoners and carters, and would expect to provide stabling and pasture for large numbers of horses. It may have been the 18th century equivalent of a truck stop and it may also explain why it quickly went out of business in the late 18th century after the introduction of canals. After the subsequent creation of railways road haulage was not to make a comeback until the 1950s.

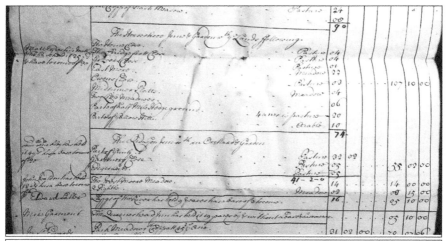

Details of the Horseshoe and Red Lyon leases, 1710

The *Three Swans* was a smaller establishment by comparison. Christopher Carter had the lease of an orchard and gardens at the back of the inn, Lamma Close and part of the Leyes to make up 12 acres. Another 24 acres of pasture leased less conveniently a mile away to the south at Greenleys. The annual rent was £67 14s.

The fifth, but rather lesser inn, the *Red Lyon* was next door to the *Horseshoe*. It was leasing, or had been leasing since 1709 36 acres, 30 of which were in Greenleys. with another 20 years to come on the lease.

The *Queens Head* was also detailed in the Radcliffe Trust document and provides us with some information about the range of services available from Stony Stratford's inns. The *Queen's Head* had no land attached and probably had limited stabling facilities, an observation borne out by the Constables accounts of 1770, which records no horses being stabled at the *Queen's Head*. In 1713 it was leased to

Michael Garment and, fortunately for our ability to assess continuity, he was still there when licensing records began in 1753. A few years later it was licensed to Mary Garment, presumably his widow, and subsequently to John Payne in 1769. A year later John Payne changed the name to the *Hare and Hounds.*

Michael Garment paid £5 10s annually to rent this property. There was no land attached. To help us understand this valuation, the mill was valued at £3 10s., The *Bull* at £37 5s., the *Three Swans* at £19 4s 6d., the *Horseshoe* at £30 10s., and the *Red Lyon* at £9 12s 6d. All of these values exclude any rental paid for land. This tells us that the *Queen's Head* was by far the smallest of the inns on the east side.

Its actual location is not obvious from the documents but it would seem reasonable to suppose that, as the northern sites had been claimed, it was at the southern end of town. It may have been on the site now occupied by the Retreat, and possibly used the name *The Gate* at an earlier date. The *Queen's Head* doesn't get mentioned until the 18th century so this chronology can work.

The last name to mention is this section is The *Nags Head.* At a rent of 17 shillings a year it was probably little more than an alehouse. It is impossible to place the *Nags Head.* When regular licensing records emerge forty years later there is no such name, but it is possible that it continued its business under another name. It is equally possible that if it was destroyed by fire in 1742 and never rebuilt as an alehouse.

The other inns on this side, the *Drum and Anchor* and the *White Horse* were on land sold off by the Longuevilles and do not appear in surviving records.

Naturally enough, there were and are inns on the west side of the road, but because there are no surviving records that go into as much detail the picture is less clear.

There were at least four mid-sized inns (if they can be so characterised) on the west side of the High Street - The *George*, an inn on the site of the present *White Horse,* the *Talbot* and an inn on the site of the Cross Keys. The *Globe*, which may have been an alehouse, was just to the north of Church Street. We can only name the *George* and the *Talbot* with certainty. In addition the Square had started to open up to the inn trade in the late 17th century as traffic increased and prime High Street locations became limited. The *Crown* and the *King's*

Head date from this period and both seem to have had an extensive yard of an acre or two.

There were also, and had been since the 16th century, a larger number of smaller inns and alehouses. We know some names and in some cases locations, but they are difficult to classify. Mostly they were alehouses in character although they may have offered limited accommodation, There is a remarkable collection of names. As well as the names listed above, you could have encountered the *Black Boy*, the *Rowbuck Inn*, the *Nag's Head*, the *White Horse*, the *Ship*, the *Angel*, the *Gate*, the *Bell*, the *Crown* - all on the East side. On the Calverton side of the street was the *Swan with Two Necks*, the *Valiant Trooper*, and in the Square, the *Plough*, the *White Lion*, the *Crooked Billet*, the *Fighting Cocks*, the *Bell*, the *Green Dragon*, the *Silent Woman*.

Stony Stratford in the 18ᵗʰ Century

The sale of the manor to Dr John Radcliffe in 1713 was an important juncture for Wolverton. While various lots, such as those occupied by the *Cock* and the *Rose and Crown*, had been sold off over the years, a considerable number of buildings on the east side of the High Street still remained under the control of the Manor, and it is due to this sale and transfer of ownership we have some surviving records, in some detail, of these properties.

The *Horseshoe* Inn, the waggoners inn, had different needs from the others. They leased three adjacent closes totalling nine acres, meadow lands near the river totalling 32 acres, and a further 30 acres of mostly arable land in the Gallows Hill area. For this they paid £107 10s annually.

The *Red Lyon*, next door to the *Horseshoe*, had an orchard and garden, but had to go some distance for pasture. They leased 30 acres in Greenleys and 5 acres in Gardeners close on the corner where the *Plough* now stands, and another 5 acres at Edy's Leyes. All horses that were not stabled would have to be led up the High Street daily. The annual lease costs amounted to £55 2s.

The landholdings of some of the inns show that they were organisations of some complexity. The horse, for those who could afford it, was the only way to travel at speed. Cartage was entirely dependent on horse-drawn vehicles. The scattering of additional pasture for the main inns in these documents must also be an indicator of the increase in travel. The medieval inns could make do with the close attached to their property. Their 18th century successors had to lease land as far away as Greenleys.

Foot travellers (and there must have been many) could stay at such inns as the *Queens Head* which had no facilities for horses.

There are a number of inn names in the 17th century which get mentioned in leases - the *Bell* (1625), the *Rowbuck* Inn (1642), the *Crown* Inn (1654) may have been the same establishment as one or both of the previous two names. The names of inns changed, although the property did not. It seems best to put this interpretation on this. There must have been a limit, even for Stony Stratford, to the number of inns it could sustain at any one time.

The *Rose and Crown* was due, under the terms of Michael Hipwell's will, to build a schoolhouse at the back in 1708. This was duly created, although the exact date of its institution is not clear. What is also unclear is whether or not the *Rose and Crown* continued to function as an inn. My reading of the will (and I am open to challenge on this) is that it was the intention that income from the inn would support the schoolmaster for the school.[35] If so it is fair to assume that an inn was continuing to function here in the 18th century. Under what sign is unknown, but it was certainly not the *Rose and Crown*.

The Great Fire of 1742

These road improvements introduced a period of rising prosperity for Stony Stratford and the relatively large number of inns in the town by the mid-century appears to affirm this. In 1742 disaster struck. A great fire destroyed most the the Wolverton side of the High Street.

Fire was an ever present hazard until quite recent times. Cooking was done over open fires and even chimneys were a late medieval development. Buildings were made of combustible material and the ability to put fires out once started was limited. Fire was a common enough occurrence in Stony Stratford

Records are scarce and for the most part do not exist before the development of newspapers in the 18th century. There is a brief record

---

35 An earlier version of his will, dated 1603, records the income from the Rose and Crown at £5 a year. This would have been just about enough to support a poor schoolmaster.

in the Radcliffe Trust papers of a fire at the *Horseshoe* in 1703. More detail is to be discovered in the Quarter Sessions records held in Aylesbury on June 13th 1703, where the Widow Eyre made application for permission to seek charitable donations to help sustain the losses experienced by the people staying there. In 1703 a system of covering such losses through insurance had yet to be devised, although in the years after this such a mechanism came into being, so that anyone with the bad luck to lose their possessions through fire often had to depend on public charity.

The Widow Eyre submitted a tally for the losses which amounted to a staggering sum of £666 18s 11 1/2d. The inn itself was destroyed but the fire had spread to other houses consuming "thirty Bayes of Building". A house might contain from three to five bays, that is a section divided by a post, so the loss was between six and ten houses. These losses were included within this total.[36]

Another fire was reported in June 1729.[37] Early on Tuesday Morning a Fire broke out in the Stable of an Inn in Stony Stratford, which destroy'd the House and most of the Furniture, as also six Waggon Horses, five Pack Horses, and a considerable quantity of Carriers Goods.

The name of the inn is not recorded but from the description it sounds like the *Horseshoe*, which was the premier inn for the wagon trade. It does appear to have been contained. There is no report of its spreading to other dwellings. However, it was this fire that prompted the Radcliffe Trust to take out insurance on the four major inns - *The Bull, The Swan, The Red Lyon* and *The Horseshoe* - for a total annual premium of £3 12s. 6d. It was a wise precaution. The tiled buildings were covered for £1,251 and the thatched buildings for £450 1s each. These were high premiums, but necessary as the Sun Fire office faced a large payout in 1742.

Stony Stratford now experienced two great fires, within 6 years of each other and between the two most of medieval Stony Stratford was destroyed and what we now see as characteristic of Stony Stratford's architecture, the imposing appearance of the 18th century facades on the east side of Stony Stratford, comes entirely from this period. The

---

36 Buckinghamshire Quarter Sessions, June 13th 1703.
37 Derby Mercury, June 19th 1729.

1742 fire became known as the "Great Fire of Stony Stratford" and was indeed sensational, but before I come to describe what happened we should perhaps realise that it was only unique in its size. Fire, as already illustrated, appears to have been common.

In 1736 an accidental fire brought the loss of 53 houses, mainly on Church Lane. That is the extent of the record. The fire may have taken out an inn on the High Street, possibly the *Globe*, and if this was the case it was certainly never rebuilt as an inn. Six years later there was a much bigger fire and we have a reported account from the Northampton Mercury of May 1st 1742.

The fire originated at The *Bull* Inn with a servant girl who was drying sheets before the fire place. One of them caught fire and

Fire insurance became a prudent necessity in Stony Stratford and most insurance companies ha an agent in the town. In the 18th and 19th centuries and insured property was marked by a sign such as the one above, which still survives in Stony Stratford toaday.

instead of smothering it, she panicked and stuffed the sheet up the chimney, hoping not to be found out by her mistress. This action compounded her problems. The chimney caught fire and then the roof. There was also a high wind on this day and the fire leapt from one building to another, not simply on the one side of the High Street, but also crossing the street, hitting a thatched roof on the other side and relentlessly catching other houses in its destructive path.

The church of St Mary Magdalene, built about 1280, was completely destroyed. It was never rebuilt, apart from the Tower, which the MP Browne Willis generously funded. There may have been good intentions to rebuild the church but the initial enthusiasm probably melted away when the citizens of Stony Stratford discovered that two churches was a redundancy and that St. Giles (an enlarged St. Giles) was adequate for their needs.

The paper also reported that the fire crossed the River Ouse and even caught some houses in Old Stratford with airborne fiery debris. 146 buildings were destroyed in total.

The precaution of insurance allowed the inns to rebuild and resume their trade during the boom years of coach travel. The rebuilding must have been very swift because on January 18th 1743 another fire was reported near the *Bull* Inn in Stony Stratford.[38] The mention of the *Bull* in the *Northampton Mercury* would indicate that it was back in operation at that date. This fire burned four houses to the ground before it could be extinguished. In the same week stables and outbuildings belonging to the Duke of Grafton were burnt, killing a large number of animals. That fire, it was reported, was thought to have been started by deer stealers.

In 1750, the *Bull* was advertising a concert. Business had clearly returned to its normal flow. By the mid century the appearance of Stony Stratford High Street took on the form that we recognise today. The *Three Swans* went out of business in 1782 and was converted into private residence. These 18th century buildings still stand proud on the High Street. The *Lyon and Horseshoe*, which closed down in 1796, was replaced in the 19th century by St Paul's School.

The *Cock* and The *Bull*, now hotels, both retain their Georgian facades and stand almost side by side in the centre of Stony Stratford.

_____

38 Northampton Mercury, Jan. 18th 1743.

Between them they dominated the coaching trade up to the arrival of the railway. They were both posting houses, that is, they were part of the network of inns which maintained teams of horses for quick changeover when the stage coaches arrived going north and south. Speed was becoming important and a team of horses could be changed in minutes so that the coach could continue, sometimes with average speeds of twelve miles an hour. Since the census records do not begin until 1841, when the railways were becoming dominant, it is impossible to estimate accurately the number of people in the employ of these two great hotels. One would guess at a team of ostlers and stable boys working round the clock as well as a complement of kitchen staff, chambermaids and serving staff at each establishment.

It would not take much imagination to realise the great rivalry between the two and we should perhaps consider whether the phrase "a Cock and Bull Story" had its origins in Stony Stratford.

A Cock and Bull Story

Almost side by side in the centre of Stony Stratford and almost the same in size and appearance, the *Cock* and the *Bull* are prominent features of the town. Whatever their origins, by the 17th century they were, with the exception of the *Horseshoe*, the two largest inns in the town, and since the *Horseshoe* was mainly an inn for wagoners, the *Cock* and the *Bull* had the quality trade between them. It is noticeable, for example, in the records of military billeting in 1770 that the officers stay either at the *Cock* or the *Bull*, but nowhere else.

The phrase "a cock and bull story" is usually applied to a story which is slightly preposterous or fanciful, a bit of a tall tale. It has certainly slipped into common language. Where did it come from? The truth is that nobody knows how the phrase came into being. Local legend certainly has it that the rivalry extended to the telling of traveller's tales, bragging rights going to the Inn that could boast the most entertaining tales. Naturally this encouraged the tellers of "tall tales" which may have started with a vestige of truth but ended with something so fanciful as to be implausible. Thus the phrase "Cock and Bull story" came to be applied to any story that you might doubt the truth of - "That's a bit of a Cock and Bull Story!"

The cock, as a figure in story telling, has a very old tradition. It

The Bull, above, and the Cock Hotel, below, as they appear today. They were borth rebuilt as they largely appear today after a disastrous fire in 1742, which originated at the Bull.

features in Chaucer and other medieval writers. Usually the tales were told in a comic tradition so the cock is never a serious figure. The bull scarcely has a literary pedigree other than perhaps the minotaur of myth and tends to be seen as a dangerous and threatening animal - not material for comedy.

Therefore the first written reference to a cock and a bull in the same sentence is found in a book entitled The *Anatomy of Melancholy* by Robert Burton written in 1621:

> Some men's whole delight is to take tobacco, and drink all day long in a tavern or alehouse, to discourse, sing, jest, roar, talk of a Cock and Bull over a pot.[39]

This does not take us very far, other than to discover the words cock and bull in the same sentence. Burton may simply offer these as examples of trivial subjects. The reference may have a sporting connotation in the context of cock fighting and bull fighting. Another quotation, about the same time, from the water poet, John Taylor:

> Wit and Mirth ... Made up, and fashioned into Clinches, Bulls, Quirkes, Yerkes, Quips, and Jerkes.[40]

The word "bull" here seems to mean a joke or jest.

So it is hard to come to a definite opinion on the matter. The Burton quotation, while within the period of travelling and staying at Inns, and when both Stony Stratford Inns were certainly in business, tells us that men are telling stories about cocks and bulls rather than in the *Cock* or the *Bull*. The explanation for the origin of the Cock and Bull Story does appear to be a concoction. It is quite possible that a tale overheard in the Bull would be repeated, with embellishments in the Cock later, but to suggest that people went back and compared notes as it were and decided that the original tale was a monstrous fabrication appears fanciful.

Why would this version develop? Why are there no George and Falcon stories, or White Lion and Red Lion stories, or White Horse and Black Horse stories? Admittedly these do not trip off the tongue and easily as Cock and Bull, but the notion that only people in the Cock and Bull in Stony Stratford made up such stories does stretch credibility.

In the days of speedy coaching services at the beginning of the 19th century, when Stony Stratford was a mere day's journey from London, these two great hotels would have enjoyed some fame throughout the land. The phrase "cock and bull story" had that kind of recognition. In time the phrase slipped into common usage and people forgot where it came from even though it did not stop them from using the

---

39 Robert Burton. The Anatomy of Melancholy, Part 2, 1621.
40 Title of book written by John Taylor, 1580-1653.

phrase.

For example you can often hear today the phrase "level playing field". Nowadays all football playing fields are absolutely flat, but two generations ago some professional football fields had a distinct slope giving an advantage to the side which was kicking downhill. Nevertheless the phrase is in common use, although no longer applied to football. Room to swing a cat is still in use hundreds of years after flogging with a cat of nine tails was banned from the navy.

There are those who argue that the phrase does not have its origin in Stony Stratford. They may be right, but why spoil a good story?

Highwaymen

The age of the highwayman tends to be associated with the 18th century, partly because improved roads and increased travel offered greater pickings to the criminal but also because of the enduring fame of Dick Turpin.

The semi-legendary Dick Turpin became the most famous of all highwaymen and the phrase "Stand and deliver!" became embedded in the language. He did exist. He was baptised in 1705 in Hempstead in Essex and hanged at York for theft 7th April 1739. He was the son of an innkeeper and butcher, John Turpin, who maintained the *Blue Bell* Inn at Hempstead in Essex. He was most likely apprenticed to the butcher's trade and some say he worked at Whitechapel, at that time a village outside London. He married and on completion of his apprenticeship opened his own butcher's shop at Buckhurst Hill in Essex. In the 1730s he became associated with a gang of deer poachers and this led on to his life of crime. The authorities succeeded in

breaking up the gang in 1735 but Turpin eluded capture and turned his hand to highway robbery. He appeared to be adept at evading capture and often his associates were apprehended while he made good his escape. After his last escape in May 1737 he hid in Epping Forest, but he was seen by one of the forest keepers, one

Thomas Morris. Turpin shot Morris dead and had to flee.

He seems to have gone north to Yorkshire where he lived for a while under the alias of John Palmer. Eventually he attracted suspicion because his income had no identifiable legitimate source and he was exposed. He was tried for horse stealing, then a capital offence, and hanged at York.

Some contemporary literature was published, of the penny dreadful type, and to a certain extent he became famous. There is little in these accounts which is actual fact.

It was however a 19th century novelist, W.H. Ainsworth, who created the romantic figure that has held popular imagination. The legendary ride overnight on Black Bess outrunning the authorities who were hot on his trail is not only pure fiction, it is physically impossible. The journey is 200 miles and no horse, however fabled, could do it.

The power of the legend inevitably draws him into a tale about Stony Stratford. According to this story Dick Turpin was staying at an inn, possibly the *Talbot*, when word comes that the authorities are on their way. After some quick thinking the landlord winched Turpin and his horse up into the roof or loft while the authorities searched the place. Once they were gone he was able to go on his way.

The same story is probably told at many inns across the land but the tale loses none of its character by changing the location. Its only interest to us today is that it is almost certainly untrue. Even if this may have happened there is no evidence that Turpin ever came this far west. His sphere of operation was north-east London, Essex and the Great North Road.

Highway robbery was not a new phenomenon in the 18th century. For as long as there were travellers on the road there were villains ready to relieve them of any wealth they were carrying.

William Shakespeare wrote some scenes in his play *Henry IV Part 1* portraying a highway robbery by Falstaff and his drinking friends. Putting aside the comedy of the scene, it was rooted in a growing phenomenon of highway robbery in late Elizabethan times. As trade increased so did the amount of commercial traffic on the road and as we have already seen from the number of innholders in Stony Stratford in 1577, road traffic must have increased since the middle ages. The very real risk to travellers meant that merchants preferred to travel in groups so that they could ward off attacks from potential robbers along the highway. The lone highwayman, the Dick Turpin type, mounted on a horse with a brace of pistols to command hapless travellers to "Stand and deliver!" was a future development. In fact the word highwayman had not been coined at this stage in history.

In fact, as the following stories will show, highway robbers were nasty and vicious characters indeed.

Some notes in the papers of Henry Montagu who was sitting as a justice in Northamptonshire in 1596, more-or-less contemporaneous with Shakespeare's play illustrate the growing problem and are specific to Stony Stratford.

In this letter, dated 14th December 1596. Montagu had just been sitting at an assize in Northampton where amongst other judgements he had ordered several executions and one man to be pressed to death, These are his notes about Stony Stratford:[41]

> Greatehead, an innkeeper in Stonistratford, a bad fellow and a common receiver, a notable bad fellow.
>
> Thomas Car, an innkeeper of Stonistratford, another receiver, and acquainted with this examinate's lewd conditions.
>
> Thomas Murfoote, a high lawyer, a robber by the highway, a guest at Greatehead's house, and sometimes comes to the Cock in Tocester.

Here were at least two innkeepers from Stony Stratford who were acting as receivers of stolen goods. They were probably in a position to effect a quick sale. Greatehead is considered by Montagu as a "notable bad fellow" which meant that he had a well-known bad reputation. The inn he kept in Stony Stratford is unknown but it is unlikely to have been one of the more reputable inns. He probably kept an alehouse and for a time kept himself a finger away from the strong arm of the law. It must have been attractive to highway robbers who could commit their robbery and quickly dispose of their goods through a "fence". Stony Stratford, just across the river, may have been an attractive place for robbers operating between Old Stratford and Towcester; they could quickly make their escape across the river out of the reach of the Northamptonshire authorities while they disposed

41 Hist. MSS. Com. i, 232. MSS of Duke of Buccleuch, Montagu House.

of their goods. It is a pity that neither Greathead nor Carr are to be found on the alehouse keepers list of nineteen years earlier, nor Mompesson's accounts of 1619, because we could then identify them with a house, but no doubt, given their inclination to criminal activity, they did not last long in the inn-keeping trade.

Thomas Murfoote, who is named here, appears to have operated between Stony Stratford and the *Cock* at Towcester. The phrase "high lawyer" is unusual but I would take it to mean a "High road Law breaker." As remarked earlier, the word highwayman had yet to be invented.

Apart from legend, Stony Stratford, or more particularly the road, attracted a number of nasty characters. In January 1729 one Samuel Adams of Towcester was in court to confess his part in a series of grisly crimes. His accomplice Edward Branson, who was apparently an extremely vicious character, was still at large. Adams confessed his part in a series of crimes, presumably hoping to get away with a lighter sentence than his murderous partner. On the 7th January they, or rather Branson, attacked Philip Bevins a gardener from Stony Stratford while he was walking his horse along the road. Branson first attacked him with a heavily weighted stick to knock him down and then proceeded to thwack him about the head until he died. The two men then emptied his pockets of 26 shillings, which they shared. Bevins skull was fractured in eight places, which will give some idea of the intensity of the attack. Adams also confessed earlier crimes. One of stealing a horse from Little Linford which he then sold to an innkeeper in London. The other, also involving Branson, was an attack on a Calverton Farmer, Daniel Hix from whom they stole £3 17s 6d. After they robbed him, Branson went back to give him some more blows so that he would not be able to talk and they left him for dead. Fortunately Hix survived to give evidence.[42]

Some of these characters ranged over some distance. William Calcot, originally from Oxfordshire robbed a jeweller between Stony Stratford and Towcester one night and ended up with quite a haul. He was apprehended in Worcestershire in October 1739 for a series of violent robberies with his then partner John Jeffreys. It was only then that the Stony Stratford crime was solved as the authorities discovered

42 Stamford Mercury 30 Jan 1729

his loot. His Worcestershire crimes were particularly violent and this led to the hue and cry which caught him. Calcott was armed with a hanger (a kind of short sword) and he did not hesitate to use it, leaving one Stratford upon Avon farmer seriously wounded and an Alcester farmer on the brink of death.[43]

On the other hand some crimes were not solved. In September 1742 the murder of a Mr Collins a wholesale button seller from Macclesfield was reported. He was found murdered and robbed in a ditch by the road between Stony and Fenny. There were no clues about the assailant. "The most diligent Enquiry after the Authors of this Tragedy has hitherto been ineffectual."

But sometime the authorities got lucky. In April 1745 somebody recognised Henry Poorman, a noted highwayman, and tipped off the authorities. On his arrest they found a brace of pistols in his pocket and he was sent to Aylesbury Gaol under armed guard.[44]

Newspapers continued to report robberies near Stony Stratford. The stretch of road around Shenley seems to have been a favourite place for attack as the road was uninhabited.

Northampton Mercury October 1st 1774

> On Thursday last, about six in the Morning, was found in the High Road between Shenly and Stony Stratford by two Men going to Work, the Body of one James Wills, a poor industrious Man, most barbarously murdered. He belongs to Woolverton, near Stony Stratford, and had been to a Statute held near Fenny Stratford selling Nuts and Cakes. His head was so terribly beat and bruised by a Slate of a Stake Rail, that on moving him his Brains dropp'd out. He has left a Wife and seven children. Diligent Search is making after the Murderers.

Some spirited characters took it upon themselves to apprehend criminals and were not shy of taking final action if need be. This reports from the London Caledonian Mercury, 2nd July 1766 makes for interesting reading:

Letter from a Gentleman at Coventry, June 25th

---

43 Stamford Mercury 25th Oct 1739.
44 Stamford Mercury 18 April 1745

"The account of the officer being robbed on the Towcester road was as follows. I happened to pass soon after and saw the dead body:

"On the Thursday the officer was riding alone between Towcester and Stony Stratford; the highwayman attacked him and robbed him of seventeen guineas; the Captain immediately galloped away to Stratford, hired a couple of post horses, and a boy to accompany him and went in pursuit of the highwayman; he overtook a clergyman on the road who agreed very readily to accompany him; they soon overtook the fellow, when the clergyman called out several times to him to surrender, which he swore he would not do, and was getting out one of his pistols to fire at him, when the post boy, who rode almost even with him, desired the parson to fire, otherwise, he said, the fellow would shoot one of them; accordingly he did so, and shot him in the back; he rode a few yards, and then fell off his horse dead. He swore, when he set off in pursuit of him, that he would have him dead or alive."

The unnamed clergyman in this account was the Rector of Tingewick, Mr. Risley and the soldier Captain Fleming who was apparently robbed near Potterspury. These further details come from the notes of the Rev. W. Cole, the Bletchley historian, who made notes about the affair as was reported to him.

Two further reports from the Northampton Mercury later in the century tell us that the problem did not go away.

Northampton Mercury 2nd March 1778

Dennis Ryan, charged on the Oath of Thomas Kelly, with having beat him on the Turnpike-Road, between Shenly and Stony-Stratford, and robbing him of one Guinea, ten Shillings, a few Halfpence, two Farthings and a thread Purse.

Northampton Mercury Monday 18th August 1783

Last Monday evening, between Nine and Ten o'Clock, as William Haddon of Pisford in this County was travelling between Stony-Stratford and Brickhill in Buckinghamshire, with a Team, he was knock'd down by two Men, who beat him in a cruel Manner, and rifled his Pockets of 8 Guineas and a

Half in Gold, between 3 and 4 Pounds in Silver, and his Watch - Makers Name Hemmen.

As the century progressed the authorities got the roads under better control. Improvements in road surfaces helped because travellers were able to move at a faster pace and as more people started to use the roads it became harder for highwaymen to make a getaway.

These factors, the increase in travellers on the road and the faster speed of travel, tended to diminish the number of highway robberies. It became less easy to effect the robbery and make a getaway without being spotted by other travellers coming up the road, and as the above example of the energetic clergyman illustrates, the consequence could be final for the highway robber.

Military Movement

The military were also great road users and if we remind ourselves that the original purpose of the road was to aid troop movement, it should not surprise us that the military continued to use the road.

Anglo Saxon and feudal armies were based on volunteer tradition of men coming forward for military service when required. Tenancy of the land, at all levels of society, was tied to a certain number of days of military service. In the later middle ages, these expectations of so many days of military service were excused by payment and mercenaries were hired instead. Some soldiers became professional in the 14th century by hiring themselves out as mercenaries. The concept of a professional standing army was a long time coming. It started with Cromwell's new Model Army, but only became an institutional part of government when Charles II came to the throne in 1660. The amateur aspect was not completely lost and men were conscripted into service and discarded when no longer required.

As another indication of its fledgling status the British professional army had little equipment of its own and had to requisition carts, horses, stabling and lodging as required. Stony Stratford's position on the Watling Street meant that many soldiers passed through, not that they were always welcome:

"Ye lowsy red-coat rake hells, ye locusts of the nation, you are dogs that would enslave us, plunder our shops and ravish our daughters, ye scoundrels"[45]

The reasons behind the practice of billeting on the local populace were three-fold; firstly the bureaucracy of the modern nation state army was in its infancy and had not yet developed the resources to cope with a barracks building programme of any scale. Similarly, at least in England, the idea of the monarch's standing army, such as held by Cromwell, was seen as a sign of tyrannical and autocratic rule. Barracks were seen as an embodiment of this threat upon English men's hard won civil liberties. Finally the main role of the army was to maintain and restore public order, suppress riots and crush civilian insurrection. By dispersing the army around the country the government had a potential company of men at hand not only as a deterrent but also as a reactionary force in every local area. Billeting troops as they moved across the country became common in the 18th century and the parish twas required to keep accounts and reclaim payment from the government. This has left us a valuable record. They are tantalisingly incomplete. The constable on the east side, who was responsible for this tally, has these records from 1770 to 1778. The equivalent book on the west side does not show these accounts. Either this job was entrusted to one other official or the record was separately kept and did not survive.

However the Constable's book for 1770 gives us some useful numbers which if nothing else tell us the relative size of the inns at that date and may even help us to determine their location.

As one would expect the established inns like the Horseshoe, the Three Swans, the Cock and the Bull were able to take the lion's share of the men and horses, with the smaller inns taking men only.

The billeting figures do help us to understand the size and scope of the various inns down the High Street. The Constable's Book of 1770 records in tabular form the numbers carried over from a lost record book. The Red Lyon and Horseshoe list 154 men and 204 horses, the Three Swans 137 men and 161 horses, the Drum and Anchor 44 men, the Cock 139 men and 168 horses, the Bull 149 men and 201 horses, the White Horse 41 men, the Red Lyon 41 men and the Hare and Hounds (formerly the Queen's Head) 38 men. The remainder of the year, which appears to go to Easter, as the last entry is April

---

45 Thomas Otway. The Sooldier's Fortune. Act I, scene i.

13th, record entries each time a group of militia come through. They appear to be distributed amongst the inns according to availability of beds. For example on January 14th 1771, the Bull takes 3, the Cock 4, the Three Swans 4, the Horseshoe 4. No horses were stabled so one assumes that the men were on foot. On May 22nd however, there was a lot of movement: the Bull accommodated 7 men and 15 horses, the Cock 5 men and 10 horses, the Three Swans 5 men and 10 horses, the Lyon and Horseshoe 6 men and 12 horses, the Drum and Anchor 2 men with another 2 men were billeted at the White Horse. What is evident from these random samples is that only the larger inns had stabling and pasture and the smaller inns, such as the White Horse and the Queen's Head were only used when the larger inns were full.

A summary page from the Constable's Book of 1770, showing the number of soldiers and horses billetted at the East side inns.

One other piece of information that comes from the accounts is the possible location of some of the inns. One tally in the Constable's Book appears to list the inns from North to South, and since we know the locations of some, this may help us to determine the approximate site of the others. The *Red Lyon and Horseshoe, Drum and Anchor, Three Swans, Cock, Bull, White Horse, Red Lyon and Hare and Hounds* are recorded from north to south, a if in order. It is therefore tempting to interpret the establishment at Number 32, known as the *White Swan* in the 19th and 20th centuries, as the site of the *White Horse*, for a period known as the *Ship*. The *Hare and Hounds*, which had only just changed its name in 1770 from the *Queen's Head*, was most likely on the site of the retreat. This was Radcliffe Trust property and leases are on record to Michael Garment who held the property for a good part of the early 18th century. This leaves the Red Lion somewhere in between. It is tempting to consider the Rose and Crown as this address. It was known as an inn in the previous century and it had been in private hands since the 16th century. The licensee for this new Red Lion, John Kingston, is first recorded in 1766. A few years later the licensee was Francis Kingston, possibly his son. In 1776 John Davis took over the license and his last license was taken out in September 1781. After this date the Red Lion is never heard of again.

This house was newly built in 1820 when it opened as The Swan. Later in the century it changed the name to the White Swan. The arrangement of the yard would indicate that there was an earlier inn on this property, possibly known as the Ship and then the White Horse, which closed in 1772.

Soldiers as temporary residents no doubt brought a set of social problems with them, They were men who were rough and tough whose only allegiance was to their paymaster, and even that at sometimes was doubtful. Desertion was a problem, although by no means confined to Stony Stratford. The Constable's book records and expenditure of 4d in 1771 on a bundle of straw to lay in the Cage for 9 deserters. The Cage was a secure lock-up on the Square which actually survived until 1862 when the Police station was built. On Monday 23rd September

1776 the Northampton Mercury posted a reward for the capture of one James Biddel who had deserted in Stony Stratford. James Biddel, colourfully described here as "carbuncle-faced", enlisted (took the King's shilling) on September 5th and deserted in Stony Stratford on the 20th. I presume that after 15 days he found the military life much less appealing than it must have seemed on the 5th of September.

> DESERTED from Captain Hamilton's Recruiting-Party, belonging to the 14th Regiment of Foot, at Stony-Stratford, Bucks, on the 20th September, 1776, JAMES BIDDEL, aged 27 Years, five Feet seven Inches 3-qrs. High, swarthy Complexion, lank black Hair, Carbuncle-faced, strait and stout made, born in the Parish of Kingston in the County of Somerset, by Trade a Gardener, insisted at Northampton the 5th inst. had on, when he went away, an old dark-blue Coat, brown Waistcoat, dirty linen Breeches, a new pair of Pumps, and a black silk Handkerchief about his Neck.

> Whoever secures the above-said Deserter, in any of His Majesty's Gaols, and gives Notice thereof to Captain Hamilton, or to Messrs Ross and Gray, Agents to the said regiment, in Conduit Street, London, shall receive TWENTY SHILLINGS, over and above what is allow'd by Act of Parliament for apprehending Deserters.

The costs to the town of travellers who had no money was not insignificant and presumably was born by taxes raised from tradesmen, not least innkeepers. In some cases there was some urgency in getting them out of town. In 1791 the charity paid a woman 1s 6d to move on because her child had small pox, and in the same year paid 2s 6d to a heavily pregnant woman "that was near to her time of lying." In 1799 they "gave the woman with 4 children to go on, two of the children being ill" 1s 6d and paid a further 1s to a waggoner to convey them. As heartless as this may sound, in an age when there was no national system of supporting the poor, the needy and the infirm, and where everything fell on the Parish, it was cheaper to move these people on rather than incur the expense of midwives or doctors or even burials.

There were some events that could not be forestalled. Here is a curious report from Northampton Mercury Saturday 19th May 1792.

> On Saturday last, another inquisition was taken at Stony

Stratford before the same Coroner, on view the body of William Pearson, a traveller, who died suddenly as he was sitting in the chimney-corner at the coach-and-horses public house in that town. - Verdict, That he died by the visitation of God.

The former 18th century inn known as the Drum and Anchor. In 1792 it changed its name to the Coach and Horses. There may have been an inn on this site prior to the fire of 1742 and there are 17th century records of a Blue Anchor.

The Coach and Horses, now a dental clinic at 106 High Street, was an old inn and has probably witnessed many bizarre incidents before this one. I assume that the man died of a heart attack, but 200 years ago they were content to describe it as a "visitation of God." The Parish bore the cost of the Coroner's inquest and his burial unless someone from the family came forward.

The practice of moving troops and armaments up and down Stony Stratford's High Street continued until the by pass road was built and passage through the High Street was no longer necessary. In the post-WWII period convoys of, mostly American troops, moved up and down the High Street. As we noted at the beginning, the road was built for military movement and the development of Stony Stratford came out of that. Accommodation for men and horses and provisioning for both turned Stony Stratford into a natural stopping place for medieval kings and magnates moving their retinues up and down the country. The practice of billeting soldiers at Stony Stratford inns continued up to the railway age.

Waggon Trade

The speedy mail coaches were at the glamorous end of the business. Just as important however was the carriage of goods and as the 18th century entered its long period of rising prosperity the carriage of goods across the country grew in importance. England was beginning to move towards a more complex manufacturing economy where goods could be manufactured in one place and transported and sold somewhere else. The local, almost entirely self-sufficient peasant economy of the middle ages had given way to something rather different.

St Paul's School, later Mr. Fegan's Orphanage, was built on the site of the former Horseshoe and Red Lyon in the 19th century.

Daniel Defoe, best known for Robinson Crusoe and an inveterate traveller himself, made this observation at the beginning of the 18th century:

> Suppose the poorest countryman wants to be clothed, or suppose it be a gentleman who wants to clothe one of his

servants...he shall, in some part, employ almost every one of the manufacturing counties of England, for making up one ordinary suit of clothes...Come next to the furniture of [a country grocer's] house; it is scarce credible to how many counties of England, and how remote, the furniture of but a mean house must send them.[46]

Pivotal to this distribution was the carrier. Carriers worked the sea routes and rivers but at some point the burden would need to be transported by road. Hence Stony Stratford provided for the carrier trade and in one instance specialised in it. The Horseshoe in particular was the waggon stop. Waggoners might have up to six horses which would need stabling, feeding and rested in pasture and the Horseshoe leased quite a large acreage of land for this purpose.

Waggons made no better time than two miles an hour, including rests, so theoretically a journey from London to Stony Stratford could be achieved in two days, if the wagons kept rolling for twelve hours a day. In practice, and especially during the shorter days of the winter months, this was impractical and it was more likely to have been a three day journey.

The carriers of the day were often depicted as rough characters, usually wearing a heavy overcoat and a wide-brimmed hat to keep the sun off their faces, and often accompanied by a vicious breed of dog. Of necessity they had to be tough. As we have seen in the section on highway robbery, the carriers were vulnerable and needed to be prepared. It is likely too that they preferred to stay with their fellow carriers at the Horseshoe rather than at the more genteel Cock, for example.

West Side

The west side has had less attention up to now due to a scarcity of ancient records, but there is no reason to suppose that the west side of the street did not develop an inn trade of long standing. The *George* dates certainly from the early 17th century and most likely was operating in the 16th century. One might predict that the site of the *White Horse*, next door to the church, is at least as old a foundation as

---

46 Carolyn Dougherty. The culture of carrying in the long 18th century. Leeds, March 2013.

the *Cock* and *Bull* opposite, and although there is no evidence for this it seems to be the right intuitive judgement. One deed which survives from the reign of Henry VIII tells of a transaction of a burgage plot on the Calverton side, lying between the burgage late of Richard Barton and the inn called *The Key*. The plot abuts Watling Street and stretches to the Market Square so one could deduce from this that the inn stood on the site of the present *White Horse*.[47] This may also be the St Peter's Keys to which Markham makes reference, rather than the *Cross Keys* site further to the north. The *Cross Keys* may well be a later name.

The George was built in the early 17th century and in 300 years the road has risen by 2 feet. It is the best living example in Stony Stratford of an inn of the period.

The 1577 list of inn holders name for the west side number five, so on the basis of later knowledge we might infer the sites of the *George*, the *White Horse*, the *Talbot and* the *Cross Keys*. Each of these sites had inn yards in later centuries. A fifth inn might have been found on the site of the *Rising Sun*, for similar reasons.

As we have seen from discussion of the development of the Market Square several inns came to life in the 17ᵗʰ century and thrived into the 19th century.

---

47 See discussion in Chapeter 5 for more detail.

Inns in those days needed land for pasture. Horses were standard for transport and drovers accompanying cattle, pigs, sheep or geese, would need to be able to pen their flock overnight so it is easy to see why inns were located where they were. Although the Market Square was a secondary location the ones on its west side still had yards of several acres that extended to Cofferidge Close, and perhaps Cofferidge Close itself was rented for pasture.And herein we may find a reason why inns did not develop along Church Street.

Two hundred years have passed since the two houses in this photograph functioned as the Talbot inn. Inn features are unrecognizable today but this inn may have a much older history than we know. It was on record as the Talbot from 1680 to 1776 when it was last licensed, but some of the interior structural elements tell us that it is a much older building, possibly medieval.

The Barley Mow and the Crown and the White Hart had sufficient land, as did the King's Head on the west side. The Fighting Cocks came into being in the 18th century and must also have had a large yard of sorts. The Plough, which Markham places at the former 2 Market Square was an alehouse.

Another inn which came to record in the late 17th century and survived for just over 100 years was the Talbot. The building is still there at 81-83 High Street, now separated, but you can see where the central entrance one existed. Little is known of its history but it seems to have expired circa 1790 when there was a great falling off of licenses in Stony Stratford. The reasons are not clear, but at the end of the century a relatively small number of inns and alehouses dominated the trade. This situation began to change in the middle of the 19th century when the Wolverton end was developed.

In 1753, the first year that licensing records survive in Bucks, we have a comprehensive list of licensees and inn names. On the east side of the High Street are the major known inns, the *Cock*, the *Bull*, the *Three Swans*, the *Horseshoe*, the *Red Lyon*, the *Drum and Anchor* (later known as the *Coach and Horses*) and the *Queens Head*. On the West side of the High Street were the *George*, the *White Horse*, the *Talbot*, the *Cross Keys*, and on the Square, the *Crown*, the *Barley Mow*, the *Crooked Billet*, the *Fighting Cocks*, the *King's Head*, the *Plough*. Other places, the *Swan with Two Necks*, the *Valiant Trooper*, the *Silent Woman*, the *Welsch Harp*, the *Sow and Pig*, the *Three Tuns*, the *Marlborough Head* cannot be located.

The age of the former Rising Sun is belied by its present appearance as the brick facing covers the original stone building. It has been dated to 1740 but there was probably an inn on this site in an earlier period. The field behind it was known as Lyon Close, which may suggest some connection with a Golden Lion which appears on record in 1619.

Chapter Seven
Inn Names: Passing and Permanent

In medieval times it was enough to raise an ale stake above the entrance to indicate to travellers the nature of the business. Later inns began to put up painted signs and before too long almost everyone, except perhaps the village alehouse, displayed a distinct sign. As time wore on these names became more diverse. Some inn names endured; others were subject to the whims of fashion, and a few were so popular that they cropped up in more than one place.

Angels and Barley Mows

The *Angel* is one of these and its use at various times and in various locations has inevitably led to some confusion. Oliver Ratcliffe, writing in the 19th century, offers this story to suggest that there were two Angels operating at the same time.

> The Barley Mow was originally the Angel, and as there was the Angel at the other end of the street, it was a jest with the soldiers who passed through, that Stony Stratford ought to be a good place, as it was guarded by an angel at each end.[48]

When we come to look at the licensing register in the latter half of the 18th century, we can discover some substance to the saying. Indeed, in the last quarter of that century, Stony Stratford did have two houses of that name at the north and south ends of the High Street. One was at 11, High Street and the other, at the very entrance to the town, at 185, High Street. The first *Angel*, the "Angel of the South" (if we may call it that), was first licensed in 1770; the second took out a license two years later.

Quite why the name was duplicated is a source of some wonder to us at a time when there were many names to choose from. This second *Angel* held onto the name until 1790, when it changed its name, not to something original, but to another name already in use in the town, the *Barley Mow*.

There was at least one earlier inn called the *Angel*. The Longueville papers show a lease from Sir Henry Longueville in 1629 to Lettice Ashby, noting that the lease was formerly held by George Walton

---

48 Oliver Ratcliffe. The Newport Hundreds. Olney, 1900.

This old postcard, circa 1910, shows the old Angel in the middle on the left hand side. It was first licensed in 1772 an operated continuosly until it was replaced by the Cofferidge Close development in 1973. The High Street seems strangely free of traffic, although at the time it was considered a busy road.

The building that was once the 18th (or possibly 17th) century Barley Mow at Number 10, Market Square.

from 1613.[49] Markham believed that it was near the site of the present *Plough* Inn, in which case it would have been a forerunner to the *Sun,* later to be renamed the *Plough.*

The Angel at Number 11 High Street was first licensed to Richard Brookes in 1770. Markham suggests that the inn may be two centuries earlier than the earliest date that he gives, 1790. If so, the house bore different inn signs.

In the 20th century the Angel had three licensed rooms, a tap room at the front, a parlour and a smoke room, which accommodated skittles and darts. There was a scullery at the back but no provision for food. Whether such provision was different in earlier centuries is unknown.

There was a complaint from the police constable in 1919 that some customers would park their cars outside the front door while the went in for a drink. The High Street is quite narrow at this point and traffic was often held up. (There were no double yellow lines back then.) For a good part of the 20th century the Brown family held the tenancy. The frontage of the Angel is preserved in the Milton Keynes Museum at Stacey Hill.

The first *Barley Mow* that we know of was on the Market Square at Number 10, on the corner of Silver Street. Judging from the detail of the auction of 1810 the property may have extended back to Cofferidge Close. The *Barley Mow* first comes to notice in 1753 when it was in the hands of the Day family. Presumably the inn was in operation years before that date. After 1770 it passed through several hands until William Holland acquired the premises in 1798. He died a few years later and on 4th July 1807 the executor of the estate of William Holland posted in the *Northampton Mercury* asking that all debts be paid immediately to his widow, Mary Holland. Three years later Mary Holland died and the premises were put up for auction. It is interesting to read this to get some idea of the scope of a late 18th century- early 19th century inn.

Capital Public-House and other Freeholds, in Stony Stratford, Bucks. To be SOLD by AUCTION, By JOHN DAY,

By Order of the Executors of the late Mr. WM. HOLLAND, on Thursday the 20th. of December, 1810, at Four o'clock in The

49 Ms. Radcliffe dep. deed 363.

Afternoon, on the premises, in the following Lots,

Lot 1. ALL that well-established PUBLIC HOUSE, now in full Trade, called the OLD BARLEY MOW, situated in the MARKET PLACE, in STONY STRATFORD, in the occupation of Mr. Marlow; comprising three Parlours, Kitchen, excellent Cellaring, several Sleeping-rooms, Brewhouse, Stabling for twenty Horses, large Yard and Garden, with a Malting granary, and other Out-offices thereunto belonging..

Lot 2. A CLOSE of excellent SWARD LAND adjoining the said Premises, containing two Acres (be the same more or less), with a Garden, Hovel, and a small Tenement adjoining. - This Lot will be sold with or without the Tenement, as agreed on at the Sale..

Lot 3. A neat DWELLING HOUSE or TENEMENT, situated within the said Market-Place; containing two Parlours in Front, four Sleeping-Rooms, Kitchen, Pantry, and Cellar, with Wood-Barn, and Stable. Yard, and Garden, late in the Occupation of Mrs. Holland, deceased.[50]

William Marlow had been running the Barley Mow for the last two years of Mary Hollands life and he was probably the successful bidder at the auction. However he may have overreached himself because by 1816 he had to declare bankruptcy. The major creditors George Brookes, a maltster of Stony Stratford, and Thomas Harris of Braunston were given the property in trust in order to settle everything. The inn continued in business but with tenant landlords until 1819 when they decided to sell it, including a vast cellar that could accommodate 100 hogsheads.

I don't know who purchased the property, but as an inn this *Barley Mow* was finished.

The Marlows were not yet done with the inn trade. Mr Joseph Marlow, possibly a son of William, become landlord of the *Rising Sun* and then in 1830, according to the Pigot Trade Directory he was the landlord of the *New Barley Mow*, and thereafter for some years to come.

The new *Barley Mow*, formerly the *Angel*, brings this story of Angels and Barley Mows full circle. It traded under that name until its final

---

50 Northampton Mercury

closure 200 years later. As can be seen in the early photograph, the tap room could be entered through two doors. This buildng, which is now a private house, still commands the northern entrance to the town and is really the first point where habitation could be built. It is protected by a ditch which was once used for boat moorings and this must have been one of the attractions for siting a house here.

This house at the entrance to Stony Stratford opened as The Angel in 1770. A few years later the name was changed to the Barley Mow, a name it held until it finally closed in the late 20th century. The house is now a private residence. The older photograph below, dating from the beginning of the 20th century shows the pub as it used to be.
Stony Stratford's High Street was infinitely quieter before the age of the motor car. The point on the right where the road widens is believed to have been the site of the Eleanor Cross.

Lions

Stony Stratford has had a number of "Lions".

The *Red Lion* as an inn name owes its popularity, if that is the right word, to the arrival of King James in 1603, when he decreed that all public buildings (which included taverns) should display his heraldic device, the Red Lion. Consequently it became the most common inn sign in England. It was not unknown before that. It had been associated with John of Gaunt, Duke of Lancaster, for example. It has, as far as we know, no local associations. The de Wolverton family used a heraldic eagle and the Longuevilles a cross of Lorraine. The Bennet family of Calverton had three silver lions on their heraldic shield, and it is possible the *White Lion* may have owed something to that. Stony Stratford also had a *Golden Lion* at one time, which had no connection with anything that we know of.

The inn which we know of as the *Red Lyon*, next door to the *Horseshoe*, does not have that as a recorded name until the 17th century.

In the prospectus for the sale of the manor drawn up in 1710, the *Red Lyon* is described in terms of its lease. It was then one of the more important inns although by no means the largest. The "yearly value of the house by supposition" was £9 12s 6d. The *Horseshoe* next door was clearly larger and valued at £30 10s 0d. Only the *Queen's Head* at £5 10s 0d was smaller.

> The Red Lyon Inn & the Grounds belonging are lett as Usuall, part of Grindley field is newly put to it well worth the Money, has had it four years at lease of 20 come.[51]

This appears to be a recent lease, dating only to 1706. In the same document there is a grouping of about 80 acres of mainly pasture described as Red Lyon leys. At this date they had been leased to

---

51 Particular of the Manor, 1713.

Thomas Penn, a farmer, in the middle of a 40-year lease. These meadows probably acquired their name in the middle of the previous century when enclosure was completed and may have been historically associated with the *Red Lion*. This may refer to an earlier *Red Lion*, a name which crops up in a dispute over William Edy's will in 1529. This was not manorial property at the time and perhaps should not be associated with the 18th century *Red Lyon*. It may have been in a different location altogether.

Around 1765 the *Red Lyon* and the *Horseshoe* amalgamated. In the 1765 licensing record the *Red Lyon* is in the hands of Edward Juffcoat (Jeffcoat) and the *Horseshoe* is not mentioned. In 1770 Edward Juffcoat is the sole licensee for the *Lyon and Horseshoe* and to corroborate that, the 1770 tabulation in the Constable's Book puts the two together. To complicate matters for us, this same book also records another *Red Lion* as billeting soldiers, although about a quarter of the number accommodated at the *Lyon and Horseshoe* during the same period. The licensee of the new *Red Lion* was John Davis.

The new *Red Lion* originated at this time and first appears in the licensing register in 1766 under the innkeeper John Kingston. The last recorded licensee was John Davis in 1781 so it probably went out of business or changed its name in 1782. There is no obvious candidate for a new name so it may have quietly expired as so many inns did in the last two decades of the 18th century. The estimated location of this house was probably between the *White Swan* near the corner of New Street and the Retreat. It did offer overnight accommodation but there was apparently no provision for horses.

The *Horseshoe* eventually dropped the joint name and the new *Red Lion* must have gone out of business completely. The 1792 records give only four licensees on the east side. However the habitual use of the joint name was slow to die. This advertisement appeared in the *Northampton Mercury*, 21 June 1794:

BLACKSMITHS

WANTED immediately, Two or Three JOURNEYMEN. Good Hands may have constant Employ and good Wages, by applying at the Red Lion and Horseshoe, Stony Stratford, Bucks.

Another *Red Lion* cropped up as a beer house in the late 19th century on Mill Lane. It closed in the middle of the 20th century and is now a private residence.

There are two other 17th century "lions" of record. The Mompesson accounts name a *White Lion* and a *Golden Lion* in 1619. The *Golden Lion* is recorded only once and may have operated under a different name in a later period. There is a "Lyon Close" on the north west side of the High Street, quite a large field stretching back to the river. This name could have originated during enclosure in the 17th century and may possibly have been associated with an inn. If we can make this tentative connection then the former *Golden Lion* might have been resurrected as the *Rising Sun* in the 18th century.

A *White Lion* is recorded in licenses from 1765 until 1783. For the most of this period the licensee was Thomas Honeybone and then his widow Hannah. After 1779 there were three short-lived licensees and nothing more is heard of it after September 1783 when Edward Knight became the last licensee. Hannah Honeybone advertised the inn for sale in 1777. Prior to Thomas Honeybone's proprietorship it had been known as the *Plough*, a holding of the Salter family for most of the first part of the 18th century. The building was demolished in the last century but was formerly Number 2, The Square.

King James succeeded to the throne of England in 1603. He was already King James VI of Scotland and had been since 1567 when he was a year old. He was the great grandson of Margaret Tudor, a sister of Henry VIII.

The Red Lion rampant was the emblem of the Scottish King and he insisted that it be used on all public buildings in England. This clearly included inns and taverns and many of them adopted this sign for convenience.

The sign of the Red Lion is still the most popular name throughout the country.

There was one Red Lion known in the 16th century in Stony Stratford which cannot be attributed to the intervention of King James. Its location is unknown.

Heads

The *Queen's Head* has already been discussed in Chapter 6. To add to this a *King's Head* opened on the west side of the Square in the 17th century, possibly as early as 1640, according to the Victoria County History. It remained in business until the 20th century. Which monarchs head was used for these two inns is not known. There is a convention that living monarchs were not used on inn signs, so it is unlikely that either Queen Mary or Queen Anne were used for the Queen's Head. It could have been Queen Elizabeth although sometimes Charles II's queen, Catherine of Braganza was used.

Charles I was often a popular sign amongst royalist supporters and there are today many public houses that use his image.

The *Marlborough Head* made an appearance in Stony Stratford, certainly between 1753 and 1762. It may have had an earlier history, but obviously no earlier than the celebrated John Churchill, Duke of Marlborough.

In this context we may as well discuss the *Silent Woman*. This was something of a cruel joke, depicting a woman as either headless or with her tongue firmly restrained. Ironically, it would seem to us, the licensee of the *Silent Woman* in Stony Stratford was a widow, Elizabeth Edwards, who held the license from before 1753 to 1761. She may have had an ironic sense of humour.

The former King's Head on the Square is the only inn in this group with a known location. The Marlborough Head, the Queen's Head and the Silent Woman once existed, but cannot be located.

its share. There is a *White Horse* today which has been there since the late 18th century. Other inns have used that same name and there was a *Black Horse* until 1782 and in the late 17th and early 18th centuries a *Nag's Head*. A *Horse and Jockey* made a brief appearance in 1754. There was a *Waggon and Horses* that may have been the forerunner of the *Black Horse*. The *Horseshoe* had a long history and there were two houses bearing the name *Coach and Horses*.

The *White Horse* was the favourite and it appears in several centuries. This has led to assumption that all these references are to the same *White Horse*. There is some evidence to make us question this.

Let us start with the present *White Horse*. Its location next to St Giles almost in the centre of Stony Stratford would argue for an inn of long standing on this site. This may be true but was it called the *White Horse*? The first license issued to an inn under this name at this location was in 1775 and in every year since. The building itself appear to date from the late 18th century and this is in agreement with the first license. We might conclude that the *White Horse* was rebuilt and

This White Horse was first licensed, at the time a new building, in 1775. There was another White Horse across the street which closed two years earlier and there are other White Horses of record in earlier centuries. This is probably a very old inn site and there is a 16th century reference to an inn called The Key which was either on this site or adjacent. Since 1775 this White Horse has opened without interruption.

opened under this new name in 1775.

Only a few years before this there was another *White Horse* on the opposite side of the street. We know this from two sources: the Constable's Account book of 1770 which records military billeting on the east side, and the annual licensing records. The licensee recorded in the Constable's Book is Samuel Gayton who had been the licensee since 1761. The last time he took out a license was in September 1771 which presumes that he continued to operate until 1772. There was a gap of about three years and then Edward Proctor took out a license in 1775 for his house on the west side under the sign of the *White Horse*.

We could make the assumption that the *White Horse* closed down while rebuilding and reopened in 1775 or Edward Proctor simply took up a name that was no longer in use after the old *White Horse* had closed down. The east side White Horse had not always held to the same name. Although it had been constantly the *White Horse* since Samuel Gayton took over in 1761, his predecessor, William Ashpole had been running the same place under the sign of the *Ship*, a change he himself made in 1754, from the *White Horse*. On this evidence one might guess that it had operated a long time as the *White Horse* and Samuel Gayton revived the old name when he took over from Ashpole.

The Constable's Book may also help in locating this inn. The billeting and stabling accounts for the inns are tabled in order, starting with the *Red Lyon and Horseshoe* in the north and ending with the *Hare and Hounds* in the south. The *Red Lyon and Horseshoe*, the *Drum and Anchor*, the *Three Swans*, the *Cock* and the *Bull* are all listed in order of their known locations so there is some confidence in believing that the next three, the *White Horse*, the *Red Lion* and the *Hare and Hounds* follow the same logic. We know that there was an inn site of long standing on the land now occupied by the Retreat. This was likely the *Hare and Hounds*. The site that later became the *White Swan* also appears as an inn yard of some antiquity in layout; therefore we might not be far wrong in suggesting that the former *White Horse* was located here. The middle one of these three, the *Red Lion*, did not have much of a history. It had a recorded life of 18 years from 1766 to 1784. It was large enough to take guests but had no provision for horses - at least the military did not stable them there. One candidate for this building may be the former *Rose and Crown*, which we only know but through Michael Hipwell's will. His intention was that the profits from the inn would be used to fund his school foundation in a building at the back but mysteriously there is no further mention of this even though the *Rose and Crown* charity prevailed. Without much confidence I put this forward as a possible site.

There was almost certainly a *White Horse* in Stony Stratford during the reign of Henry VIII as there was a dispute between the wardens of the Guild and the lessees of the *White Horse*. Unfortunately the record of the proceedings of the Star Chamber are undated so the existence of the *White Horse* could be any time between 1509 and 1547. The wardens probably acquired this property in 1481 or 1482 when a significant donation was made by three prosperous Stony Stratford businessmen, John Edy, John Hayle and Thomas Rokys. Now the site could be anywhere in Stony Stratford but one may not be too far off the mark to assume that it was adjacent to or near the Guild House itself. It does not feature in manorial documents of the 17th or 18th centuries since it had been granted at an earlier date. Continuity of inn names, that is names tied to the same establishment, seems to be more rare than common, so this 16th century *White Horse* may not have any connection with the mid 18th century *White Horse*.

The *Black Horse* may have been a name change from the *Waggon and Horses*. In 1753, 1754 and 1755 John Davis is the licensee for the *Waggon and Horses* and for the next 8 years he is recorded under the sign of the *Black Horse* before he disappears from the record. So either the *Waggon and Horses* morphed into the *Black Horse* under John Davis's stewardship, or the *Waggon and Horses* closed down and Davis found employment in another inn. The location is unknown.

There was also a *Black Horse* in Old Stratford at the northern limits of the village, and even a field named after it. The site was redeveloped in the 20th century.

Stephen Eales makes a fleeting appearance in history as the licensee of the *Horse and Jockey* in 1754 only. Neither he nor the inn sign are ever recorded in the area again. This must have been a very early use of this particular sign and no doubt Mr Eales wished to attract a sporting crowd. He may have been disappointed.

In this context was the *Nag's Head*, mentioned elsewhere, and leased to a Mr. Wagstaff for 17 shillings a year. It is only recorded between 1710 and 1718. The word "nag" has punning potential, but we would not for one minute dare to suggest any association with the *Silent Woman*.

The *Horsehoe* was one of the great and ancient inns of Stony Stratford and was located on the site which was developed as St Paul's school in the 19th century and which became Mr Fegan's Homes in the 20th century. There are earlier references but it is in 1710 that we discover a detailed account of the lease and the inn's leaseholdings, which included a substantial amount of land. The *Horseshoe*, one of the manor's major tenants, was an established inn for waggoners, an early truck stop if you like. Such an inn would have to accommodate horses and waggons and hold pasture lands. The inn did not survive the 18th century and closed down in 1796. Apart from the surviving *White Horse* the last inn to be concerned with horses was named the *Coach and Horses* in 1792, after being known as the *Drum and Anchor* for many years. It held on to the new name for the remainder of its functioning life.

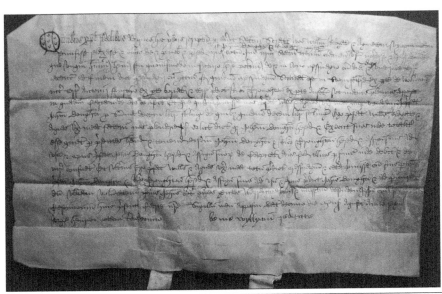

This 16th century deed describes the location of an inn called The Key, which appears to be either on, or very close to, the site now occupied by the White Horse.

Swans

The *Swan Inn* was located on the land now occupied by 92-94 High Street. its history probably dates back to medieval times although there is little record of it. There was probably a new building on the site in 1687, but to judge from Christopher Carter's complaint below, the outbuildings were much older. The late 17th century inn did not last long because it was destroyed by the great fire of 1742. Its replacement you can see today, and part of it is once more a hotel.

Formerly the Three Swans, this building dates to after 1742, when the previous building was destroyed in the great fire of that year. The previous inn may only have been built in 1687 and that replaced either a 16th century or late medieval building. It was simply known as the Swan until the late 17th century. It went out of business in 1782.

During the 17th and 18th centuries it was known as the *Three Swans* and may have been renamed after 1687.[52] In the 16th century and possibly earlier it was simply the sign of the *Swan*. Browne Willis believed that it was regarded as the premier inn of Stony Stratford in earlier centuries but in the 18th century it clearly lagged behind the *Cock* and the *Bull* in status. The *Three Swans* leases fewer acres of meadow and pasture than its rival the *Bull* down the road and are paying a lower rent. Nevertheless it was still an important inn throughout its life in the 18th century.

---

52 Deduced from an inscribed stone on the site.

At about this time Christopher Carter was the innkeeper of the *Three Swans*. In 1726 he was not a happy man. Part of his inn was falling into disrepair and despite promises made to him 12 years earlier the work had not been remedied.

According to his account, Dr. Radcliffe visited the inn soon after he made his purchase in 1713 and ordered that a dilapidated part of the building be torn down so that it could be replaced by a new structure. This was most likely an outbuilding which pre-dated the late 17th century inn.

However Dr. Radcliffe died the following year and this may have left Carter in limbo. His Trustees needed time to organise and familiarise themselves with the manor and establish priorities. Since they only met twice a year on the average it was probably difficult to get decisions.

Eventually, after 12 years he submitted a petition to the Trustees which was, to judge by the neatness of the script and the language, drawn up by a lawyer. The Trustees were minded to listen and allowed him some relief on his rent.

> That the buildings that were taken down consisted of six bay containing a shuffleboard room and severall other chambers and their not being built up again was a very great damage and disadvantage to your petitioner the buildings being demolished in such a manner as did not only render the said roomes useless but gave the inn such an ill report that Gentlemen and Travellers who were Strangers would not come to itt and severall Gentlemen after they had turned into the yard and saw in what condition the inn was in have went out again and gone to other Inns.
>
> And that the brewhouse which was under part of the said roomes was so bad and ruinous that your Petitioner could not brew therein without great difficulty and hazard and oftentimes had his drink damaged by mortar and other rubbish falling into it from the walls of the said brewhouse.[53]

One can easily imagine the reaction of customers who found clumps of mortar in their ale.

By 1730, Christopher Carter was facing insolvency and was unable to pay his rent. He made a further plea to the Trustees who did give the man relief from his debts and immediately took on another tenant - R. Wilmer in 1730.

The *Three Swans* would have been caught up in the great fire of 1742 and

---

53 Letter to Radcliffe Trustees, 1726.

was presumably rebuilt. It stayed in business until 1782 when it was converted into a residence.

The medieval inn had probably gone by 1687 when, according to the discovery of a foundation stone inscribed "W.E. 1687" it was rebuilt. Perhaps the name changed to the *Three Swans* at that date.To judge from Christopher Carter's complaint above, many of the outbuildings had not been updated. This building only had a relatively short life until it was burned down in the Great Fire of 1742.

The last lessees were the Whittakers - William Whittaker until his death in 1764 and his widow, Anne, until she finally retired in 1782. There was apparently no interest in continuing the inn trade and in a great three-day sale Mrs Whittaker was able to sell up and retire.

Everything that could be moved was sold: the furniture, the sheets and mattresses, the table linen, the barrels of wine and beer, the glasses, the crockery and cutlery and the silver plate, which was reserved for the third day of the sale. We might gather from this inventory that Mrs Whittaker had 30 bedrooms at the inn.

The *Swan/Three Swans* has sometimes been confused with the *Swan with Two Necks*, which was a different place altogether. *(See the discussion in Appendix 5.)*

After 1782 the use of the *Swan* sign lay dormant in Stony Stratford until a newly built house was opened at 32 High Street in 1823. It was called the Swan until it changed its name in 1877 to the *White Swan*. It now operates as the *Kardamom Lounge*.

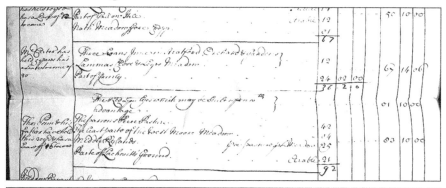

Lease particulars for the Three Swans in 1710.

The *Swan* revived the name in Stony Stratford in 1820 when a new house of that name opened. What it replaced is unknown, but the configuration of the yard suggests that it may have been an inn. Some possibilities are discussed elsewhere in this text and in the Compendium in Part Two. The distinctive half-timbered appearance makes it look older but it is very much a 20th century building because it was once more rebuilt in 1915.

In 1877 new owners modified the name to the *White Swan*, a name which it held until it had a brief excursion as the *Stratford Arms* at the end of the twentieth century.

This view of the High Street, taken circa 1907, shows a very different frontage for the White Swan, in the middle distance on the right. Also visble here is the boy's school, a National School founded in the early 19th century. National schools were Church of England foundations, and as this was not acceptable to other denominations another school was founded on the corner of the Wolverton Road for "dissenters."
The White Swan was rebuilt in 1915 to give it a half-timbered appearance that was fashionable at the time.

In the meantime the *Swan* at Old Stratford has demonstrated more longevity. It made its first recorded appearance in 1823 in a trade directory, although it is certainly older than that. It remains in business today, more visible now that some of the surrounding buildings on the corner have been cleared..

In the 18th century there was a *Swan* very much active in Calverton. It is still in business today, but under the name of *Shoulder of Mutton*, a name it has held since 1779. It was known as the *Swan* until 1767 when it changed to the *Green Dragon*.

113

Two survivors from the 18th century, and both originally known as the Swan.
The Old Stratford Swan (above) has kept its name for over 200 years.
The Shoulder of Mutton at Calverton, (below) is still in business today after more than
250 years, was first called the Swan and then the Green Dragon.

Chapter Eight

Neighbours: the Unusual case of the Royal Oaks

After the Battle of Worcester during the English Civil War, the defeated Prince Charles escaped the scene with the Roundheads in pursuit. He managed to reach Bishops Wood in Staffordshire, where he found an oak tree, known locally as the Boscobel Oak. He climbed the tree and hid in it for a day while his obviously short-sighted pursuers strolled around under the tree looking for him. The hunters apparently did not look up and eventually gave up the search. Prince Charles later climbed down and escaped to France. Nine years later he became Charles II on the Restoration of the Monarchy. To celebrate this good fortune, his birthday 29 May was declared Royal Oak Day. After that innkeepers who were caught with patriotic enthusiasm put up inn signs for *The Royal Oak*.

With this in mind we should not look for any of the Stony Stratford Royal Oaks until after 1660. The first *Royal Oak* of record appears in the 1753 licensing records for one year only. The licensee was Diana Williamson. This is a fragmentary record since the surviving licences in Buckinghamshire began only in that year, but from this we may reasonably assume that the inn had some prior history. We might guess that Diana Williamson was a widow who had taken over from her deceased husband and operated the inn for a few years until either she found it too much for her or died in harness, as it were. This inn or alehouse may have gone out of business in 1754 or may have changed its name under a new innkeeper. Its location is unknown.

After that, no *Royal Oak* makes an appearance until 1776, and then to confound us all, a second *Royal Oak* emerges in 1780. One of them, the *Royal Oak* on Horsefair Green we know about because it had a life until the 20th century; the second has a surprising location.

Let me mention here that the old parish boundary followed a line from the Watling street down the middle of Horsefair, tuning north along Silver Street to Horn Lane and then down Horn Lane to the river. Everything to the south and west of this line was once within the parish of Calverton.

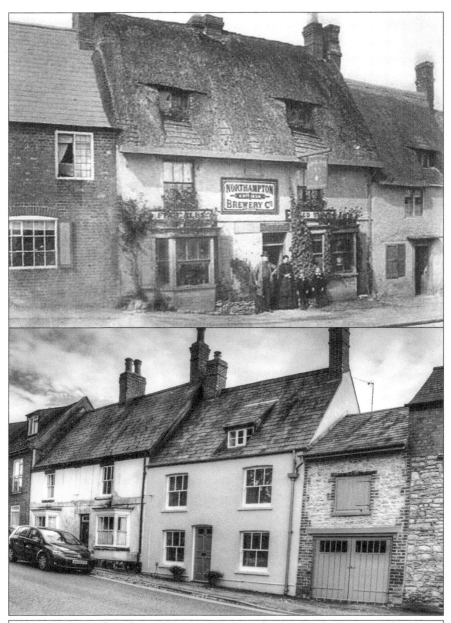

The top photograph, at least 100 years old, shows the Royal Oak that survived into the 20th century and the cottage next door that was known as the "Old Royal Oak" until it closed circa 1830. The modern photograph shows the two houses as they appear today. The two houses opened for business in 1776 and 1780 respectively. That the second to open chose the same name as the first is bizarre and remains unexplained.

Both *Royal Oaks* appear in Calverton's licensing records. In 1753 there were three licenses held in Calverton - Francis Cave, who had no inn sign and only lasted a few years, Comfort Roberts, who was at the sign of the Cheshire Cheese until 1756. And Edward Samson (sometimes written as Sampson, Simpson, Sympson) who was at the sign of the Swan until 1767. For a decade he was the only licensee in Calverton and then he was joined by Henry Nokes, a new licensee in 1765. Nokes was only in the picture for three years and since no inn sign was recorded it is impossible to deduce anything from these entries.

From other evidence we can deduce the location of the Swan. Today it is known as the *Shoulder of Mutton*. There are no clues as to the location of the *Cheshire Cheese*, except that, given the population distribution of Calverton, it was likely found close to Horsefair in Stony Stratford, perhaps on the site of one or other of the later *Royal Oaks*.

By 1768 Calverton is back to a single licensee, Sands (Alexander?) Johnson, who emerges a few years later when the recorder returns to noting the name of the inn, as the proprietor of the *Green Dragon*. In 1776 Mary Ganthorne is the licensee of the *Green Dragon* and the *Royal Oak* makes its appearance in that year with John Jeffs as the landlord.

This now looks straightforward. The *Green Dragon* continues until 1778 and in 1779 a new landlord William Maydon makes his entrance as the landlord of the *Shoulder of Mutton*. John Jeffs is still at the *Royal Oak*. Therefore we are not pushing the evidence too hard to conclude that the *Green Dragon*, previously the *Swan*, became the *Shoulder of Mutton* in 1779. It bears this name today. If this is so then Calverton's second inn would most probably be found at the Calverton End of Stony Stratford. Horsefair and Cow Fair were lightly populated at the time but if, as seems possible, the Calverton parish had more benign regulations for alehouses, there would certainly be an advantage to setting up on the border of St. Giles parish.

It would therefore be easy to identify the *Royal Oak* opened by John Jeffs in 1776 as the pub which was still there in the 20th century but for an anomaly which crops up only a few year later in 1780 when George Lineham established another *Royal Oak* in Calverton. John Jeffs' Royal Oak is now described as the "*Old Royal Oak*". Quite why the new house would want to take the name of an existing house is something I will try to address a little later.

To make matters more confusing the licensee record in 1781 records Jeffs at the *"New" Royal Oak* and Lineham at the *"Old" Royal Oak*. However, for the next few years no such distinction is drawn between the two and they are both simply *Royal Oak*. In 1786 Jeffs disappears for a year but is back in 1787 as the *New Royal Oak*, leaving Lineham with the claim to the old. This became the settled distinction.

In 1798 Thomas Palmer replaced George Lineham at the *Old Royal Oak* and John Jeffs continued at the *New Royal Oak*. In the 19th century new landlords come and go but the designations which were established in 1787 were fixed by the tradition established in 1781.

The last mention of two Royal Oaks is in the 1830 Pigot Trade Directory: *The New Royal Oak*, Thos Powell; *The Old Royal Oak* Jas. Ridgeway.

One of them had closed by 1841 when Bartholemew Higgins is listed in the census as an innkeeper. He is also in the 1844 Pigot as the landlord of *The Old Royal Oak*. Thereafter there is only one Royal Oak.

To sum up this confusing story, the first and at one time the only *Royal Oak* in the Calverton Place area, was opened by John Jeffs in 1776. In 1780 a second *Royal Oak* appeared, nearby. After a few years jockeying for precedence the John Jeffs' *Royal Oak* became the *New Royal Oak* and George Lineham's *Royal Oak* became the *Old Royal Oak*. These designations continued to the 19th century until one of them closed in the 1830s. The survivor (for years known as the *New Royal Oak*) was briefly styled the *Old Royal Oak* and then settled into becoming the *Royal Oak*. This one we know about and its location. It is the double-fronted house on the west side of Horsefair Green.

As to why this unusual duplication came about we can only speculate. Possibly there was some rivalry between Jeffs and Lineham, perhaps even a vendetta. Lineham's choice of the same name for his neighbouring house must have been deliberate and perhaps was intended to spite Jeffs. Jeffs was certainly the first licensee to use the name but Lineham must have felt some entitlement. He may have been a descendant of the Williamson family of the previous generation and believed that this family had first claim on the name which John Jeffs had usurped. The evidence we do have does suggest that they agreed that Lineham could use the "old" designation. After years passed and landlords changed this no longer mattered but the names stuck and no one made any effort to change them.

This advertisement from 1824 describes a more extensive establishment than could have existed next door at the "Old Royal Oak".

> Northampton Mercury Saturday 16 October 1824

> Lot 3. An old-established PUBLIC HOUSE, situate in the Parish of CALVERTON, and immediately adjoining the town of Stony-Stratford called "THE NEW ROYAL OAK", with the Brewhouse, Stable, Yard, and Premises thereto adjoining, now in the occupation of John Hutton, who had a Lease of the same Premises four years and a half of which are now unexpired.

> For further particulars apply to Mr. John Billington, Grocer, Stony Stratford, Mr. Beasant of Wolverton Mill; or to Mr John Congreve, Solicitor, Stony Stratford.

The surviving *Royal Oak* building has undergone much change and renovation. The original thatched roof has been replaced and bow windows were added at the front. There is evidence from the wall at the back that the original was timber framed with brick infill. This building is now a private residence. The adjoining cottage to the north, sandwiched between the former *Royal Oak* and Burnham House, is also a private residence but at the back is a rubble stone building which was once a brewhouse. Could this have been the other *Royal Oak?*

The cottage is small and does not easily sit with our present day notions of a public house, but in the 18th century the parlour would have functioned well enough as an alehouse. Indeed it must have been here. The large house on the corner of Horsefair Green and next to the *Royal Oak*, Burnham House (formerly known as **The Coppers**), is a large early 18th century house with stables already occupying the property before the licensing if the second *Royal Oak*. At that date these are the only properties on that side of Silver Street.

So we are forced to the astonishing conclusion that the two Royal Oaks co-existed side-by-side for about 50 years.

There is a 1724 deed that refers to a Red Cow on Horsefair and while this cannot be definitely associated with either Royal Oak, if it did exist at one of these locations this might offer a plausible explanation as to why one of them claimed to be the older house. One must also bear in mind that the earlier Cheshire Cheese might have been at one of the locations.

There is however a good deal of information from this period about the surviving Royal Oak. There were several changes of landlord but within the family. Bartholemew Higgins, as noted above, was the landlord in 1841 and his successor was probably a nephew, Charles Higgins, aged 25 in 1851 and the son of a Stoke Goldington farmer, who went on to become a farmer himself in Tattenhoe a few years later. John Bliss, who was most likely a relative of Charles Higgins' wife, Caroline, succeeded and was followed by Francis H. Bliss.

We may get some idea of the extent of the brewing activity here when the landlord Henry Willison in 1877 styles himself as a publican and brewer. Presumably he was brewing on a small scale for some of the beer shops in Stony Stratford and district.

In 1883 Mrs Emily Smith was the landlady and she was succeeded by George Banton who held it until 1895, when Thomas Gee entered possession. The Gee family were there until 1911 when Frederick Washbrook took over. Harry Gable was the landlord in the 1920s until Joseph Jelley, former manager of the Co-op, purchased the property in 1928 as a retirement project. One of his sons, Percy, carried on until the 4th August 1961 when the licence was allowed to lapse, thus concluding its almost 200 year history as a licensed public house.

Chapter Nine

The Golden Age of Coaching

Elizabeth Richardson was a very busy woman. As Stony Stratford's post mistress she opened her office on the High Street at 8 am every morning and kept it open until 9 pm at night. The mail was collected and delivered at inconvenient times. The London coach arrived at 2:30 am and the Liverpool mail coach came in at midnight. In addition, the 1830 Pigot trade directory noted that there were coaches passing through the town hourly, from London, Birmingham, Manchester, Liverpool and Coventry.

> Letters from LONDON every morning (Monday excepted) at half-past two, and are despatched every night (Saturday excepted) at twelve. - Letters from LIVERPOOL, MANCHESTER, DERBY, CHESTER, and the northern parts of England, arrive every night at twelve, and are despatched every morning at half-past two. - Office opens at eight in the morning and closes at nine at night.[54]

This was a small part of the traffic; carriers operated from the Rising Sun and the Cross Keys and had regular routes to London, Banbury, Brackley, Northampton, Towcester and Newport Pagnell.

This period came to be called the Golden Age of Coaching. It lasted for twenty years, from about 1820 when coaches achieved their highest speed, to the creation of the London and Birmingham Railway which almost overnight destroyed the coaching trade,

It is trite to observe that horses are not tireless and long journeys were constrained by the need to rest horses. The delivery of packets and letters in an organised way began in Tudor times and young people, often boys, were hired for the task of travelling at an average speed of two to three miles an hour along difficult roads from post to post - hence the term 'post' came into common usage. In the 18th century it was a highly uncertain business. Highwaymen frequently preyed on the post boys and suspicions grew that some post boys colluded with the highway robbers. Delivery was therefore unpredictable and a system grew up where the postal charge was laid on the recipient

---

54 Pigot & Co.;s Directory of Buckinghamshire, 1830. p.92.

rather than the sender so as to introduce some incentive for delivery. Senders of banknotes adopted the precaution of cutting the notes in half and sending each half by a different post boy.

Royal Mail coaches set standards of speed and safety by which all other travel was judged. The blunderbuss and four pistols of the guard and driver gave excellent protection from highwaymen, and the coaches could outrun many pursuers. In 1800 dozens of Mail coaches set out from central London promptly at eight p.m. every night, carrying mail to 320 destinations across the country. The guard on each coach was provided with a watch that had just been checked and locked, and at the end of the trip he was required to provide a written explanation of any delay that occurred. Although as many as seven passengers were allowed on a coach, the primary concern of the guard and driver was the safety and speed of the mail. Mail coaches were not required to stop and pay at a toll gate, and circumstances sometimes allowed a Mail coach to hurry through a town at its top speed of 10 miles an hour, picking up and dropping off mailbags without even slowing down. Schedules allowed only five or six minutes for changing horses at a posting station, and some ostlers actually learned how to change out a four-horse team on a Mail coach in sixty seconds. On the four hundred mile trip from London to Edinburgh the Mail coaches often arrived within five minutes of their scheduled time.

The Mail coaches operated in all weathers and in stormy conditions in winter. If the coach broke down there was little to be done but wait for daybreak.

As can be seen from the advertisement at the beginning of this chapter, the mail coaches arrived in Stony Stratford in the dead of night. This meant that any passengers would also have to put up with the inconvenience of night travel. The poet Samuel Coleridge introduces us to the phrase "coach-stunned" after a Mail coach trip. He began his letter the following day, November 23rd, 1807:

> I arrived here in safety this morning between seven and eight, coach-stunned, and with a cold in my head; but I had dozed away the night with fewer disturbances than I had reason to expect . . . which I attribute to the easiness of the mail. [55]

Nevertheless, the mail coach afforded some comfort and he was

55 E.H. Coleridge, ed. Letters of Samuel Taylor Coleridge, Vol. II. p. 519.

able to sleep

Out of this system grew the post or posting house, an inn which could provide fresh horses and quick, turnaround services. After the Royal Mail stagecoaches were introduced in 1784 the system moved into high gear. Each stagecoach could take on fresh horses at each stage, while the tired horses were put to pasture. Thus teams of horses were constantly being moved up and down the Watling Street. By the 19th century Stony Stratford had three posting inns, the Bull the Cock and the George. After the railways came into being the George withdrew immediately and the Bull dropped out of the system by the mid 1840s. Only the Cock stayed in the system and continued to advertise itself as a "posting and commercial hotel" until the mid 1880s, although that era had long gone.

This development was revolutionary. Earlier mail packets had been carried by "a very low or worthless boy, mounted on a miserable hack . . . too often suspected of being in collusion with the robber." Post boys were robbed so frequently that a contemporary account described the mail as:

> very unsafe, and to avoid loss, people generally cut Bank Bills in two, and send the parts by a different post. The Postmasters General advertised directions to the public how to divide a bill, in such a manner as to prevent its being of any use to a robber.[56]

Mail coaches began to lose passengers in the 1830s to commercial stage coaches. Better law enforcement led to a reduction of highway robbers, and commercial stages (just as safe, less hurried, and offering travel in daylight) began to flourish. The last stagecoaches disappeared when railways covered the land.

Travel by stage-coach was very expensive; only the wealthy could afford it, and only the very wealthy could go by mail or post coach. The London to Chester route, which passed through Stony Stratford was 188 miles. At the peak efficiency of the mail coaches this was accomplished in just under 24 hours. It required tremendous organisation. The daily service in each direction needed:

> 4 stage-coaches, (at any one time, one coach was travelling south, another travelling north, and a spare coach was kept at each end

---

56 Samuel Pratt. Gleanings in England; descriptive of the countenance, mind and character of the country, Vo,. IV. p. 73. 1798.

of the route to allow for maintenance, breakdowns, etc.)

188 horses, (a team of four every eight miles, horses rested every other day, a simple equation that works out at one horse per mile of route.)

8 coachmen (drivers, 50 miles each per day)

4 guards (each did 24 hours on-duty then 24 hours off)

Payment of stage-coach tax (a sum per mile)

Payment of road tolls (charges for each section)

The High Street in the 1860s.

In addition, the posting houses at Stony Stratford had a platoon of workers to help to change the team of horses, effect any repairs to the coach, and look after the refreshment needs of the passengers. In addition, our Stony Stratford Postmistress, Elizabeth Richardson, or her deputy, would have to be on hand to receive incoming mail and deliver the outgoing packages.

Passenger numbers varied. A full load on a mail coach was 5 passengers, a post-coach (i.e an express) carried 4 or 6, and an ordinary lumbering stage-coach piled up 16 - inside, on top and astride some of the horses.

Travel by coach was never comfortable. Those who could afford it took a seat inside. There, passengers (some of whom may have been less than savoury company after nights on the road) were crammed into a tiny space, and banged and jolted together for hours or days. The less well-off travelled outside at half the inside fare. It was rarely a pleasant experience.

The weather was not the only hazard. Highway robbers were still on the road and that was an occasional risk, but one of the most serious was falling off the coach. It was often fatal.

Tired and weary passengers, either sitting on the outside of the coach or one of the leading horses might easily find drowsiness overtake them and a bump in the road might easily pitch the unwary sleeper into the ditch. It is said that the phrase "dropping off to sleep" originates from this time when sleep overtook the unfortunate individual who was unable to save himself when dropped off the coach. These contemporary newspaper reports illustrate some of these cases.

This first accident describes the accidental death of a woman who was riding on one of the horses pulling the coach. This was a common enough practice; in order to take more passengers, people were placed on top of the coach and a light person, such as a woman, could be placed on one of the leading horses.

> On Monday last a young woman on a journey from St. Albans to Cheshire, to see her mother, who was ill, riding a horse belonging to a stage-waggon, fell backward off the horse, between Fenny and Stony Stratford, and the wheels of the wagon running over her, killed her on the spot.[57]

Here is a similar story, with an equally tragic outcome.

> Wednesday night was buried one of the outside passengers who fell off one of the early stages that went through the town the preceding morning, and at day break was found dead with his skull fractured; the coachman he went with did not miss him until he came from the next stage, by whom we hear that he was a half pay officer and lived at Stony Stratford.[58]

James Burnham, Coroner for Bucks., presided over this inquest:

> On Monday 24th November, an Inquisition was taken at Stony Stratford, Bucks, before James Burham, Gent. His Majesty's Coroner for the said County. On view the body of James

57 *Derby Mercury 1st November 1754.*
58 *Stamford Mercury 8th May 1766.*

Connelly, a Sailor, one of the Passengers in the Basket of the Liverpool Stage Coach, who, being intoxicated with Liquor, fell out of the Basket, of which Fall he languished about 20 Minutes, and then died. The Jury brought in their Verdict, Accidental Death.[59]

This report describes another, less fateful accident.

On Sunday morning last, about Three o'clock, Banks, the driver of one of the Chester coaches, by a sudden Jolt of the Carriage, was thrown from the Box, near Stony Stratford, by which Accident both his legs were broke. The Horses went on with the Coach through Stony-Stratford and brought it safe to Old-Stratford, notwithstanding they passed a Waggon on the Road, without the Passengers knowing Any Thing of the Accident.[60]

Golden Age

The so-called "Golden Age of Coaching", a period of 20 years before the coming of the railway was a high point for the industry but it may not necessarily have been a high point for the inn trade in Stony Stratford. In terms of numbers, that high point may have been reached in the 18th century. In the middle part of that century the number of inns in Stony Stratford was at a peak. From brief historical glimpses we can deduce that the number of inns and alehouse at any one time was a constant figure from the 16th to the 18th centuries. In 1577 there were 28 licenses and in 1753, 27. In the closing years of that century there was a dramatic falling off in licenses. After the Horseshoe closed in 1797 that number was down to 18, including the two Royal Oaks in the Calverton parish.

Quite why this should be so cannot easily be explained. The population of Stony Stratford and Wolverton was constant during the century; in fact, Wolverton's village and farming population had not changed since Domesday. It is possible that the growth of inns along the road offered competition to Stony Stratford. The weary traveller could find a place to rest at Loughton, for example, rather than push on to make the extra miles to Stony Stratford. Canal transport, from bout 1780 onwards, even though the Grand Junction Canal was some

---

59 Northampton Mercury of December 8th 1783.
60 Northampton Mercury of Saturday April 19th 1788.

years away from Wolverton and Stony Stratford, began to eat away at the road trade. A carter, who might employ up to two men and six horses on a waggon, must have experienced loss of trade to the new canal system, and this may explain why the Horseshoe closed its doors in 1796.

Nevertheless, despite this consolidation, we must assume that the Cock and the Bull flourished during these years. Unfortunately, this can only be inferred. The first record which might offer some means of assessing their prosperity come in the 1841 Census, three years after the new railway system had brought about its revolution in travelling distances. That census reveals five female and two male servants at the Cock and a single female servant at the Bull. Both hotels must have maintained a larger household before 1838. For comparison purposes, the railway Refreshment Rooms at Wolverton employed 29 full-time staff.

Decline of Coaching Inns

The old coaching inns were certainly suffering. The Bull in particular seems to have struggled.

In 1851 it records Henry Wilmin as the victualler with only two servants. In 1841 it was kept by Samuel and Sarah Rich. They had four daughters, aged between 14 and 23 living there, with one servant. There is no hint of guests.

When the Bull was put up for sale in 1843 it was the brewery in the back yard which was calculated to attract buyers, not the hotel, which is offered in this advertisement as a house only.

We can derive more information from this advertisement.[61]

TO BREWERS, &c. - TO BE LET

FOR A TERM OF YEARS OR SOLD,

A COMPACT BREWERY, most eligibly situated at Stony Stratford, Bucks, within three miles of Wolverton Station, on the London and Birmingham Railway.

The Brewery has been constructed about three years. The plant was designed by Messrs. Pontifex, London, and the whole is in a most perfect and complete state of repair.

There is a spacious dwelling house adjoining, heretofore used

---

61 Bucks Herald, April 19th 1843.

The High Street (above) at the beginning of the motor age. The Cock and the Bull have both adapted to the new traveller by displaying large signs advertising garage services. The former Three Swans shown below has preserved the central entrance to the inn yard, which was probably typical. The decline of coaching caused many inns to fill in the central passage and create a hotel lobby, as seems to have happened at the Cock. Later, in age of the motor car, new access was needed and the Cock had to acquire property at the side for rear access.

On the next page, the Bull Hotel, the facade of the Cock, and the access passages for the Bull and the White Horse.

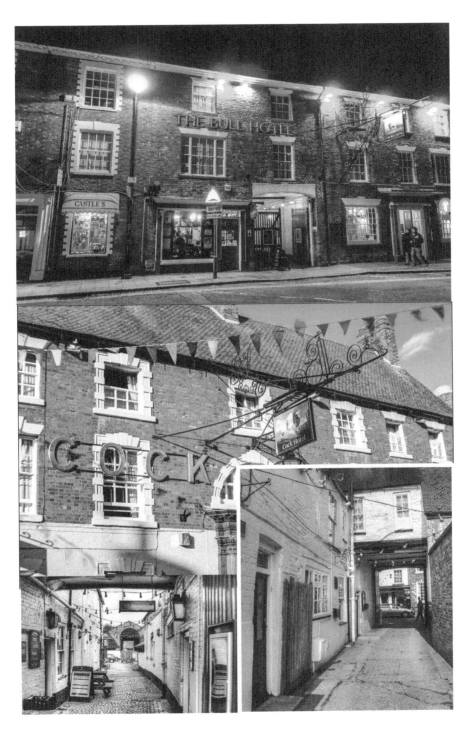

as the Bull Inn, (to which the licence is continued). And there are capacious granaries, store-houses, stables and buildings adjoining, which may, at a trifling expense, be converted into maltings.

The Owners of these premises are joint-owners of the two public houses at Wolverton Station, which have the SOLE AND EXCLUSIVE right of selling beer within the station.

The Tenant will be required to take the plant and fixtures.

Immediate possession may be had.

To treat for a Lease or purchase of the premixes apply to Mr. Congreve, Solicitor, Stony Stratford.

The picture of long term decline is reinforced in the 1861 Census, where the *Bull* employs a single servant in addition to family members.

The Cock weathered the downturn rather better.

The 1841 Census shows the Cock kept by John Battams and his wife, with seven staff. The 1851 Census, which is a bit more specific, shows it in the hands of the widow Mary Chapman. Her staff include a barmaid, House Maid, Waitress, Kitchen Maid, Post Boy, Porter and an Ostler. She also had five guests staying there that evening. Yet next door, John Reeve the Grocer (who also had a branch at Wolverton) was also employing six live-in staff, adding a detail line that noted he was employing 3 men and 1 boy indoors and 11 men and boys outdoors. In 1851 the grocery was a bigger business than the coaching inn!

But the Cock appeared to hold its own. In 1861 the hotel was still able to employ, in addition to family members, a barmaid, a cook, a waitress, a chambermaid and "boots."

By the 19th century all of these inns were in private ownership. The Radcliffe Trust was subject to Land Tax but a new act in 1799 and later in 1802 allowed them to redeem their taxes with a lump sum payment. The lump sum payment would earn interest at 3%, which would in turn be applied against taxes. Accordingly they decided to sell some of their Stony Stratford properties, especially the inns, which were put up for auction. Their land agent, Thomas Harrison, who never appeared to be short of funds to invest in property, accordingly obliged and successfully bid on The Bull. From this time on the managers of these hotels were either tenants or employees, which may explain the turnover. Thomas Harrison and his son probably did well out of this establishment until the forced sale of 1821.

Despite this downturn, these three establishments have survived into the 21st century as hotels with impressive facades onto Stony Stratford High Street. Today it is no longer a busy thoroughfare as the A5 now bypasses Stony Stratford

Across the road the Cross Keys limped along until 1870 when it closed finally as an inn. The George managed to stay in business throughout the century, although for a lengthy period in the 20th century it did business as a tea room and coffee shop.

The cause of this decline was plain. Railways offered journey times of hours instead of days. The time from Euston to Wolverton dropped from 3hrs 15 minutes to about 1 hour over the 19th century as engine power and reliability improved. Stony Stratford was transformed. Its heyday as a premier coaching town was over.

The new railway, originally connected Liverpool and Manchester. It was extended southwards to Birmingham in 1837, and London in 1838. The early trains travelled between Liverpool and London in 11 hours, compared to 24 hours by the fastest stage-coach.

"Railway Mania" hit the country. New railways were proposed everywhere. It took some years to extend railway coverage over the whole country. Some new stage-coach routes were started to act as feeders to the railway, but in general, wherever the railway went, stage-coach routes closed. The image of coaching had changed. From being the fastest mode of transport, the smart way to travel, coaches came to be seen as slow and old-fashioned. Engine Drivers, not Coachmen, were the new working elite.

As stage-coach routes closed, tens of thousands were put out of work. Drivers, guards, ostlers, farriers, toll-keepers, innkeepers, booking-clerks, cooks, waiters, chamber-maids, coach-builders, harness-makers, providers of fodder, disposers of dung, most would lose their jobs. A similar thing happened to hundreds of thousands of horses.

The main roads changed from bustling highways full of fast long-distance travellers, to sleepy backwaters serving only local traffic. The turnpike trusts fell apart as their main source of revenue dried up and, short sightedly, at the beginning of the motor age, they hit motorised vehicles with penal tolls and restrictions, stifling innovation in the UK, and allowing Germany and France to take the lead in developing road transport. The immediate future of transport in the UK belonged to the railway.

Stage-coaches struggled on in gaps left by the railway. There were occasional revivals for sentimental reasons, or when the railways abused their monopoly powers, but for most people stage-coaches soon became a thing of the past.

Fortunately, the railway company chose Wolverton as a site for a maintenance depot rather than simply using it as a station to serve Stony Stratford and Newport Pagnell. In consequence Stony Stratford grew at a rate not seen since the 13th century. This expansion of the workforce and population led to the opening of a steam tram shuttling from the Forester's Arms to Wolverton Station. Apparently able to accommodate 100 passengers, it ran until replaced by motor buses.

But the old inn trade had gone and the town became more notable for its public houses than its inns.

In this old photograph, dating back over 100 years, the Bull has adapted to "modern times" by offering garage space for automobiles. Nevertheless, horse-drawn transport was still much in use, as illustrated here.

Chapter Ten

The Railway Age

The Rise of the Beer House

In the middle of the 20th century Stony Stratford had a plentiful supply of drinking houses. The word inn and alehouse had gone out of fashion and most of them were known as public houses - pubs. The Bull and the Cock were still pre-eminent but were now hotels, offering accommodation and restaurant services and function rooms for receptions, club dinners and meetings.

The newest pubs developed quickly after the 19th century expansion along the Wolverton Road. Two of them took their names from Queen Victoria's eldest sons, Albert Edward, the *Prince of Wales* and Alfred, the *Duke of Edinburgh* The latter was the second son and was named Alfred. He was created duke in 1866 and retained this title until his death in 1900. His son pre-deceased him and the title became extinct until it was revived for the present holder in 1947. The pub happily retained this name until recent times when it was changed to the *Duke of Wellington* after a brief outing under the sign of the *Dog and Gun*, presumably because nobody had any notion of the identity of the 19th century Duke.

In 1871 it was in the hands of William H Cowley and his wife Esther. Cowley was a stone mason as well as a publican so one might guess from this that the income from the pub was not sufficient on its own to support his family. The same was true of Walter Sykes and his wife Ellen who were there in 1881. They were both in their mid-thirties with five children and a domestic servant living at the premises. Sykes was also a commercial traveller as well as a licensed victualler.

The *Case is Altered*, a little further towards Wolverton, was also a sideline. John Franklin, the first licensee was a bricklayer and only at the Prince of Wales does Thomas Gregory seem to be able to list himself solely as a publican..

The *Case is Altered* is a rare pub name, although it is found in

Two of the beer houses that opened in the Wolverton Road in the 1860s. Both were named after Queen Victoria's eldest sons: The Prince of Wales, below, and the Duke of Edinburgh, above. The Prince of Wales closed in the 20th century and is at present a Funeral Home. The Duke continues in business but has been renamed the Duke of Wellington, after a short spell as the Dog and Gun.

This corner was developed in the 1840s, at the beginning of the Railway age. The Forester's Arms (the three-storey brick building) closed in 2014, and, at the time this photograph was taken, was being refurbished to re-open as a restaurant.

The corner buildings were erected in the 1840s as a non-conformist school.

The Case is Altered, one of the new beer houses to spring up on the Wolverton Road in the late 1860s. It closed down in 1956 or 7. In the middle distance you can see the Duke of Edinburgh. It is now called the Duke of Wellington.

The Fox and Hounds (above) was originally a beer house at 87 High Street which later acquired 85 next door and combined the premises. A fire destroyed Number 87 and it was rebuilt as a single storey house. Ether or both houses at 85 and 87 High Street may have had older associations with inns, but these are unknown.

Below is the house that opened as a beer shop in the 1860s on Mill Lane. It acquired the name of the Red Lion before it closed in the mid 20th. century.

places other than Stony Stratford.[62] The name itself originates with an Elizabethan lawyer, Edmund Plowden and referred to the impact of new evidence in a case he was pursuing. The phrase became the title of a Ben Jonson play, written in 1597. It is a somewhat haphazard play of intertwined comic plots and is thought by some critics to be the work of several authors. Quite why this title should resurface four centuries later as a pub name may not be easily explained except that the phrase slipped into the language as a sort of catch phrase. The Case is Altered got its first license in 1867.[63]

David Leslie, a former resident, contributed this description:

> The Case is Altered (No 83 Wolverton Road) was our family home from 1957 until 1976. It was bought by my parents Derek and Irene Leslie, and my sister Pat brother James and I grew up there. From memory the pub was only ever a beer house. I believe it was built as a pub because the beer cellar runs the full width of the house, and had a single gas mantle to light it. The front door as shown on the original photo went into a small vestibule with doors either side and a serving hatch for the off licence "jug and bottle". The left door led into the lounge bar and the right to the public bar. Beneath the left of the two windows the Lounge bar was the cellar trap which was covered over by my Dad to stop the rain flooding the cellar. It was a great house to grow up in with masses of room to hide and play. We visited a couple of years ago and it is now 4 separate dwellings, the old garage and what was our kitchen and dining room have been demolished. I can remember also finding various flags and bunting in the attic which must have hailed from the Coronation of Queen Victoria.

---

62 Some claim that this name was brought back by soldiers from the Peninsular War in Spain. In colloquial Spanish, Casa desaltar means "House for Jumping." Others say that it is a corruption of the Spanish Casa Alta (High House). In both instances the name has been anglicised. The derivation of the name will fire pub arguments for many years to come.

63 Closer to the period was the notorious Red Barn murder of Maria Marten in 1827. The murderer, William Corder, could not be prosecuted because no body was found and it was possible that she had left the district. However, the body was discovered almost a year later and the "case was altered." Corder was hanged for the crime.

The other two houses date from the same time. All three were in business by 1871.

The *Forester's Arms* probably dates to the time of the building of the short return from the corner of the High Street. It was known as Chapel Street for a short time before becoming part of the Wolverton Road. William Russell appears as a Victualler in the 1851 census. He was something of a property developer. He purchased two cottages on the corner in the early 1840s from the Inwood family and set about redevelopment. At that time the property stretched all the way to what was then known as Back Lane. Once Russell had developed his new properties and sold land for the school and chapel on both corners. Back Lane eventually became known as Russell Street.

In the 1860s after the demise of the old *Red Lion* on the High Street an enterprising man opened up a beer shop on Mill Lane. Later he got a full licence. The pub eventually closed in the 1950s. It is now a private residence. In the same period another beer shop opened at 87 High Street, later to be known as the *Fox and Hounds*. It is still in operation today, although now expanded to include the house next door.

This expansion only met the needs of local consumers. None of these new houses offered accommodation or even much of a range of alcoholic beverages. They were pubs, locals.

Public Houses

This 19th century expansion led to the development of the area to the south along the London Road. It was a late development in Stony Stratford's history and for centuries was a field known as Gardners Close. There may have been some cottages on the corner which were torn down to build the new school, but next door, possibly uncomfortably so, was a public house called the *Plough* which could not be torn down and continued in business. A house had been established at least in the 18th century when it was known as the *Sun*, and may even have been there in 1613 when a transaction involving the *Angel* was recorded.

In the early 19th century it passed from the Colliers to William Barter, who is named in the 1830 Pigot Directory. The Barter family still had it in 1847 and again in 1854.

One story of petty crime from this period was reported in the Bucks Herald October 20th 1838

> Jane Gooding was charged with stealing a silver watch, on the 2nd. August, the property of Samuel Sheppard, in the parish of Wolverton.
>
> Samuel Sheppard, lives in Wolverton, in Northamptonshire. - Was at Stony Stratford on the 22nd of September; about 9 o'clock went up the town to a public house called the Plough; had a glass of gin; the landlord did not serve me; some women came in while I was standing at the bar; one of them snatched my watch out of my pocket; went out and fetched a constable; saw the prisoner take my watch; gave her in custody; I was not drunk; saw the prisoner in the street; did not speak to her before I went to the public-house; they asked me to treat them; told the landlord to give them a glass of gin each; have not seen the watch since.
>
> William Barter, landlord of the Plough, at Stony Stratford. - Remember the fair; in the evening, about 9 o'clock, heard a voice say, "give these women a glass of gin each;" saw the prosecutor push two women into my house; he said something behind the door, but what it was I cannot say; heard him say that he was robbed of his watch.
>
> Verdict - Not Guilty.

The *Plough* continued at this location until 1936 when the school was vacated and sold to the owners of the public house next door. Photographs of the original *Plough* from the 1930s and earlier do not show an obviously 18th century building. Perhaps it was remodelled with bay windows, or it may have been substantially rebuilt.

The late 19th century building now occupied by the *Plough* was designed by the distinguished Stony Stratford architect Edward Swinfen Harris as a school to replace the old National School, which had grown from the *Rose and Crown* charity on the High Street. The new school building was part of the new development of church and vicarage for the new parish of St Mary's, itself carved out of the Wolverton parish to accommodate the new inhabitants of that part of Stony Stratford. It was popularly known as "Wolverton St. Mary's."

Although the tram went all the way to Deanshanger for a period, its effective terminus was at the corner of the High Street and Wolverton Road. These two photographs shw the ticket office on the corner and below, in the coloured post card, the very long tram and the steam engine which pulled it all the way to Wolverton Station.

The Forester's Arms is behind the steam engine and on the left hand side of the top photograph is another view of the Angel.

The Plough has been at this corner since about 1936 when it moved into the vacant school building from its former site next door, which has since been replaced by a garage. The Old Plough was formerly The Sun and there has probably been and alehouse or inn here for about 300 years.

Below, the older photogrpah shows the old Plough, with its double fronted bay windows, on the left hand side. The buiding had probably been much-changed over the years and it is very difficult to date it from this photograph.

Both sides of the Watling Street

As we have discussed Stony Stratford grew up along the road which divided the manors of Wolverton and Calverton. Towards the end of the 12th century this cluster of properties began to form its own identity on both sides of the street and by 1290, when Queen Eleanor's funeral cortege passed through, it was an identifiable town, in name if not in status. While not the principal focus of this book we should consider the other inns and alehouses that met the needs of the village population of Wolverton and Calverton.

Calverton developed four or five small population groupings - at Upper Weald, Middle Weald, Lower Weald, and the western edge of Horsefair and Cowfair (later Silver Street) This part of what was generally considered to be Stony Stratford remained in the Calverton parish until 1920 when the Wolverton Urban District Council was formed. Thus the *Royal Oak* on the western edge of Horsefair Green was considered part of Calverton even though to most of us it was obviously in Stony Stratford.

A similar anomaly exists with Wolverton. The east side of the Watling Street was Wolverton until the Stony Stratford part was sectioned off. This still left everything from the Plough corner to Brick Kiln Farm as part of Wolverton. For this reason inns like the Plough and its predecessors were always licensed in the Wolverton parish.

Old Stratford, across the river, always struggled to build its poulation, but it did establish inns and roadside services, which will be considered below.

Wolverton

The old Wolverton village most likely had an alehouses until the village was abandoned after the 17th century enclosures. There may also have been an alehouse on the Wolverton Road/London Road corner in the 18th century. Nothing can be pinned down with certainty.

There was a recorded house in Wolverton in 1577, licensed to one Martin Hawse. This may have been in the old village, or it may have been at or near the *Plough* corner.

In the early 18th century there is record of a lease to the *Nag's Head*. At 17 shillings a year it would have been an alehouse at best. It may have been in Old Wolverton village or on the east side of the High

A view of the wharf at Wolverton and the Galleon.

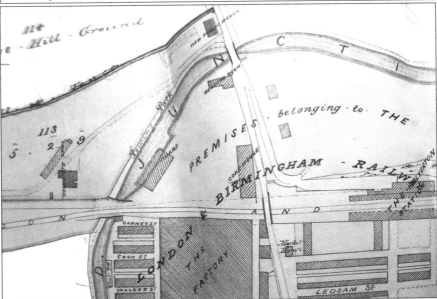

This plan of New Wolverton in 1847 shows the site of the original Radcliffe Arms in 1939 and the proposed second Radcliffe Arms at the side of the Stratford Road. The first pub was converted into four tenements. Both were demolished in the late 1870s to make way for the new loop line and the recreational park.

On the next page the former Royal Engineer built in 1841 and above, the Galleon, opened as a wharfside pub called the Locomotive circa 1840.

The former Royal Engineer, built in 1841, is now one of Wolverton's oldest buildings. Below the North Western, built circa 1864. When originally built the North Western had coach access to the yard on either side, but, as the importnce of horse travel declined these lanes were filled in by small properties. The central doorway to the house has also been removed in recent times.

Street. There is no way of knowing.

The mid 18th century licensing records offer some names although not much precise detail. There is a house called the *Sun* licensed to Edward Barnbrook in 1753 and subsequently to William Hackett, when the name changed to the *Plough*. It came into the hands of William Collyer in 1772. This was the house more or less next door to the present *Plough*. It is possible that an inn on or near that corner has a long history.

There are other licences in Wolverton in the period - the *Packhorse*, the *Half Moon* and the *Chequer*. The *Chequer* shows between 1754 and 1759, after which date it makes no reappearance. The *Packhorse* was last licensed in 1761 and the *Half Moon* may have survived until 1771. At least one of these may have been located in Wolverton village itself.

The arrival of the canal ought to have encouraged the development of a pub in Wolverton, but it appears not. The sole licensee in Wolverton until the coming of the railways was the *Plough* and then the Barter family opened up the *Locomotive* on their wharf at Old Wolverton. At the opening of the maintenance depot in 1839, New Wolverton still had no housing stock to speak of, so all the cottages at Old Wolverton were soon crammed with lodgers, swelling its population. A new licensed house appeared necessary. This house changed its name to the *Galleon* in the 20th century and is still in business.

While the canal had led to an increase in Wolverton's popultion in the first decades of the 19th century, the coming of the railway in 1838, overwhelmed the old manor. The potential was quickly spotted by two Stony Stratford entrepreneurs, Joseph Clare of the *Cock* and John Congreve, a solicitor, teamed up to build the *Radcliffe Arms* opposite the first station in Wolverton. It was quickly constructed and open for business in 1839. A year later the rug was pulled from under the feet of this fledgling business when the railway company built a new station to the south of the Stratford Road on land they had recently purchased from the Radcliffe Trust. Clare and Congreve were predictably outraged and they prevailed upon the Trust to allow them to build the *Royal Engineer* on an acre of land just outside railway property. This opened in 1841. Subsequently a new *Radcliffe Arms* was built on the Stratford Road near to the site of the present station and

The Victoria Hotel, Wolverton. It was built in the 1860s, about the same time as the North Western, when the Radcliffe Trustees finally agreed to the expansion of Wolverton. Wolverton quickly grew along the new streets - Church Street and the Stratford Road.

The Craufurd Arms on the Stratford Road, Wolverton, opened circa 1908 and was operated by the People's Refreshment House Association. The organisation was headed by Colonel Craufurd, hence the name.

the former building converted to housing. The *Radcliffe Arms* quickly acquired the nickname of *Hell's Kitchen*, a name which appears to have stuck, because the four tenements in the former public house were so described in the 1871 Census. Many of Wolverton's new arrivals were single men on good wages, who had little else to spend their money on but drink. Its original bad reputation persisted, and eventually it expired in the 1870s.

It was a condition of the railway purchase that no licensed premises were allowed on railway property; however once Wolverton began to expand westwards in 1860 this argument could no longer be made and the *North Western* opened in 1864, followed shortly after by the *Victoria Hotel.*

When the *North Western* was built the public were still dependent on horse-drawn carriages and the new property was built with street entrance on either side to the yard at the rear, as indeed was the *Royal Engineer.* At the close of the century horse travel became less relevant and the passageways on either side were filled in by two smaller properties, as can be seen in the photograph.

The *Victoria Hotel* occupied a large lot on the corner of Church Street and Radcliffe Street. The large yard had stables and at one time accommodated a blacksmith's premises. For many years it held on to the status of Wolverton's premier hotel. In recent years it has struggled and has experienced a number of closures and re-launches.

A Working Men's Club opened on Church Street in the 1880s and they were able to build their own premises on the corner of the Stratford Road and the then new Cambridge Street in the 1890s. Curiously, as Wolverton expanded to the south and west no new licences were granted. There was one attempt to open one on Green Lane the late 1890s but that came to nothing, probably because of a reluctance on the part of the JPs to grant new licences, and it was not until the *Craufurd Arms* was built in 1908 as a project by the curious People's Refreshment House Association that Wolverton got a new licensed establishment. With the exception of the "Top Club" (the Wolverton Central Working men's Club), built around the same time, this was to be Wolverton's last.

The Radcliffe Trustees and Stony Stratford commercial interests probably had a strong influence on this. The Trustees had always been against the idea of licensed premises in railway Wolverton and the first two, as we have seen, were built outside New Wolverton. In 1860 when the railway acquired new land for expansion this policy was relaxed and the *North Western* and the *Victoria Hotel* were permitted. After that the *Craufurd Arms* was permitted in 1908, possibly due to the PRHA policy of encouraging temperance and sobriety.

During the same period in the 19th century Stony Stratford acquired new licences at the *Red Lion*, the *Foresters Arms*, the *Fox and Hounds*, the *Case is Altered*, the *Prince of Wales* and the *Duke of Edinburgh*. That was a total of six extra licences while New Wolverton, putting the two Working Men's Clubs aside, was never allowed more than four public house licences at any point in its history. New Bradwell in the same period sprouted the *Railway Tavern*, the *Foresters*, the *Cuba*, the *County Arms*, the *Morning Star*. Both communities were much smaller than the burgeoning Wolverton.

The Shoulder of Mutton today. The building may date from the 17th century and in the 18th Century it was known as the Swan and the Green Dragon before it changed its name to the Shoulder of Mutton in 1779.

Calverton

The *Shoulder of Mutton* has been at Calverton at its present location since 1779. Prior to that it was known as the *Green Dragon* and in the middle of the 18th century was called The *Swan*.

The other Calverton pub was The *Royal Oak* on Horsefair Green, discussed in Chapter 7. The *Chequers* also features in the licensing register in the 1750s and 1760s. Its location is unknown, but given that the *Swan* was licensed during the same period it may either be a forerunner of the *Royal Oak* or somewhere near the site.

Old Stratford

Stony Stratford's cousin across the river in Northamptonshire lived somewhat in the shadow of its neighbour to the south. Nevertheless there were at leat four roadside hostelries in the small village. Today only the *Swan* survives near the crossroads.

At one time Old Stratford had at least four inns: the Swan, the Falcon on the north side of the Cosgrove Road, the Black Horse on the hill at the edge of Old Stratford and the Saracen's Head, which was on the site occupied by this car dealership. It was converted into a private school in the 19th century.

The *Black Horse* was at the top of the hill on the very edge of Old Stratford on the west side. There was a field up there named after it which suggests that it had its origin in pre-enclosure days. However, it does not appear on record until the Musson and Craven Trade

Directory of 1833. It closed after WWI and was demolished in the 1930s for a new housing development.

The *Falcon* was built on the north east corner of the crossroads and had origins going back at least to the middle of the 18th century. It was demolished when the road was widened.

The *Saracen's Head* was another 18th century establishment and may have been older. In the 19th century the site was turned into a school known as Belvedere Academy. It later acquired the name of Trinity House. Since it closed as a school it has been a truck stop and a car dealership. Trinity House still stands but retains little evidence of its earlier origins.

Malting and Brewing

For most of its history ale making in Stony Stratford was made in house, that is each alehouse or inn would make their own ale. The process, which had originated in these parts in Anglo-Saxon times, was well-understood and could be effected at room temperature with relatively simple equipment. The only difference between brewing at home and in a brewery is one of scale. The essential ingredients - barley, yeast and water - were readily available and usually a selection of herbs was added to the mix, partly for flavouring and partly as a preservative. Hops, at first imported from Flanders, replaced the native herbs in the 17th century and the taste eventually supplanted English ale in popularity and the product became known as beer. From medieval times until the 19th century, when water supplies could be better guaranteed, a low alcohol fermentation, known as small beer, was the liquid intake of choice for everyone, including children. Although they did not know the cause of water-borne diseases they did know that water could bring about unaccountable diseases and that the fermented drink was safer. Thus home brewing was common.

Brewing was still a home based activity in the 18th century. The auction of the belongings of Richard Rands of Wolverton in 1784 may illustrate this. Apart from the livestock, farm implements and household goods the sale also included "a Hogshead Brewing Copper, Brewing Vessels, Beer-Casks."

The quality of beer was variable. Changes in temperature and procedures could affect the final product as did the keeping of the product which only had a "shelf life" of a few days. Even in the twentieth century, when beer was delivered in pressurised casks from the large breweries, the quality of the product could vary from house to house depending on how it was kept. Sometimes there were risks to the drinker, as this cautionary tale on a gravestone in the grounds of Winchester Cathedral relates:

In Memory of Thomas Thetcher

a Grenadier in the North Reg. of Hants Militia, who died of

a violent Fever contracted by drinking Small Beer when hot the 12 May 1764. Aged 26 Years.

In grateful remembrance of whose universal good will towards his Comrades, this Stone is placed here at their expence, as a small testimony of their regard and concern.

Here sleeps in peace a Hampshire Grenadier,

Who caught his death by drinking cold small Beer,

Soldiers be wise from his untimely fall

And when ye're hot drink Strong or none at all.

This memorial being decay'd was restor'd by the Officers of the Garrison A.D. 1781.

An Honest Soldier never is forgot

Whether he die by Musket or by Pot.

Beer with a higher alcohol content was fermented for inns and for special occasions and this was known as strong beer, although even that might be regarded as weak by today's measures. The intermediate stage between the harvesting of the barley and its fermentation was making malt. Malting is the process of partial conversion of the starch to sugar and then arresting this initial fermentation so that it can be resumed later in the beer making process. There is some complexity and skill in malting and it became the part of brewing that was farmed out early to the specialists. Malt making begins with the barley harvest and light threshing to ensure that the husks are retained. The grains are then dried and stored for about six weeks. Once dry these grains are soaked in water over two or three days until they start to sprout. At this stage they are transferred to the floor of the malt house and turned over periodically until dry. The last stage in the process is to kiln dry the grains. Under floor pipes in the malt house carried heat from a fire's smoke which was channelled through the building. Longer heating times produced a darker malt which added colouring and flavour to the final beer product.

Specialised malt makers in Stony Stratford preceded specialised brewers although we have no way of knowing when they emerged but given the size of the inn trade in Stony Stratford and its population of over 1000 it would be surprising indeed if there were not malt makers in the town by the 16th century. One will in probate in 1558 describes William Wodecrofte as a *brewer and maltster*. We can infer that he was practising during most of the years of Henry VIII's reign, and of course he may not have been the only one. In the 17th century more sporadic references appear. There was a malting in Lyon Close, which was the field behind the 18th century house known as the *Rising Sun*. In 1615 it was in the hands of Thomas Boughen and in 1653 William Boughen. In 1663 a man called John Botteswill had a malthouse there and in 1683 John Botteril (probably the same man) is recorded as a maltster.

There was almost certainly a malthouse in the yard of the *Plough* on the Market Square as a fire was reported there on 17th May 1736. Edward Salter, the landlord of the *Plough* was listed as a maltster in 1727 in his will of that year, and his son Edward continued in that line as well as operating the inn. The Plough was renamed the White Lion after a new tenant started up in 1765. It was last licensed in 1783 but it is possible that the brewhouse, which backed onto the George yard continued to be used for some years.

Thomas Willeat, who was the licensee at the *King's Head* until his death in 1773, built a house at No 9 Horse Fair Green in 1764. It is still there today and was built with an archway on the west side, presumably so that wagons could gain access to the yard. This has now been filled in but the structural arch is still visible. I am told by a former resident that there were many scrapes on the wall from wagon wheels trying to squeeze through the narrow space. Willeat built a malt house backing onto Cofferidge Close that was still used for its original purpose in the 19th century. In the 1830 Pigot Trade Directory George Wilkinson was listed as a Maltster on Horse Fair Green, probably at this address, although as the farmer at Brick Kiln he may not have lived there, instead either renting the maltings or letting the house to his employee who did the specialised work. The 1841 census shows Thomas Payne as a maltster on Horse Fair but after that there is no further reference to any malting on Horse Fair.

The house at 9 Horsefair Green was built by Thomas Willeat who established a maltings in the back yard. In the 20th century the passageway was filled in to create more living space, but the former arch is still visible.

By this time there was one specialist maltster and two breweries who incorporated malting.

William Golby, listed on the High Street in 1847 as *farmer, maltster and merchant* in 1847 was in the malting business for at least thirty years. His sons took over but appear to have extended their activity into brewing. They are listed in the 1869 directory as Golby Brothers, brewers. There is no mention after that, an indication perhaps that the era of small brewers was quickly disappearing. At any rate the Golbys were probably established in the 18th century in this trade. On the street map of 1806 Mr Golby shows as the owner (although not the licensee) of the *Cross Keys* and also at the house which is now part of the *Fox and Hounds*, at Number 85 High Street. It is difficult to ascertain whether this was simply a residence for William Golby who carried on his malting activities behind the *Cross Keys* or whether this was the actual site of the malt house. The census of 1851 lists him as a maltster but of course does not determine that he was practising that trade at his house. Next door to Mr. Golby, at Number 87, (also part of the *Fox and Hounds*) was Richard Ball. His occupation is unknown although there is evidence that it was at one time a bakery. Both houses date from the middle of the 18th century and the previous buildings may have been damaged after the Great Fire of 1742.

When the *Northampton Mercury* advertised a sale of the Cross Keys on 25th March 1848, all the fixtures and fittings, including the brewing plant and equipment, were featured in the promotion and in fact the brewing plant was the headline for the sale rather than the old inn itself, which is an indication of how far downhill its trade was and it appears that the licensee, Henry Scaldwell was in financial difficulties. This doesn't quite square with the Golby Brothers listing themselves as brewers in 1869 so their activities may after all have been carried on at 85 High Street. The Cross Keys did not last long as a pub after that and 1865 was its last year in that line of business.

There are a surprising number of properties advertised for sale in the late 18th century in Stony Stratford which have a brewhouse attached. Although ale was brewed for domestic consumption the provision of a brewhouse on its own for the family and domestic servants seems a bit much. It is more than likely that these were once inns and as we have already seen those numbers did dwindle in the late 18th century.

There is evidence that some of the known pubs brewed their own beer. The *White Horse* is recorded as having a brewhouse in 1824. A brewhouse at the *George* is mentioned in 1821 and again in 1830. When it went on sale in 1877 brewing equipment included "a large brewing copper, mash vat, brewing tubs and wood spouts."

Breweries

The 19th century was a period of transition in the practice of brewing and over this period in-house brewing eventually ceased in favour of having barrels delivered weekly by specialised brewers. As with all these enterprises a lot of small outfits gradually merged into larger more centralised breweries, a process that continued throughout the 20th century. Newport Pagnell managed to retain its brewery until 1920 but the Stony Stratford breweries had a relatively short life before being obliterated by the larger breweries. By the end of the 19th century Stony Stratford pubs were served by either of the two large Northampton breweries, Phipps and NBC, or by the Newport Pagnell brewery, which was taken over by Charles Wells of Bedford in 1920.

Two operations in this period seem to have made the transition from an in-house brewery to something on a larger scale. One was associated with the *Bull* and the other with the *White Hart* on the Square.

The outbuilding on the right in the Bull yard and adjoining Odell's property may have been the brewhouse for the Britannia Brewery. There was once a door to Odell's side which was blocked off in the 19th century. This presumably gave access to Edwin Revill who was the previous owner of the property before James Odell and who also owned the Britannia Brewery until his death in 1856.

The first specialist brewer of record was Thomas Carter. He is described as a "Common Brewer" in the 1841 census and is listed as a Brewer in the 1844 Pigot Trade Directory. He was also listed as the proprietor of the Bull and as a beer retailer in New Wolverton. It is probable that the brewery was in an outbuilding at the back of the Bull or at the back of one of the adjoining properties. When the Bull was up for sale on 26th July 1832 the brewhouse was described as "lately considerably repaired." He did not live at the Bull but instead at a house further down the street, Number 46, presently occupied by a bookmaker. There is no reason to suppose that brewing took place at this address.

The two Wolverton Public Houses were the *Radcliffe Arms* and the *Royal Engineer*, both presumably in the early days of Wolverton selling great quantities of beer to the new and growing population. The Bull may not have been doing so well and it seems that the prime asset was the brewery. The owners, John Congreve and Joseph Clare, may have been interested in realising some capital from this, but would also settle for a lease. The brewery must have been state of the art for the time and by being able to supply three houses began a trend that saw future breweries increasingly tying houses to their brand.

Edwin Revill had the ironmonger's shop next door and it is possible that George Thorne's drapery business was in the shop on the other side of the Bull, now occupied by the Vaults. They formed a partnership and, as well as continuing their main business activities, established the Revill & Thorne Brewery, later known as the Britannia Brewery.

Edwin Revill senior died in November 1853 and was succeeded by his son, also Edwin. His father's death may have been the stimulus to bring in Thomas Phillips to manage the brewery.

The Phillips family had extensive brewing interests across the country and founded several major breweries. Thomas Phillips was from the Bicester branch of the family. He moved to Stony Stratford in 1854 and it appears that his brother William established an agency for this brewery in Northampton in November 1855. In November 1857 Thomas Phillips, together with his brothers William and Arthur founded the Northampton Brewing Company and he moved there the following year. His association with Stony Stratford was therefore brief.

And this history of the Britannia Brewery in Stony Stratford is sketchy indeed. Apart from this record in the Phillips family archive the Britannia Brewery is mentioned in one trade directory, that of Musson and Craven, which made one appearance in 1853. There was also an advertisement in the Northampton mercury on Saturday May 12th 1855 offering the Wheatsheaf at Loughton for let and asking applicants to *apply to Mr. T. Phillips, Britannia Brewery, Stony Stratford.*

He was still in Stony Stratford at that date.

The brewery does not appear to have survived Phillips' departure because no more is heard of it. A few years later, the younger Edwin Revill sold the ironmongery business to James Odell, which business is still in the same family.

Northampton offered greater opportunities to Thomas Phillips and within a year or two the Northampton Brewery Company had been founded. In the years that followed NBC, together with Phipps, came to dominate beer sales in Stony Stratford. Only the Newport Pagnell Brewery had a toehold in the town, supplying the Plough.

In 1875 two of the Phillips brothers sold their share of the business. One was Thomas who then moved to Newport in Monmouthshire where he bought the Newport Brewery. One of his sons, Frederick, who was born in Stony Stratford, entered and continued the business.

7 Market Square was once the home of William Tomkins and later his son who had a brewery on the premises until 1880.

The other brewery of significance was operated by William Tomkins at 7, Market Square. He owned the *White Hart* next door which must have been his principal outlet.

He was listed as a brewer and maltster and Joseph Rogers was recorded as the licensee for the *White Hart*. Tomkins' will of 1856 makes clear that he owned the property and he described the *White Hart* as "partly occupied by me and partly occupied by Joseph Rogers". He makes his first appearance in 1847 in the trade directory. After his death in 1856 one of his sons, John Tomkins took on the brewing business and the *White Hart* continued to be leased to tenants. The brewery certainly satisfied the thirst of the customers of the White Hart, which, according to Markham, "brewed the best beer in town," an endorsement of Tomkins' expertise as a brewer.

One assumes that Tomkins also provided other houses with his ale and made the business viable. This brewery stayed in business until about 1880. By 1883, this business seems to have gone for good. It is a similar story with the Golbys, who appear to have taken up the brewing mantle after Revill & Thorne dropped the ball. Their last entry is in the trade directory is 1877.

In the same period the *Royal Oak* was also characterised as a brewery. This brewing business was taken over by Samuel Nichols in the 1870s but it does not appear to have had much of a life after that.

William Whiting was another "cottage brewer" of the period, plying his trade on the High Street in 1851 and then on Church Street in 1861. The ready movement of men like Carter and Whiting is an illustration of how simple brewing was on this scale in the 19th century; they were able to pick up and move with some ease.

By 1880 larger breweries in Newport Pagnell and Northampton were able to service pubs in Stony Stratford.

Thereafter Stony Stratford public buses were entirely dependant on breweries further afield and as these larger breweries became richer they began to buy up public houses and either let them to a tenant or install a manager, thereby creating the "tied house", ensuring that only their products could be sold.

Most of the Stony Stratford pubs were tied to the Northampton breweries, either Phipps or NBC, The single exception appears to have been the Plough, which was served by the Newport Pagnell Brewery and was probably at the end of its run.

In 1915 the Newport Pagnell Brewery was still a going concern and

The dray acccident of 1915

on February 1st of that year two men, Job Griffin and Henry Stanton, set out with their dray loaded with barrels for delivery to Bradwell, Wolverton and Stony Stratford. Their vehicle, interestingly, was steam operated.

On the way back to the depot at 1:30 pm., presumably having completed deliveries to Stony Stratford, the vehicle skidded on the rise going up from Creed Street to the bridge going over the former railway line, now McConnell Drive. The report described the road surface as "greasy" but it does not say what was on the road to cause the skid. As the vehicle was not loaded down with heavy barrels the back wheels went out of control and the lorry crashed into the corrugated iron railings on one side of the bridge.

The vehicle crashed down some 20 feet onto the railway line pinning the men beneath the wreckage.

When the crane arrived to lift the wreck they found Henry Stanton already dead and Job Griffin with serious injuries. he was taken to Northampton Hospital where sadly he died four days later.

An inquest was held into the accident later at the North Western Hotel. Griffin had a reputation as a careful and experienced driver and no fault was found.

The Newport Pagnell Brewery was later acquired by Charles Wells of Bedford and they continued to supply the *Plough*.

Working Men's Clubs

The Working Men's club was a by-product of 19th century industrialisation. Men were living and working in more densely populated towns, often in a single industry, and were on the whole better paid and better educated and able to organise their own institutions.

Wolverton established the first of such clubs in a terraced house on Church Street. In the 1890s they had the resources to build the

Wolverton Working Men's Social Club on the Stratford Road. In the next decade the Wolverton Central Club was built on the new Western Road development.

New Bradwell also established two similar clubs, although only one survived to the 21st century.

Stony Stratford opened a Working Men's Club at the former White Hart on the Market Square in the early part of the 20th century and after 1948 moved to the London Road. This has recently closed. In this context, the Conservative Club on the High Street, performs a similar function, although its affiliation is obviously different. This organisation is still going after 100 years.

Wolverton Social Club, the fisrt Working Men's Club in the district. It had its origins in a terraced house on Church Street in 1872 and in the 1890s the club was able to move to a new, purpose-built facility on the Stratford Road.

These clubs brought new standards to social drinking. Members were expected to behave themselves. The clubs had educational aspirations; they ran some adult education classes and operated lending libraries long before there were public libraries in the district. They had access to indoor games, such as billiards and snooker and some clubs ran sporting teams. Drinks were reasonably priced. On Saturday night they often promoted concerts and variety entertainments.

Beer Shops

In 1830 the government passed the Beerhouse Act with the intention of liberalising licensing in the UK. Under its provisions anyone could brew and sell beer on the premises on payment of a fee of two guineas. Up to that point licensing was in the hands of local magistrates who tended to be very restrictive in such matters. It certainly opened things up. By 1841 there were some 45,000 commercial brewers in the country plying their trade mostly through beer shops. Oddly this new act had little impact on Stony Stratford, possibly because the community was already well served with licensed premises and because the beer shop licence could not be obtained by anyone who had a licence before 1830.

By 1844 Thomas Scaldwell had one on the High Street. He was also a leather dealer, so this must have been an additional activity. Similarly the butcher William Patison became a beer retailer,

William Russell, who developed the corner of the Wolverton Road to the chapel and built what became later the Foresters Arms also operated under a beer licence. During his tenure it was called the Engineer but for most of its history the Foresters Arms has endured as a public house until its very recent closure.

The new Wolverton Road pubs also began life as beer shops and they have already been discussed. The *Red Lion* started out on Silver Street in 1866 in a similar fashion. It first appears as a public house in 1891 when Richard Holman was the licensee. The full license may have been dropped after his death because it once more reverts to a nameless "beer retailer" in the trade directory until 1939, when it is once more listed as a public house under the name *Red Lion*.

William Marlow, a chimney sweep, is listed as a beer retailer on Horn Lane in 1869. This appears to have been a short-lived enterprise and almost nothing is known about it.

New Wolverton attracted the most interest, because, as mentioned earlier, the Radcliffe Trustees made it a condition of sale that no licensed premises should open on railway property. Hence the two licensed outlets that Wolverton had, The *Radcliffe Arms* and the *Royal Engineer*, were both outside Wolverton as it was at that time. The railway company turned a blind eye to beer shops. They were outside the control of the magistrates and the railway board were probably not too concerned as they were technically legal. There were three beer shops in Wolverton in the 1840s, and one was listed to Thomas Carter who was a Stony Stratford Brewer.

However there was some controversy about the premises operated by George Spinks. Spinks was an early arrival in Wolverton and opened up his Locomotive Eating House at the north end of Bury Street in 1840. For a time he showed no interest in selling beer but after a few years he began brewing and selling beer. He must have been successful because the public house owners were making representation to the Radcliffe Trustees to put pressure on the LNWR Board to close him down. The railway company's heart wasn't really in it and Spinks seemed to carry on. There was more correspondence until the issue was finally resolved by a board decision which had nothing to do with licensing. In 1855 the railway Board decided to demolish three northern streets, including Spinks' eating house/beer shop for workshop expansion and Spinks was no longer able to rent premises. He left town.

The famous Refreshment Rooms at Wolverton Station was an anomaly. The premises were licensed and they did a brisk business, employing almost 30 staff. Whether or not local people were allowed to drink there is not known.

In the 1860s Wolverton expanded and the addition of the *North Western* and the *Victoria Hotel* and a beer shop at the end of the Stratford Road, later known as the *Drum and Monkey*, seemed to satisfy Wolverton's drinking needs. Curiously George Spinks assured the very young and probably impressionable Hugh Stowell Brown in the early 1840s that he was very much in favour of the temperance movement. Clearly commercial interests made him change his mind a decade later.

On the subject of Temperance, Stony Stratford had a "Temperance hotel" in the 20th century. It appeared to have lifespan of about 20 years from 1915 to 1935. It was known as the Victoria Homeland operated from the premises at 73 High Street. The Becks family also used the premises as a retail confectionery and in the end this side of the business came to dominate and the hotel was quietly closed. Later the business was bought by Thomas Haseldine under which name it is now better known.

Chapter Eleven

Pubs, Hotels, Restaurants and Coffee Shops

Pubs have sentimental associations. We can all remember our first pint, our favourite "local", landlords we liked, and landlords we didn't. We recall the days of good fellowship, occasional drunkenness and hangovers but when all is said and done they are businesses and subject to economic cycles. Our survey has shown times when inns were very numerous and periods when they were in decline. As mentioned in an earlier chapter, there was a dramatic falling off in licences at the end of the 18th century, only for there to be an expansion in the 19th century. Some places such as the *George* had periods when they ceased to be licensed premises only for them to be revived some years later.

But over the last 50 years the prevailing trend has been to reduce the number of licensed premises in Stony Stratford, and Wolverton too. Few if any are locally owned (The *George* appears to be the lone exception.) and are often one of a plethora of properties held in the portfolio of an investment firm.

When Sir Frank Markham was born in Stony Stratford in 1898 these premises were licensed in the town:

Coach and Horses, Cock, Bull, White Swan on the Wolverton side of the High Street; the *Barley Mow*, the *Rising Sun, Fox and Hounds*, Stony Stratford Working Men's Club, *White Horse* and the *George*, and the *Angel* on the west side;

The *Royal Oak* on Horsefair and the *Red Lion* on Mill Lane;

The *Plough* on the London Road;

The *Foresters Arms*, the *Duke of Edinburgh*, the Case is Altered, and the *Prince of Wales* on the Wolverton Road

The *Crown* and the *King's Head* on the Square.

In 1948 when he compiled his survey of Stony Stratford's inns there were these public houses:

Starting from the very north end, the *Barley Mow*, the *Rising Sun*, the *Fox and Hounds*, the Conservative Club, the *White Horse and the Angel*. On the eastern side, the *Cock*, the *Bull*, the *White Swan*, the *Foresters Arms and the Plough*. In the Market Square, the *Crown* and the Working Men's Club. The *Royal Oak* prevailed on Horse Fair Green and along the Wolverton Road, the *Case is Altered* and the *Duke of Edinburgh*.

A few years before this the George had transformed itself into a coffee house.

Today the number has diminished further although some have returned to being licences premises.

The *Cock* and the *Bull* are the outstanding long term survivors and both command the High Street after being rebuilt after the fire of 1742. The *George* is once more a hotel and public house and also has a history that extends back to the early part of the 17th century. Curiously the old *Swan* has come back into play as the *Hotel Different Drummer*. The *Plough* too, although it has only been in its present premises since the 1930s also has a long history stretching back to at least the early 18th century when it was known as the *Sun*. The *White Horse* was rebuilt in the late 18th century and has continuously operated under that name since that time, although it is highly likely that another inn under different names occupied that site since medieval times. The *Fox and Hounds* emerged in the 19th century, although it may have had an earlier history. On the Market Square the *Crown* is a long term survivor, almost certainly dating from the middle of the 17th century. The Conservative Club has survived for over a century, as has the *Duke of Wellington* on the Wolverton Road, formerly the *Duke of Edinburgh*, and briefly the *Dog and Gun*. The *Forester's Arms* closed while we were compiling this book, and has now re-opened as a restaurant.

The *Shoulder of Mutton* prevails at Calverton as does the *Galleon* at Old Wolverton, although both have experienced rocky times. Wolverton town has lost the *Royal Engineer* and one Working Men's Club. Old Stratford has lost the *Black Horse*, the *Saracen's Head* and the *Falcon*.

There are always fashionable cycles. The coffee shop was a popular meeting place in the 18th century. it looks as if a 21st century version of this has returned to our High streets. The history of the *George* can illustrate this. It started life as an inn in the 17th century and became a posting house and hotel in the 19th century. In the middle of the 20th century it operated as a coffee shop. Now it has returned to its innkeeping roots serving its public as a pub, hotel and restaurant.

Some of the old inns, now hotels, appear to be managing. There is always a demand for accommodation and the Milton Keynes area seems to be doing well in this regard. Pubs, however, have suffered.

Stony Stratford High street in a more leisurely age.

Above: The motorised omnibuses which replaced the steam tram outside the Cock Hotel.

Below: A photograph from earlier in the century looking towards the Bull. Horse and cart and motorised vehicles were co-existing at this time.

There is more competition for people's leisure time and supermarkets offer alcoholic beverages at lower prices. Pubs in the meantime have to contend with increased regulation and have chosen instead to go out of business. We don't know at the time of writing if this will continue or if pubs, with their long heritage will prevail in the long term. We suspect they will.

Over 2000 years there have been taverns, inns, alehouse, hotels and public houses along this famous road. Over time they have adapted to changing economic circumstances. Over time they have survived. Over time they have been subject to hostile regulation and punitive taxation. At certain times monopolies have threatened to strangle the life out of them. As we go to press, legislation to curb the system of tying pubs to high rents and high costs of beverages through effective monopolies is working its way through Parliament. This is by no means the first time that government has felt impelled to intervene to restrict monolpolies.

This historical survey is intended to be comprehensive, but it is not complete. More evidence is bound to emerge in the future which will help to confirm some findings, support some educated guesses, produce alternative conclusions and fill some gaps in our knowledge.

We hope this is not the last word.

Stony Stratford High Street today.

Part Two
A Compendium of Inns, Taverns, Alehouses and Public Houses

A Compendium of Inns, Taverns, Alehouses and Public Houses

A lot of inn names have been unearthed as a result of this research. In some cases there is a name or date only, in others there is a complete history. This compendium presents a summary of what is known and includes inns, alehouses, beer shops, wine shops, off licences, clubs, breweries and maltings. For the purpose of completeness, all premises that were within the Wolverton Urban District are included here, although not necessarily discussed in the text. This list include Old Stratford, the Parish of Calverton, Wolverton, New Bradwell and, because of its proximity, Old Bradwell.

The Angel (11 High St.)

Location: 11 High Street
Period: 18th to 20th Century
First reference: 1770[1]
Commentary: The Angel was a small house on the west side and the first on the High Street. There was a saying that originated in the 18th century that Stony Stratford was guarded by angels at both ends making reference to this house and the other Angel at 185 High Street, which later became the Barley Mow. The licensing records of 1770 mark its first documented record although Markham suspects that it may have had a longer history. He notes that the building was at least 17th century in origin so it may have operated under a different sign in an earlier period.

The building was demolished in 1970s to make way for the Cofferidge Close development. The frontage of The Angel is preserved in the Milton Keynes Museum as a shop front.

The Angel (185 High St.)

Location: 185 High Street
Period: 18th to 20th Century
First reference: 1772[2]
Commentary: See details under Barley Mow.
See Barley Mow.

---

1 Register of Licensed Victuallers, Bucks. 1753-1828.
2 Register of Licensed Victuallers, Bucks. 1753-1828.

The Angel (East side)

Location: High Street, East side
Period: 17th Century
First reference: 1613[3]

Commentary: Our only knowledge of this house comes from a lease from Sir Edward Longueville to one Lettice Ashby in 1629. From the same document we learn that it had also been leased in 1613 to George Walton. Because we know the name of the landlord we can say with some certainty that it was located on the east side since most of Stony Stratford on this side of the Watling Street was still part of the Wolverton Manor. Exactly where it was located cannot be determined. "The Angel" in this context is never heard of again and if it continued its function as an inn it changed its name.
See Plough.

Barley Mow (Market Square)

Location: 10 Market Square
Period: 18th to 19th Century
First reference: 1753[4]

Commentary: The first recorded entry is discovered in the licensing records of 1753. It was then licensed to Elizabeth Day and in the following year to Sands Day, who continued to hold the licence until 1771. If he was the son of Elizabeth this might suggest that his father may have held the licence for 20 or more years prior to that date. When it was sold in 1810 it was a substantial property with a brewhouse, stables, several other outbuildings and two acres of pasture, indicating that it probably had a field which extended back to Cofferidge Close. There is no proof of this but one can surmise that its life as an inn went back at least to the 17th century when the other inns on this side of the Square were built.

In 1798 William Holland and his wife Mary became the licensees and purchased the property four years later when Lord Salisbury was disposing of property to relieve himself of the Land Tax. They continued to operate it as an inn. William Holland died in 1807 and his widow took on William Marlow as a tenant. She died in 1810 and everything was put up for auction. Marlow was the successful bidder, but he may have been less successful in his financial affairs because in 1819 he was bankrupt and the property was sold to pay creditors. This was the end of the Barley Mow and since that time the building has served as a shop and private residence.

---

3 Ms. Radcliffe dep. deed 363. 1629
4 Register of Licensed Victuallers, Bucks. 1753-1828.

Barley Mow (185 High Street)

Location: 185 High Street
Period: 18th to 20th Century
First reference: 1772[5] (The Angel), 1790 (The New Barley Mow)
Commentary: The Barley Mow, at the very northern entrance to Stony Stratford has a history which is older than its name. As far back as 1317 there is a reference to an inn on or near this site. (See Grilkes Herber) The four centuries following are a complete mystery.

The present building is 18th century. This piece of land, known as "Gregg's Arbour" in the 18th century was still part of the Wolverton Manor in the early 18th century when the privilege of mowing was given to the miller William Perry for 15s a year. It is not clear if there was a house on the property, and indeed Greggs Arbour might actually have been the strip of land between the Barley Mow and the river. The deeds to the present Barley Mow property show that it was sold by the Marquess of Salisbury, at that time Lord of the Manor of Calverton in 1807. This suggests that it was always part of the Calverton manor and had never belonged to the Wolverton estate. The deeds to the property offer no earlier dates.

All we can say with certainty that this building was an alehouse in 1772 when it opened as The Angel. In 1790 it changed hands and name and was known as The Barley Mow and distinguished from the existing inn on the Square of the same name by being known as the New Barley Mow. When the Old Barley Mow closed in 1819, this one remained until 1970.

See Angel (185 High Street)

The Bell (Market Square)

Location: 16 Market Square
Period: 17th Century
First reference: 1713[6]
Commentary: This property was sold by William Perry to William Gilpin. Markham believes this to be Number 16. The property has been used as a shop for a number of years and is presently a hairdressing salon. The present brick frontage is late 18th century but the building may well be of an earlier date.

The Bell is also a licensed inn from 1775 to 1780. In the first five of these years the licensee was John Parsons; in 1780 it was John Harrison. It is by

---

5 Register of Licensed Victuallers, Bucks. 1753-1828.
6 Deed of sale: William Perry to William Gilpin.

no means certain that was at this address; if so, its life as an inn under this name was brief.

Apart from this reference the inn or alehouse has no history before or after. If it did continue in this line of business it must have used another name.

Bell (East side)

Location: East side
Period: 17th Century
First reference: 1625[7]

Commentary: Sir Edward Longueville leased this property to Thomas Rawbone in 1625 for 22s 8d per annum and two fat capons at Christmas. The last condition is curious and suggest a feudal tribute, which might further tell us that the lease for this property had its origin in medieval times. The annual rent indicates that it was a small house and was most likely an alehouse rather than an inn. Typically, inns named The Bell were often found close to churches and may even have started their life as a hostelry run by the clergy. In which case it might have been in the vicinity of St Mary Magdalen, but this is guesswork and its location is unknown.

Bell (Bradwell)

Location: Abbey Road, Old Bradwell
Period: 18th to 20th century.
First reference: 1753[8]

Commentary: This was probably the oldest inn or alehouse in the village of Bradwell, although its history is obscure. It first appears in the licensing records when they begin in 1753, which suggests an older history. In the early 19th century it is listed as the Old Bell in directories, although it reverts to the Bell later in the 19th century. The house was located on Abbey Road at the corner of what is now Primrose Road. It closed in 1953.

Black Boy

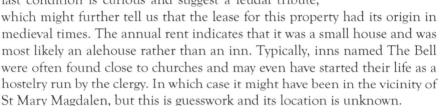

Location: East side
Period: 17th century
First reference: 1625[9]

Commentary: Here is another inn which only makes a brief appearance, under a name which would not be

---

7 Ms. Radcliffe dep. deed 359. 1625.
8 Register of Licensed Victuallers, Bucks. 1753-1828..
9 Ms. Radcliffe dep. deed, 302. 1625.

acceptable nowadays. The location is unknown, apart from inferring that it must be on the east side. The document, found amongst the Radclffe Trust papers held in the Bodleian Library, records the conveyance of the inn from Michael Boughey to John Parsons. Michael Boughey came from Michael Hipwell's inn holding family and was probably at this time the Innholder of the Swan with Two Necks. This looks very much like the passing on of a lease and the property remained in the hands of the Longuevilles.[10]

Black Bull

Location: The Bull Hotel
Period: 18th century
First reference: 1777[11]
Commentary: The licensing register records a Black Bull in 1777. This is almost certainly The Bull. The licensee John Coates appears for the Bull in the years before and after.
See Bull.

Black Cock

Location: Unknown
Period: 18th century
First reference: 1757[12]
Commentary: The Black Cock appears in licensing records from 1757 to 1761, licensed to Thomas Cattle.
See Three Tuns.

Black Horse

THE
BLACK HORSE INN

Location::   North end of Old Stratford, west side.
Period: 19th to 20th century
First reference: 1830[13]
Commentary: The Black Horse Inn was once the first or last (depending upon your direction) pub in Old Stratford sitting at the high point of the road. The buildings were quite extensive and behind them was a large field known as

10 Here is a transcription of the document, dated 1625:

Michael Boughey of Stony Stratford, inn holder, and Margaret his wife, convey to John Parsons of Passenham, County Northampton, Gent., an inn called The Black Boy in Stony Stratford in the Parish of Wolverton.

11 Register of Licensed Victuallers, Bucks. 1753-1828..
12 Licensing records.
13 Pigot's Diectory, 1830.

Black Horse field. This field is now divided by the by-pass road.

Its relatively remote location probably did it no favours because the house developed a poor reputation and in 1920 the Northampton Licensing Committee refused to renew the licence. Compensation was paid to Phipps Brewery Company, which then owned the house, and to the tenant. In 1922 Phipps sold the property. The Black Horse buildings were demolished in the 1930s and developed into a row of semi-detached houses.

Black Horse (Stony Stratford)

Location: Unknown
Period: 18th century
First reference: 1756[14]
Commentary: It was probably the Waggon and Horses previously but changed its name in 1756. It was out of business in 1782.

See Waggon and Horses

Blue Anchor

Location: East side
Period: 17th century
First reference: 1678[15]
Commentary: This is a most unusual name for an inland pub. While this name is often found at coastal towns, it is a rather odd find in Stony Stratford. But here it is.

It appears in a lease to Robert Edge, who was named in the deed. He was a gardener by trade and his alehouse provided him with an additional source of income. What he gets in this deed is "all that messuage, or tenement, with the appurtenances situate on the east side" and "a pyghtle of pasture" - meaning a small plot of land. A "messuage" is Norman French, still in use in the 17th century, for a house, any outbuildings and the yard.

There is no apparent entry in the estate documents 30 years later that would match the Blue Anchor (unless it became the Nag's Head). The property may have been sold in the intervening years.

From the description the Blue Anchor sounds more like an alehouse than an inn. However, the emergence of the Drum and Anchor in the next century does suggest a connection and one might look for the former Blue Anchor on this site.

See also Drum and Anchor and Coach and Horses.

14 Register of Licensed Victuallers, Bucks. 1753-1828..
15 Ms. Radcliffe dep. deed, 319. 1678

Boot

Location: Unknown

Period: 18th century

First reference: 1721[16]

Commentary: One Thomas Miller was recorded in 1721 as the landlord of a house known as The Boot. There is no other reference.

Bradville

Location: Bradwell Road, New Bradwell

Period: 20th century to Present

First reference: c. 1950

THE

BRADVILLE

Commentary: The Bradville estate was started in the 1930s and further developed after WWII with pre-fab houses. The new public house on the corner was named after the estate and still stands on the Bradwell Road.

In the late 1970s it was re-named the Jovial Priest. In 1986 Halley's Comet made a return to our night skies and the pub was again re-named. It is still known as that today.

See also Halley's Comet, Jovial Priest

Bull

Location: High Street

Period: 17 to 21st century

First reference: 1619[17]

Commentary: The Bull, together with the Cock, became one of the two great posting houses of Stony Stratford. Both were rebuilt after the great fire of 1742 which originated in the Bull and both present imposing 18th century facades to the High Street. The earliest historical reference is 1619 when Sir Gyles Mompesson fined Micheall Boughen £5 on the 16th July of that year. The Mompesson account book lists it as the *Bull Head* but there is no reason to suppose that it was a different place. A manor document of 1710 tells us that the Bull had been leased "eighty years" which would place its origin at 1630; however that date may be an estimate only so the earlier date can be taken with confidence.

Was there an inn on this site before the 17th century? Certainly the Bull sits on one of the three earliest plots that date back to the foundation of Stony

---

16 From notes by Mike Brown, author of ABC: A Brewer's Compendium.

17 Account Books of Sir Gyles Mompesson, 1619-20.

Stratford in the last years of the 12th century. Educated guesswork should tell us that there was an inn on the site at an earlier date. It may have borne the sign of the Bull, but there is no record to be able to say one way or another. From its known history from the early 17th century it became a great rival to the Cock and the other great inns at the north end of town, like the Swan, the Horseshoe and the Red Lyon. It outlasted all of them with the exception of its close neighbour the Cock

For many years it remained a property of the Wolverton Manor and contributed large rents to the estate until the Radcliffe Trust decided to sell the property to help manage the Land Tax in 1802. It was bought by Thomas Harrison of Wolverton House who was also Land Agent to the Trust. Presumably, nobody saw a conflict of interest in those days.

It changed hands a few years later, presumably at a profit for the Harrisons and again in 1813. Ownership was not stable in the 19th century and it periodically came up for sale. Like all coaching inns it was hit hard by the arrival of railway travel in 1838.

The following advertisement from 1815 describes the establishment in some detail.

Northampton Mercury 3 June 1815
Bull Inn, Stony Stratford.

To be SOLD by AUCTION,

On the Premises, In the Month of June, in Lots, unless an acceptable Offer should be made for the Whole by Private Contraction or about the 5th Day of June next,

ALL that old-established Inn, called the BULL INN, in complete Repair, situate in the HIGH-STREET, of STONY-STRATFORD, in the County of Buckingham, on the Great West Chester Road, and now in the Possession of the Proprietor, who is now retiring from the public Business.

The House consists of thirteen best Bed-Rooms on the first Floor, seven Servant's Bed-Rooms on the second Floor, two large Dining-Rooms, four Parlours, Kitchen, Back Kitchen, Brewhouse, four Cellars, Laundry, Mangling-Room and Soldiers'-Room. In the Yard - Stabling for 60 Horses, with capital Granaries over the same; two Coach Houses, and other convenient Out-offices. Also a very productive Garden inclosed by a Brick Wall; and about seven acres of very rich Meadow Land nearly adjoining, together with a large Farm-Yard, Manure Yard, Cottage-House, and capital Stone-built and tiled barn, the whole surrounded by a Stone Wall coped with Yorkshire Paving.

Possession to be given at Michelmas next, and if the Estate is sold together, the Purchaser may be accommodated with the Chaises and Horses, and also a very choice Stock of Wines, Liquors, Furniture, &c. At a fair Valuation. For a view of the Estate, apply to the Proprietor; and for further Particulars to him, or to Messrs. WORLEY, Solicitors, Stony Stratford.

19th May, 1815.

We can get some clue as to how the loss of the coaching trade affected the once proud coaching inn of the Bull. The premises were up for let or possible sale in April 1843, but, and here is the interesting piece, the inn was no longer the principal selling point. Instead it was the brewery in the back yard that was more likely to generate income and profit. The inn itself was offered as accommodation.

The joint owners at this time were Joseph Clare of the Cock Hotel and John Congreve a Stony Stratford solicitor. They had already built the Radcliffe Arms and Royal Engineer at Wolverton and these premises were tied to the Bull Brewery. In other words there were two thirsty and profitable outlets notwithstanding the decline of the Bull itself.

Case is Altered

Location: Wolverton Road
Period: 19th to 20th century
First reference: 1867[18]

Commentary: This was one of three new pubs that opened in the late 19th century as the Wolverton Road developed. For many years it only held a beer licence. Judging from the census it was originally one house on the corner which later incorporated the adjoining house.

The Case is Altered is a rare pub name, although it is found in places other than Stony Stratford. Quite why it was ever adopted as a pub name will probably remain a mystery.

The phrase originated with an Elizabethan lawyer, Sir Edmund Plowden, who died before 1585. He was called upon to defend a gentleman who was charged in those sensitive religious times with hearing Mass. This was against the law, but Plowden discovered that his client had been set up and the man conducting the mass was not an ordained priest. therefore he argued, if there was no priest there could be no mass. "The case is altered!" he triumphantly declared and all of Elizabethan England was buzzing with the news. The phrase slipped into the language as a sort of catch phrase and frequently

18 Post Office Directory, 1867.

in tavern disputes a man would assert the rights of his argument by saying, "The case is altered!" It later became the title of a Ben Jonson play, written in 1597. This play is a somewhat haphazard confection of intertwined comic plots and is thought by some critics to be the work of several authors. It has no special bearing on the naming of a pub in Stony Stratford.

Quite why this pub name should resurface four centuries later may not be easily explained. Possibly by this date the phrase had come into general usage as a way of asserting one's rights in an argument.

The first landlord was John Franklin, a bricklayer by trade. It closed between 1956-7.

Castle

Location: 131 High Street
Period: 17th century
First reference: 1789[19]
Commentary: There is one reference only to this name, in 1789 to a licensee called Henry Harris. Since Henry Harris was the licensee of the Rising Sun the year before and after, one supposes that he changed the name in that year but a year later regretted than decision.

See Rising Sun

Chequer

Location: Wolverton Parish
Period: 18th century
First reference: 1724[20]
Commentary: The Chequer was advertised for let when one Henry Nicholls was the licensee in November 1727. It was, according to the advertisement, "noted for its fine ales." The Chequer was again offered for let in 1750 with details available from either Thomas Woodhead, grocer of London or Michael Garment at the Queen's Head. Might this suggest that the Chequer was adjacent to the Queen's Head?

This sign was licensed to Daniel Parrott for three years only - 1757 to 1759. He was licensed in the parish of Wolverton which could place in it the village itself or on the London Road.

See Queen's Head.

---

19 Register of Licensed Victuallers, Bucks. 1753-1828..
20 From notes by Mike Brown, author of ABC: A Brewer's Compendium.

Chequers

Location: Old Bradwell
Period: 18th century
First reference: 1753[21]
Commentary: When licensing records began in 1753 the Chequers was one of two licensed houses in the parish of Bradwell. Its location is unknown. It may have been in the village but it could also have been further north on the Newport road beside the toll gate. It closed in 1803. Throughout this period it was run by members of the Mortimer family.

Cheshire Cheese

Location: Calverton Parish
Period: 18th Century
First reference: 1753[22]
Commentary: The Cheshire Cheese shows in Calverton parish licensing records between the years 1753 and 1754. The licensee was Comfort Roberts. As the Swan (later Shoulder of Mutton) was licensed at the same time, there is good reason to suspect that it was on or near the site of the later Royal Oak.

Coach and Horses

Location: 106 High Street
Oeriod: 18th to 20th century
First reference: 1792[23]
Commentary: The Coach and Horses was formerly the Drum and Anchor and possibly the Blue Anchor before that.

The Coach and Horses began its life under that name in 1792 and continued under this name until it closed just before the first World War. It presently serves as a dentist's surgery. The house dates from the early 18th century according to the listed buildings survey but it would have been gutted by fire in 1742 and therefore rebuilt. There was a house on this site in 1487 and there was a lane running along side which in the 19th century was known as Coach and Horses Lane. These facts tend to point to a medieval establishment. Whether or not it was an inn we do not know.

Northampton Mercury Saturday 19th May 1792

21 Register of Licensed Victuallers, Bucks. 1753-1828..
22 Register of Licensed Victuallers, Bucks. 1753-1828..
23 Register of Licensed Victuallers, Bucks. 1753-1828..

On Saturday last, another inquisition was taken at Stony Stratford before the same Coroner, on view the body of William Pearson, a traveller, who died suddenly as he was sitting in the chimney-corner at the coach-and-horses public house in that town. - Verdict, *That he died by the visitation of God.*

See also Blue Anchor, Drum and Anchor

Cock

Location: 72-74 High Street
Period: possibly 13th to 21st century
First reference: 1529
Commentary: The Cock may be the oldest foundation in Stony Stratford. It is one of three burgage plots established in the last two decades of the 12th century.

It does not feature in any of the 13th century deeds of the Wolverton manor leaving us to deduce that it was granted early, probably to a retainer of the Baron of Wolverton. We have to wait until 1520 for any written reference to the Cock Inn. We can reasonably infer that it was a commercial establishment very early. An acre of land was not worth a great deal in 1200 unless, as in this case, it was ideally situated to profit from travellers. So while there is no actual proof as such, it would be difficult to challenge any claim that the Cock, under whatever name it may have had, was among the first of Stony Stratford's inns.

The inn was gutted by the great fire of 1742 that originated in the Bull and therefore like every other part of Stony Stratford north of the Bull it was rebuilt with its impressive 18th century facade. Nothing of the medieval inn remains.

Its greatest age of prosperity was during the coaching age which came to an abrupt end in 1840 after the railways came into being. The hotel survived the downturn and the 19th century censuses show that it consistently had a larger staff than the Bull.

Into the 21st century the Cock does not look like losing its status as one of Stony Stratford's premier hotels. (See appendix 3 for a full discussion of the origin of the Cock.)

County Arms

Location: Corner Pin, New Bradwell
Period: 19th century to present.
First reference: 1869[24]

---

24 Post Office Directory 1869.

Commentary: The County Arms was built around the time of the Caledonian Road development, probably around 1865. It first appears on record in the Post Office directory of 1869. This district is known as Corner Pin as the Newport Road took a sharp bend here before beginning a winding ascent up to Wolverton. The County Arms has continuously operated under the same name until the present.

Craufurd Arms

Location: 59 Stratford Road
Period: 20th century to present
First reference: 1908

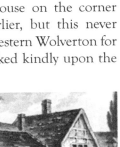

Commentary: The Craufurd Arms was built by the People's Refreshment House Association, which in essence was a temperance movement modified by common sense. They encouraged the drinking of less harmful beverages but did not prohibit alcohol and fostered an environment where tea and coffee could be served alongside alcoholic drinks in a more genteel environment. Colonel Craufurd was a leading light in the PRHA and this house was named in his honour.

There had been a move to build another public house on the corner of Green Lane and Radcliffe Street a few years earlier, but this never materialised and when the Radcliffe Trust opened up western Wolverton for development at the beginning of the century they looked kindly upon the PRHA's application.

Crooked Billet

Location: Market Square
Period: 17th - 19th century
First reference: 1684[25]

Commentary: Joseph Malpas bequeathed the Crooked Billet property to his son William, who was by that time resident in Stony Stratford, in 1796. It was purchased from someone with the last name of Lover; a blank is left for the first name with the intention of filling it in later. It never was. This name never appears in licensing records so we must assume that all the licensees from 1753 were tenants. They include: Francis Miller (1753-1772), Francis Clutton 1773, Martha Reynolds (1774-1782, John Meakins and his son William (1783-1808), Benjamin Wise (1808-9), John Garner (1810-1813), John Ludgate (1814-1817), Joseph Norman (1818-21)

---

25 Calverton Manorial Rolls

Sir Frank Markham said that it had a very seedy reputation, the "haunt of tramps, hucksters, vagabonds, and soldiers" and has found a reference to it as early as 1684 when it was leased by the lord of the manor, Simon Bennet. It was located in a small group of cottages on the south side of Church Street, more or less opposite Number 36 today. The Crooked Billet was auctioned on March 10th 1821 "together with another tenement adjoining; a four stall stable, offices etc."

These buildings were demolished in 1937.

It may have been called the Sun and Moon in the 17th century.

See Sun and Moon

Cross Keys

Location: 95-7 High Street
Period: Medieval to 19th century
First reference: 1773[26]
Commentary: The former Cross Keys buildings present to the casual eye an almost perfectly preserved medieval inn. It is a low two storey building with an archway entrance to a spacious yard. The buildings, now separate properties, have been rebuilt, repaired and modernised over the centuries but they still retain some 15th century timbers. Excavations in 1936, as a by-product of building work, revealed the medieval inn yard some 2 feet below the present surface. At the same time evidence of a banqueting hall was exposed.

This building is undoubtedly medieval in origin and the configuration of its buildings strongly suggests that it was an inn. Its former names are lost.

The name Cross Keys is not so ancient. It first appeared in a licence register in 1773 and ceased to trade as a public house in 1870. For some years in the 20th century half of the building was a tea room, trading as Ye Olde Cross Keys.

Markham suggests it may have been known as St Peter's Keys, but we have to take that suggestion with care. As is apparent with many inn names there is no continuity.

Crown (Market Square)

Location: 9, Market Square
Period: 17th century to present.
First reference: 1666[27]
Commentary: The Crown on the Square appears in the Parish registers after 1666. It was licensed to John

26 Register of Licensed Victuallers, Bucks. 1753-1828..
27 St. Giles' Parish Register.

British (Briddis) in 1753 and has been annually licensed thereafter. This gives it a continuous history under this name for 250 years. Only the Cock and the Bull of today's survivors have a longer history. Prior to the late 17th century we know nothing. It could have had another name prior to the late 17th century or it may simply have opened with that name,

The Crown has a similar history to its neighbour The White Hart, which also arose in the 17th century. In the 19th century it is listed as a tavern or alehouse. Was it ever a coaching inn? The central doorway might indicate that there was once a passage through the middle and that it was filled in after the coaching age died.

Crown Inn

Location: High Street East side
Period: 17th century
First reference: 1654[28]
Commentary:
This was leased in 1654 by Sir Edward Longueville to James Barnes together with "parts of Mill Meadow and Bridge Meadow, totalling two roods." It was short lived, at least under this name, because it does not appear in the documents of 1710-15 which detail all the leases associated with the Longueville estate.

Cuba

Location: Newport Road, New Bradwell.
Period: 19th-21st century.
First reference: 1864[29]
Commentary: The Cuba does not show in the 1861 Census but is listed in the 1864 Post Office directory; therefore it must have been built during these years as the Newport road was populated. The first landlord was William Harding. The name is unusual and the reason for its choice has been forgotten. We might note that Julia Ward Howe, who wrote the words to *The Battle Hymn of the Republic*, published a book called *A Trip to Cuba* in 1861. We have no idea at all if there is any connection The house closed in 2014 after just over 150 years of continuity in business.

28 Ms. Radcliffe dep. deed, 238. 1654.
29 Post Office Directory

Dog and Gun

Location: 61 Wolverton Road
Period: 20th century
First reference: 1990
Commentary: The Duke of Edinburgh was re-named the Dog and Gun.
After five years it was re-named the Duke of Wellington.
See Duke of Edinburgh, Duke of Wellington.

Dog and Monkey

Location: London Road/Wolverton Road corner
Period: 19th century
First reference: 1799[30]
Commentary: Markham says it was near the corner
of the Wolverton and London Road, part of a row of
cheap cottages that were cleared in 1870 to make way
for the new school. He believes it was an off licence and poor lodging house
and he discovered a mention in Plumb records. However there is no record
of anything like this in the censuses from 1841-61, nor does it appear in any
licensing records. It may well have existed "under the radar".

Drum and Anchor

Location: 106 High Street
Period: 18th century
First reference: 1753[31]
Commentary: The Drum and Anchor appears under
the name of Francis Lambert in 1753 and thereafter
Lambert, whose name is sometimes written as Lambourn.
He may have been a descendant of Michael Lambourn who was prominent
in the early 17th century. It should be added that the Lambourns were related
to Michael Hipwell who founded the Rose and Crown Charity.
Fortunately the house has some continuity and held this name (apart from
one bizarre record in 1789 when it is recorded as the "Tong and Ancre"
under the management of one Charles Wasse) until 1792 when John
Marshall, who had taken over the previous year, changed the name to the
Coach and Horses. Marshall liked to change names. He was landlord at the
Windmill a few years earlier and in his second year changed the name to the
Ducks and Drakes. The original name was restored the following year, one
presumes after an outcry.

---

30 Plumb's records - Markham
31 Register of Licensed Victuallers, Bucks. 1753-1828..

Nevertheless the Coach and Horses stuck and this house continued throughout the 19th century. At one time the lane beside it was called Coach and Horses Lane.

For this reason we can identify the location of the Coach and Horses and its former namesake the Drum and Anchor, at least from 1753, and the building is still there at 106 High Street. The house will have an older tradition but there is no evidence to attach it to any other name. There was a 17th century house called the Blue Anchor that may possibly have a connection with the later name. The Blue Anchor was certainly on the east side.

The Coach and Horses continued in business until the early part of the first world war, possibly a casualty of restricted opening hours. Since that time it has either been residential or other commercial premises.

It is tempting to tie the Drum and Anchor to the earlier reference to the Blue Anchor which occurs in a deed dated selling the house called the Blew Anchor and a "pyghtle of pasture" to Robert Edge in 1678. If we do make that connection the house as an inn, alehouse, public house had a history of about 250 years.

See Coach and Horses, Blue Anchor

Drum and Monkey

Location: Stratford Rd, Wolverton
Period: 19th to 20th century
First reference: 1891[32]
Comentary: The house at Number 44 Stratford Road was Number 1 in the 19th century and on the western edge of Wolverton. An additional house was built on the back of the lot in the 1870s and by 1891 the occupant was Sanue Sinfield, a beer retailer. Under later licensing acts this became an off-licence and continued to serve through a "hole in the wall" throughout most of the 20th century. It was popularly known as the Drum and Monkey, although it never displayed a sign.

Ducks and Drakes

Location: 117 High Street
Period: 18th century
First reference: 1789[33]
Commentary: In 1789 John Marshall became the tenant at the Windmill and promptly renamed it the Ducks and Drakes. The following year it was back to

---

32 1891 Census
33 Register of Licensed Victuallers, Bucks. 1753-1828..

the Windmill so it would appear that the regular customers did not like the name change. John Marshall like to change names. When he came into the Drum and Anchor a few years later in 1792 he changed the sign to the Coach and Horses.

See also: The Windmill

Duke of Edinburgh

Location: 61 Wolverton Road
Period: 19th to 21st century
First reference: 1869[34]
Commentary: It has now been re-named the Duke of Wellington, presumably because the name is more meaningful than the Duke of Edinburgh (not the present holder) who was the second son of Queen Victoria.

See Dog and Gun, Duke of Wellington.

Duke of Wellington

Location: 61 Wolverton Road
Period: 19th to 21st century
First reference: 1869[35]
Commentary: See Duke of Edinburgh above.

See Dog and Gun, Duke of Edinburgh

Engineer

Location: 3 Wolverton Road
Period: 19th century
First reference: 1847[36]
Commentary: The builder and developer was William Russell who purchased the large lot on the corner of the High Street and the Wolverton road from the Inwood family. There was a house, some cottages and a chapel on this land. All the buildings except for the chapel were pulled down and the school and the present pub and other buildings were developed. Russell appears in the 1847 trade directory as a beer retailer and stonemason. In 1864, with a full licence, the place is listed as The Engineer. Russell sold the premises in 1870 to Coales and Allen and the name was changed to The Foresters Arms.

See Forester's Arms

---

34 Post Office Directory 1869
35 Post Office Directory 1869
36 Post Office Directory 1847

Falcon

Location: At the Old Stratford crossroads on the
                 north east Cosgrove Road.
Period: 18th to 20th century
First reference: 1734[37]
Commentary: The Falcon was in a prime location and
may have been quite a large inn. It was demolished together
with other properties as part of a road widening scheme.

Fighting Cocks

Location: 14 Market Square
Period: 18th century
First reference: 1760[38]
Commentary: The house at Number 14 on the
Market Square has double-fronted bow windows at
ground level with a central doorway. It is three stories
and quite a substantial 18th century property. There is
some history to the house. In 1725 Henry Potter purchased the property and
manufactured brass pins for lace workers in an outbuilding to the rear of the
property. The front of the house was used as a shop. It is not clear whether
the Church street fire of 1736 reached this part of the Square but there may
have been some damage and it looks as if the front of the house was rebuilt
and possibly enlarged at this time, adding a third story and possibly a flatter
roof. The origins of this house are not known but there are indications that
older parts of the house may date from the 16th century.

It can be inferred from the licensing records that James Richardson
purchased the property either in or before 1760. This is the first time the
name appears in the licensing register. Richardson took out his last licence
in 1784. We know that Joseph Malpas purchased the property from James
Richardson because this is stated in Malpas's will of 1796, but the date is
uncertain. We do know that Mary Sales was the licensee from 1785-1788
and that William Ebblethwaite succeeded her but it would be a good guess
to assume that Malpas acquired the property during that period. The last
licence was taken out in September 1793. This may have coincided with
the Malpas acquisition and he may have decided not to continue its use as
unlicensed house.

The Fighting Cocks therefore had a 34 year definite history.

Northampton Mercury 12th April 1794

---

37 Act for the Repair of the Highways, 1734.
38 Register of Licensed Victuallers, Bucks. 1753-1828..

To be SOLD by AUCTION

By George Knibb

At the Fighting Cocks, in Stony-Stratford on Friday the 25th Day of April, 1794 (unless previously disposed of Private Contract, of which Notice will be given in this Paper) the following *Freehold* ESTATES, viz.

Lot 1. ALL that new-erected MESSUAGE or TENEMENT, situate in the MARKET-PLACE in STONY-STRATFORD aforesaid, called the Fighting Cocks, now in full Trade, and in excellent Repair. The Premises comprise a good Kitchen, two Parlours, an exceeding good Cellar, Brewhouse, three Stables, and other convenient Offices, with a large Garden adjoining.

Lot 2. All that other new-erected MESSUAGE or TENEMENT, called the *Drum-and-Anchor*, situate in the HIGH STREET, in STONY-STRATFORD aforesaid, in good Repair and full Trade, with good Cellars, Brewhouse, and other convenient Offices.

Lot 3. A CLOSE of rich PASTURE-LAND; containing three Acres, or thereabouts, well bounded by live Hedges in good Condition, lying in the Parish of CALVERTON, contiguous to the Town of Stony-Stratford now in the Tenure of Mr. Collingridge.

For further Particulars, or to treat by Private Contract, apply to Mr. James Richardson, at the Fighting Cocks, in Stony-Stratford or Mr. Lucas, Attorney at Law, Newport Pagnell.

N.B. Part of the Purchase-Money may remain on a Security of the Premises if required by the Purchasers.

Fleur de Lys

Location: East side
Period: 16th century
First reference: 1526[39]

Commentary: This name occurs in a transaction between William Taylor and William Payton amongst the manorial documents in the Bodleian library. The year was 1526. An extract from the deed records this: "William Taylor to William Paieton of Stony Stratford, tenement in Stony Stratford, called the Fleur de Luce, situated in the parish of Wolverton, and various parcels of land."

---

39 Bodleian, Deed 1526

Forester's Arms

Location: 3 Wolverton Road
Period: 19ᵗʰ to 21st century
First reference: 1847[40]
Commentary: The Forester's Arms probably dates
to the time of the building of the short return from
the corner of the High Street. It was known as Chapel
street for a short time before becoming part of the Wolverton Road. William
Russell appears as a Victualler in the 1851 census. This Russell was something
of a property developer. He purchased two cottages on the corner after the
previous owner died in 1836. At that time the property stretched all the way
to what was then known as Back Lane. Once Russell had developed his new
properties and sold land for the school and chapel on both corners, Back
Lane eventually became known as Russell Street. He opened up a beer shop
at these premises. It was probably built shortly after the school. This short
road was first called Chapel Street. The place is called The Engineer in 1861.
After Russell retired it was renamed The Forester's Arms. It closed in 2014
and re-opened as a restaurant.
See also Engineer.

Foresters Arms (New Bradwell)

Location: Newport Road, New Bradwell
Period: 19th century to present.
First reference: 1861[41]
Commentary: The Forester's Arms opened circa
1860 as part of the second phase of New Bradwell's development to the east
of the Bradwell Road. It appears in the 1861 Census with Thomas Copson
as the Publican. North Street and parts of Harwood Street were under
development at this time. There was still a toll bar on the Newport Road
at this junction and this may have influenced the location of the Forester's
Arms. It is a survivor and remains open today.

Fox and Hounds

Location: 85-7 High Street
Period: 19th century to present.
First reference: 1854[42]
Commentary: It does not have a distinctive name in

40 Post Office Directory 1847.
41 1861 Census, Bradwell and Stantonbury.
42 Post Office Directory 1854.

the trade directory until 1864, when it is called the Fox and Hounds. It is operated as a beer shop by William Pattison, who was also a butcher.

At least from 1790 - 1839, the premises were not licensed. There are relatively few in Stony Stratford in these years and all have been identified. However, there were many more in the middle of the 18th century, so it is possible that one part of this building has been licensed before. Both buildings are certainly old enough, and were rebuilt between 1742 and 1772.

The Fox and Hounds at first only occupied Number 87, and a fire reduced this to a single storey. Today it occupies Numbers 85 and 87.

Galleon

Location: Old Wolverton
Period: 19th century to present
First reference: 1841[43]
Commentary: This was built beside the canal wharf in 1840 and named the Locomotive. It was known as such for almost 100 years when the name was changed in the late 1930s to the Galleon.
See Locomotive

Gate

Location: 12 High Street
Period: 17th century
First reference: 1700
Commentary: We know of this inn only because this property was sold in 1700 by Sir Edward Longueville to Joseph Bird. Markham believes that it was at 12 High Street and at one point was known as the Wicket Gate. It may also have borne other names in the 18th century. It was no longer an inn in the 19th century and in 1872 was redeveloped as alms houses.

George

Location: High Street
Period: 17th century to present
First reference: 1619[44]
Commentary: This is now one of Stony Stratford's oldest public houses, although it has had periods when it was unlicensed. The building was one of three houses on this site bequeathed by Michael Hipwell. The income from these houses

43 1841 Census, Wolverton.
44 Account Books of Sir Gyles Mompesson, 1619-20.

was intended to fund a gaol at Buckingham, although it appears that the trustees found other uses for the money. He did not give any of these houses a name but an inn known as The George very definitely existed in 1619 when Frances Eve, wydowe, was fined by Sir Gyles Mompesson. Michael Hipwell did specify two inns in his will, the Rose and Crown on the east side and the Swan with Two Necks on the west side. We could therefore infer that the George did not exist at that date but became an inn shortly thereafter. The building is certainly early 17th century.

The George is however an old name and dates to the crusades when the crusaders discovered St George and adopted him as their saint and in turn this saint and his red cross was adopted as the patron saint of England. Often inns named the George started off as St George and became abbreviated over time. For a period in the 20th century it operated as a tea house and restaurant. Today it is known as the Old George.

Globe

Location: possibly 69-71 High Street
Period: 18th century
First reference: 1704[45]
Commentary: The   Bridge   and   Street   Charity
Accounts leave us with this record:

> "Dec 6 1704: Spent at ye Globe with ye
> neighbours: 1s."

Markham has suggested that the Globe may have been at 69-71 High St. The existing buildings are late 18th century and replaced whatever was there in 1704.

Golden Lion

Location: unknown
Period: 17th century
First reference: 1619[46]
Commentary   The sole record of this establishment was a fine administered to William Hudson in 1619 by the rapacious Sir Gyles Mompesson. There is no other mention of it anywhere.

Green Dragon

Location: 5 or 6 Market Square
Period: 17th - 18th century

---

45 Bridge and Street Charity Accounts
46 Account Books of Sir Gyles Mompesson, 1619-20.

First reference: 1619 or 1741[47]

Commentary: The Green Dragon lies on record from 1753 to 1755 and was licensed to Martha Cooke or Cook. However, some deed for the property deposited by E.T. Ray, Solicitors, in the Centre for Buckinghamshire Studies give a fuller history. In 1720 it was an alehouse in the hands of Robert Collet. Benjamin Ingram, a victualler from Winslow, and Thomas Ingram of Old Stratford take over in 1741. After Martha Cole it may have been put to other usues. Joseph Kitelee (Kightley) has a lease/release in 1789, and Thomas Bates is recorded as a butcher later. He died in 1824 and it passed to his son Benjamin.

The Mompesson accounts of 1619 record a fine against Thomas Whitnell of the Green Dragon. This may or may not have been the same Green Dragon. The property was at either 5 or 6 the Square and has since been demolished.

Green Dragon (Calverton)

Location: Shoulder of Mutton Calverton
Period: 18th century
First reference: 1764[48]

Commentary: The Shoulder of Mutton has been running continuously under that name from 1779, but before that it was known as the Green Dragon. It was licensed under this name from 1764 until 1779 and previously known as the Swan.

See also Swan (Calverton), Shoulder of Mutton.

Green Man

Location: Unknown
Period: 18th Century
First reference: 1753[49]

Commentary: The Green Man first comes to our notice in 1753 along with so many others. The licensee was William Hawkins who died two years later and was buried on 6th August 1755. Since his burial was recorded in the St Giles parish register we can infer that he lived on the west side and that the Green Man was most likely a west side inn. It survived a number of years after William Hawkins, firstly under his widow Mary until 1764 and then (presumably a daughter) Elizabeth Hawkins, until 1770 when John Cardwell

47 Mompesson accounts 1619; Deeds Centre for Buckinghamshire Studies. D/RY/2.19.
48 Register of Licensed Victuallers, Bucks. 1753-1828..
49 Register of Licensed Victuallers, Bucks. 1753-1828.

takes over.

Now John Cardwell married Mary Hawkins in 1770, probably another daughter, so the Green Man was still in the family, as it were. Cardwell died only five years later. John True or Tree became the licensee in 1776. I have not discovered a family connection to the Hawkins but there may have been one.

He was the landlord for five years and was succeeded by Mary Tree for two years. The Green Man does not appear in records after 1782.

"Grilkes Herber"

Location: at the causeway near 185 High St.
Period: 14th century
First reference: 1317[50]

Commentary: From a 14th century deed dated 1317 we know that there was an inn on this site - "Grilkes Herber". Herber is a corruption of the French word "auberge' which even today means an inn. Grilkes is a corrupt spelling of Grik's (Greek's). So from this slight references we can construe that there was once an inn either on or near this site. Although on the very edge of Stony Stratford we can make some sense of the location if we associate the place with a toll bar which almost certainly operated here on market days and perhaps other occasions. Toll bars needed to be manned and Greek's Inn may have been a natural offspring of this duty. Nicholas le Gryk and William le Grik appear in other deeds about this time and may be associated with this inn. The name stuck to this piece of land, although in later centuries it was written as "Gregg's Arbour."

There is no evidence of continuity and there may not have been another inn here until the Angel (later named the Barley Mow) was opened in the late 17th century.

See Angel and Barley Mow (185 High Street).

Half Moon

Location: Wolverton Parish
Period: 18th century
First reference: 1753[51]

Commentary: It appears in the licensing register in the first year of record in 1753 and the licensee is Henry Baldwin. He was then in the Stony Stratford list. In 1756 he appears as Henry Bardon in Wolverton and in the years thereafter. In 1757 his name is

50 Ms. Radcliffe dep. deed, 250.
51 Register of Licensed Victuallers, Bucks. 1753-1828.

written as Henry Barding. In each instance this must be the same man. The last year he was the licensee was in 1759. There is no further record of the Half Moon.

One might guess that it was on the London Road since it was for one year recorded as a Stony Stratford licence.

Halley's Comet

Location: 101 Bradwell Road
Period: 20th century to present
First reference: 1986
Commentary: This pub opened as the Bradville around 1950 and briefly was known as the Jovial Priest in the 1970s. When Halley's Comet came close to earth in 1986, the pub adopted this name.
See Bradville, Jovial Priest.

Hare and Hounds

Location: See Queen's Head
Period: 17th - 18th century
First reference: 1770[52]
Commentary: John Payne took over the Queens Head from Mary Garment and changed its name. By 1781 there is no record of John Payne as a licensee nor of the Hare and Hounds. there is no obvious replacement name so it may have gone out of business. The location of the Queen's Head is unknown except that it must have been on the Wolverton side of the High Street.

Markham suggested that it may have been an earlier name for the Fox and Hounds.
See also Queen's Head

Horse and Jockey

Location: Unknown
Period: 18th century
First reference: 1754[53]
Commentary: There is a single year record of a licence. In 1754 it was licensed to Stephen Eales. Neither Eales nor an inn of this name is ever mentioned again. The name was topical. The Jockey Club was founded in 1750 and horse racing

---

52 Register of Licensed Victuallers, Bucks. 1753-1828.
53 Register of Licensed Victuallers, Bucks. 1753-1828.

started to come under common rules. It was probably an alehouse that failed.

Horseshoe

Location: 92-4 High Street
Period: Medieval to 18th century
First reference: 1619-20[54]

Commentary: Although we cannot find a reference before 1619 it is likely that the establishment was 16th century or earlier. This inn was at the north end of town and appears to have been an inn favoured by wagon drivers. There is no firm evidence but the collective impression is that it was at least a 16th century foundation. In the manorial records of 1710 and later it is presented as a substantial establishment which leases a lot of land for pasture and meadow crop. The 1770 Constable's Book records the stabling of many more horses than the other inns, as one would expect for a waggoner's halt. Later in the 18th century it merged with its neighbour the Red Lyon and became known as the Lyon and Horseshoe.

It closed in 1797 for reasons that are not clear. Possibly canal transport was taking a lot of traffic off the road.

Key

Location: Possibly the site of the present White
                 Horse
Period: 16th Century
First reference: 1522[55]

Commentary: This is another inn name which occurs only once in a deed. Sir Frank Markham suggested that it might be associated with the later Cross Keys, but a careful reading of the deed reproduced in part below would seem to indicate that it backed onto the Square, possibly on either of the sites now occupied by the White Horse and the George.

"William Turville of Stonystratford, Buck, and John Wyke, miller, of Wyke Hamond (Wicken), Northants, releases to Peter Percevall of Newport Pagnell, Bucks, all right and claim in a messuage in or burgage in Stonystratford on Calverton side, lying between the burgage of the late Richard Barton and the inn called le the key and stretching from the Royal Road called Watlingstrate to the square, with lands and buildings etc., adjoining in fields of Calverton."

15th June, 13, Henry VIII.

54 Account Books of Sir Gyles Mompesson, 1619-20.
55 Ms. Radcliffe dep. deed 295. 15 June, 13, Henry VIII.

Kings Head

Location: 11 Market Square
Period: 17th to 20th century
First reference: 1678[56]
Commentary: The Victoria County History proposes
1640 as the earliest date for this inn, although the source
of this information is not specified. That date seems
likely as it is during the 17th century that inns begin to expand to the Square
and Stony Stratford entries start to appear in 1678 in the Overseer's Account
Book. When licensing records start to appear in 1753 the King's Head is
continuously recorded until its closure in the 20th century. Since that time
it has not been licensed.

Markham points out that it was held by copyhold from the Lord of the
Calverton Manor, which in itself points to an origin in medieval times,
although not necessarily as an inn. Copyhold was the term given to a lease
which was copied without change from one tenant to the next. Thus the
original rents and dues of service to the lord were undertaken by the new
tenant. Usually these copyholds were passed down through the family from
generation to generation and the new copyholder was required to pay an
entry fine. As he relates the copyholder in 1802 was George Brooks. He
was never the licensee it should be noted and the house had a succession
of licensees, who were presumably sub-tenants of George Brooks, some of
whom only lasted a year.

One colourful story relates to Ann Constable, who was licensee from 1809 -
1822. Her son was caught sheep stealing, which in those days was a hanging
offence. Accordingly he was tried, found guilty and hung at Aylesbury. His
grieving mother brought the body back from Aylesbury but the commercial
possibilities of the property she now had didn't quite desert her and she
exhibited her son's body before burial and charged 1 penny per view to the
curious.

Jovial Priest

Location: 101 Bradwell Road
Period: 20th century to present
First reference: 1986
Commentary: Originally called the Bradville, the
owners decided on a more dynamic name in the 1970s
and came up with the Jovial Priest. It is said that they
had the Reverend Newman Guest, the eccentric vicar of St. James in mind

---

56 Overseers accounts, Stony Stratford, St. Giles. 1678

when they came up with an inn sign depicting a priest on a bicycle with his cassock flapping in the wind. True or not, the name did not last long and the house was renamed in 1986.

See Bradville, Halley's Comet.

Locomotive

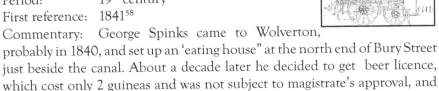

Location: Old Wolverton
Period: 19th century to present
First reference: 1841[57]
Commentary: The arrival of the railways swelled Old Wolverton's population. Most of the newcomers were young men who slept four to a room in lodgings. The Barter family, who owned the wharf, decided to build a new public house and they called it the Locomotive. It held this name until the late 1930s when it was changed to the Galleon.

See Galleon

Locomotive Beer Shop

Location: Bury Street , Wolverton
Period: 19th century
First reference: 1841[58]
Commentary: George Spinks came to Wolverton, probably in 1840, and set up an 'eating house" at the north end of Bury Street just beside the canal. About a decade later he decided to get beer licence, which cost only 2 guineas and was not subject to magistrate's approval, and began to serve customers under the name of the Locomotive Beer Shop.

This rankled among the licensees of the Radciffe Arms and the Royal Engineer, since it was a condition of the railway land purchase that there be no outlets for alcohol on railway property. Representations were made to the Trust and letters written to the railway board, whch did not appear to be much bothered.

Another unrelated decision brought the Locomotive Beer Shop to an end. The Railway company decided to demolish the northern houses to make room for new workshops and Spinks' shop and a few others were pulled down in 1856. Spinks and his family left Wolverton for Liverpool.

See Radcliffe Arms

---

57 1841 Census
58 1841 Census

Marlborough Head

Location: Unknown
Period: 18th century
First reference: 1753[59]

Commentary: This name appears once in 1753, obviously named after the famed Duke of Marlborough. It most likely predates 1753 but it was not destined to last very long. Its last license was taken out by Thomas Turner in 1761.

Beer Shop, William Marlow

Location: Horn Lane
Period: 19th century
First reference: 1869[60]

Commentary: William Marlow was a chimney sweep who must have acquired a beer license in 1868 or 1869. This enterprise appears to have been short lived and almost nothing is known about it.

Morning Star

Location: Newport Road, New Bradwell
Period: 20th century
First reference: 1907[61]

Commentary: The Morning Star was the last pub to be built on the Newport Road in New Bradwell and the first to close. It was built at more-or-less the limit of where anything could be safely built on the Ouse flood plain. It is no longer there. It was left derelict after a fire in the 1960s and pulled down in the 1970s.

Mother Redcaps

Location: Unknown, Old Stratford
Period: 18th century
First reference: 1702[62]

Commentary: In 1702 the Mansel family of Cosgrove purchased some lands in Old Stratford, including " a messuage and 2 acres called the burr yard, a messuage called Mother Red Caps in Cosgrove or Furthoe". Markham suggested that it may have been an alehouse. Its precise location is unknown but it may have been near the crossroads. The name has been adopted by a

---

59 Register of Licensed Victuallers, Bucks. 1753-1828.
60 1869 Post Office Directory
61 1907 Post Office Directory.
62 Hyde & Markham. A History of Stony Stratford. 1948. p.190.

Women's Morris Dancing group in Stony Stratford.

Mother Redcap crops up in folklore as a witch or an alewife. One camp follower of the Duke of Marlborough's army was known as Old Mother Redcap. The Monthly Magazine of 1812 printed this rhyme:

"Old Mother Redcap, according to her tale,

Lived twenty and a hundred years by drinking this good ale,

It was her meat, it was her drink and medicine beside,

And if she still had drank this ale, she never would have died."

Nag's Head

Location: East side
Period: 18th century
First reference: 1710[63]

Commentary: This first comes to notice in the "Particular of the Manor" which was originally prepared for its sale in 1710, and was updated a few years after that. The Nag's Head property, which included a small close or back yard let for 12d. per annum cost Mr. Waggstaff the princely sum of 17 shillings a year which would suggest that the Nag's Head was neither very large nor prosperous and may have been not much more than an alehouse. After this entry the inn disappears from record in the 18th century. Was it renamed? Possibly. The name never again appears in Stony Stratford's history.

New Inn

Location: New Bradwell, beside the canal
Period: 19th century to present
First reference: 1804[64]

Commentary: The New Inn is one of the oldest surviving pubs in the district. The canal brought a wharf and new jobs to this unpopulated part of the `Bradwell manor.

Like most pubs which have "New" in the title, the New Inn is actually old - over 200 years and pre-dates the town of New Bradwell. It was built as a canal-side hostelry in 1804 to serve the bargees on the Grand Junction Canal and the residents at the wharf, which itself had only been operational since 1800. It is a stone rubble-built building with thick walls.

The house did function as an inn during the 19th century and the censuses of that period do record paying guests.

---

63 Particular of the Manor. Ms. Radcliffe dep. deed
64 Deeds.

A bill for its sale in 1828 boasts "a large and commodious wharf, Stables for 30 horses, Corn Granaries, Coke and Salt Houses, Pigsties, Brewhouse, Wash-house, other detached Offices and a large garden." The house had a "spacious Kitchen, Bar, large Dining-room, Back Kitchen with pump and a good Well of water." There was cellarage for 100 Hogsheads, which seems an optimistic amount of beer to consume in a week. The "offices" was a contemporary euphemism what we would now describe as toilets. The fortunes of the house have fluctuated over the centuries but after more than two hundred years it is now the oldest surviving pub in Bradwell.

North Western

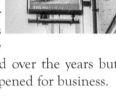

Location: Stratford Road, Wolverton
Period: 19th century to present
First reference: 1864[65]
Commentary: The Stratford Road was opened for development in 1860 and one large lot was taken for the new hotel. At one time there were street entrances to the stables and yard, but these have subsequently been filled in by small shops. The facade has changed over the years but otherwise the building is much as it was when it first opened for business.

Old Boar

Location: Unknown
Period: 17th century
First reference: 1697[66]
Commentary: This inn makes a one-time appearance in the Parish register of 1697.

Pack Horse

Location: Wolverton Parish
Period: 18th century
First reference: 1754[67]
Commentary: This name appears in the licensing records of 1754 and is last licensed in 1761. However, it is a Wolverton parish entry, one of three at this period so it is difficult to locate. Wolverton village or the London Road would be two possible locations.

65 Estimated date.
66 Hyde & Markham. A History of Stony Stratford. 1948. p.190.
67 Register of Licensed Victuallers, Bucks. 1753-1828.

Peacock

Location: Unknown
Period: 17th century

First reference: 1619[68]

Commentary: Oliver Ratcliffe, the Olney printer and local historian, mentions this name in his book The Newport Hundreds, based on hearsay information. The Mompesson account books confirm this hunch. At that date the inn holder was William Taylor.

Plough

Location: Corner of Wolverton/London Road
Period: 18th century to present
First reference: 1753[69]

Commentary: This house has had both a change of name and location. In 1937 it occupied the school which had been designed by Edward Swinfen Harris. The school had moved to a new building the previous year and the owners of The Plough next door took this opportunity to move. The Plough continues in business.

Older photographs show the former Plough, a more modestly designed building with bay windows. This building no longer exists.

This house was at one time known as The Sun and from 1753 was licensed to Edward Barnbrook in the Wolverton Parish. The licence was continued by his widow Mary until 1768 when William Hackett took a license under the name of the Plough. This is the name it has held from this date.

Its origins may be older still, going back to 1613 when it may have been called the Angel.

See also The Sun, The Angel (East side).

Plough (Market Square)

Location: 2 Market Square
Period: 18th century
First reference: 1753[70]

Commentary: The south side of the Market Square once contained buildings numbered 1 to 9 and The

---

68 Account Books of Sir Gyles Mompesson, 1619-20.
69 Register of Licensed Victuallers, Bucks. 1753-1828.
70 Register of Licensed Victuallers, Bucks. 1753-1828.

Plough was at number 2. The house had a brewhouse and a small paddock at the back. It was last licensed as the Plough to a man called Edward Salter who last took out a licence in 1764. It appears that the house was renamed the White Lion in the following year

Part of the Plough backed on to the George Yard and in an 1821 advertisement there is mention of a brewhouse formerly in the yard, formerly known as the Plough yard.

See White Lion

Prince Albert

Location: Vicarage Road, Bradwell

First reference: 1841[71]

Commentary: The Prince Albert is at the heart of the village on Vicarage Road. It probably opened under a beer licence circa 1840, as the name would suggest. Queen Victoria married Prince Albert in that year. This public house has operated continuously since that date.

Prince of Wales

Location: 68 Wolverton Road

Period: 19th to 20th century

First reference: 1871[72]

Commentary: The house was first opened by William Cowley, a mason, who named it after Queen Victoria's eldest son who later became Edward VII. The pub closed before the first world war. It is presently a funeral home..

Queen's Head

Location: High Street, East side.

Period: 17th - 18th century

First reference: 1710[73]

Commentary: We have some useful information about this place, with the exception of its location. It first appears in a document listing all the properties owned by Sir Edward Longueville, together with the tenant's name and the rent.

Michael Garment was the tenant of The Queen's Head Inn and in 1710 was paying £5 10s. a year in rent. We can only assess prices by comparison with

71 1841 Census
72 1871 Census.
73 Particular of the Manor. Portland papers.

other costs at the time, but none of the other figures are helpful. A house on its own, rented for 10 to 13 shillings a year, whereas the the Bakehouse Cottage with some land rented for £8. One might observe that land was worth more than property.

So £5 10s a year for a commercial property was probably about right. This comprised the inn itself and several out buildings - stables, brewhouse, kitchen and privies. Michael Garment had been renting on a year-to-year basis since 1694 so one assumes that he was successful.

It was definitely located on the east side of the High Street as it was part of the Wolverton Estate. Since most of the land in the centre and north of the town had either been sold or was identified by lease, it was most likely to be found at the south end, possibly in that section that ran from Ram Alley (New Street) to the Wolverton Road.

It might also have been at the same location as one of the Angel Inns recorded later in the 18th century. Sir Frank Markham believed that this might have been at the site now occupied by The Retreat.

Which Queen the inn was named after will remain another mystery. As a name, The Queens Head has never been popular in Stony Stratford and this is its only known instance.

In 1770, after a change of leaseholder, the name was changed to the Hare and Hounds. It ceased trading in 1782.

See also Hare and Hounds

Railway Tavern

Location: New Bradwell
Period: 19th to 20th century.
First reference: 1854[74]
Commentary: The new community on the manor of Bradwell (later called New Bradwell) started with three terraced streets in 1854. The Railway Tavern on Glyn Street was the first to open. It closed in 1958.

For many years it was known as the Railway Inn until it changed to the Railway Tavern circa 1911.

Red Cow

Location: Possibly 34 Horsefair
Period: 18th century
First reference: 1724[75]
Commentary: This appears in deeds as the house of

---

74 LNWR Works Committee Minutes.
75 Notes from Mike Brown, author of ABC: A Brewer's Compendium.

the widow Godfrey. There is a hint, but not yet an established fact, that this house may have been the precursor of the house that was later known as The Old Royal Oak in the later 18th century.

Red Lion

Location: Mill Lane
Period: 19th - 20th century
First reference: 1869[76]

Commentary: This house, now a private residence on Mill Lane, first opened with a beer shop licence. In this regard no inn sign was required and the trade directories consistently list the proprietor as a beer retailer until 1939 when it obtained its first full licence. The proprietor was then, and had been for some years, Thomas E. Culley. It is quite possible that the house had been known informally as the *Red Lion* for many years but the only sign that would be legally required was the name of the licensee

The first licensee was Edward South.

Red Lyon

Location: Unknown
Period: 15th - 16th centuries
First reference: 1529 [77]

Commentary: The name first occurs in a dispute about the will of William Edy, who died in 1529, in the recordings of the Court of Requisitions of Henry VIII. We can infer an earlier foundation. Some commentators have suggested that this Red Lyon was the same Red Lyon that was next door to the Horseshoe in the 18th century, but that Red Lyon was leased from the Lord of the Manor and could not therefore have been William Edy's property in 1529. Therefore the earlier Red Lyon must have been in another location.

Red Lyon

Location: Part of St Pauls/Fegan's complex
Period: 17th to 18th centuries
First reference: 1710 [78]

Commentary: By the 18th century it was substantial enough but smaller than its neighbour the Horseshoe and the Three Swans and the Cock and the Bull. The inn was

---

76 1869, Post Office Directory.
77 Ct. of Req. bdl. 2 no.186; Feet of Fines Bucks. Mich . 21 Hen VIII.
78 Particular of the Manor, 1710.

destroyed by fire in 1742 and rebuilt and those buildings were demolished in the 19th century to build St Paul's school. There are, to our knowledge, no drawings of this inn.

Around 1769 the Red Lion was taken over by its neighbour, the Horseshoe. Edward Juffcoat (Jeffcoat) was the landlord. It the continued as the Lyon and Horseshoe until it closed in 1797. Its use after that is not known. *See also Horseshoe.*

Red Lyon (South)

Location: Possibly between the site of the later White Swan and the Retreat

Period: 17th to 18th centuries

First reference: 1766[79]

Commentary: Stony Stratford has a habit of duplicating inn names (see Angel, Barley Mow, Plough, and Royal Oak) and from 1766 to 1781 another Red Lyon was in business while the old Red Lyon continued to operate. This Red Lyon was opened by John Kingston. It was not very large and although it accommodated people overnight there were no stable facilities. The Constables book of 1770 makes no record of horses. It was probably located between the site of the former White Swan and the Retreat and it is tempting to adduce the former Rose and Crown as a potential location.

Rising Sun

Location: 131 High Street

Period: 18th to 20th Century

First reference: 1753[80]

Commentary: The Rising Sun at 131 High Street has a continuous history from 1753 (and probably before that date) to the late 1970s when it closed for good. At the same time there was another inn called the Sun.

The building has been standing for almost 300 years, although the precise date of its construction is unknown. Archaeological surveys suggest a date in the 1740s, based upon construction techniques and written documentation which starts to appear in 1753. The house is stone built but was faced with brick at a later date, which gives it its present appearance.

The first owner of record was a man called Solomon Barley whose principal occupation was a carrier. The running of an inn or alehouse may have been a sideline and was possibly only undertaken after he married Ann Willcocks

79 Register of Licensed Victuallers, Bucks. 1753-1828.
80 Register of Licensed Victuallers, Bucks. 1753-1828.

in 1748. At any rate their interest in the property did not last long because they sold the property to John Fletcher, a shopkeeper on February 13-14, 1753, who quickly passed it on to William Hutson or Hudson on 16/17 November of that same year. It is quite possible that Fletcher did not even move into the premises. Solomon Barley is recorded as the licensee of the Rising Sun in September 1753 (the first year we have these records) and William Hudson in the following year. This suggests that Solomon Barley was still in residence until Hudson took possession. Lease and release.[81]

William Hudson's time as landlord of the Rising Sun was short lived. On 2/3 April 1755 he sold the property to Joseph Mycock, an inn holder from Daventry. Mycock was a more durable proposition and continued as the licensee until 1779. He was succeeded by Daniel Adkins, a tenant licensee in 1780 for two years and then the property was acquired by Henry Harris in 1780. He sold the property in 1807 to John Williams of Greens Norton, who quickly re-sold it to Thomas Green of Stony Stratford in 1809, although Williams continued as tenant until 1812.

It continued throughout the 19th and most of the 20th century as an established public house. It is now a private residence.

Did it have an earlier history as an inn? Probably, but there are few clues to construct a theory. It can be noted that the field behind it was once known as Lyon Close. Could this have been associated with the Golden Lion (qv) recorded in 1619, at which, quite coincidentally I am sure, was a landlord called William Hudson?

See Castle, Golden Lion.

Radcliffe Arms

Location: Wolverton Park
Period: 19th Century
First reference: 1839[82]

Commentary: Upon the advent of the railway John Congreve, a Stony Stratford solicitor and Joseph Clare, the owner of the Cock, teamed up to persuade the Radcliffe Trust to lease a four acre field on the east side of the new railway line opposite the first railway station. They wasted no time and in 1839, before many of Wolverton's first houses had been completed, they opened their doors. It looked like a winning proposition but in 1840 the railway company built a permanent station to the south of the Stratford Road and

81 Lease and release was a legal device used around this time to convey property. A lease was signed on one day and the following day a release was given for a sum of money. It was in effect a sale.
82 MS. Radcliffe, dep. c. 54. Bodleian.

the Radcliffe Arms was stranded in a remote position. Congreve and Clare then appealed to the Trust to reduce their rent (which they did) and asked to build a second public house in a more suitable location. The trustees agreed and allowed them one acre on the Stratford Road, at that time outside Wolverton Station. They then erected the Royal Engineeer (qv).

The original Radcliffe Arms must have fallen on hard times because around 1847 they built a second Radcliffe Arms on the Stratford Road, just to the east of the canal bridge. The original building was converted to four apartments.

The Radcliffe Arms quickly earned a rough reputation and was popularly known as "Hells Kitchen".

In the late 1870s both properties were demolished to make way for the loop line and the new Wolverton Park.

See Royal Engineer

Rose and Crown

Location: 26-28 High Street
Period: 16th to 17th century
First reference: 1603[83]
Commentary: The first record of this comes from Michael Hipwell's will dated 1609, where he famously granted the inn to a charity which, after 99 years would support a schoolmaster and a school at the back of the property. Unfortunately, outside this context, the name Rose and Crown never appears again and we have no way of knowing how the house was used. Did it continue as an inn under a different name or was it converted to other purposes?

The house contains a late 16th century fireplace and some Tudor mouldings on one doorway. The frontage is 18th century brick and the exterior is rendered.

It is reputed to be the inn where Prince Edward stayed when he was arrested by Richard of Gloucester in 1483 but there is no evidence that has been found in the building that would support the idea that it existed in 1483, let alone that Edward stayed there.

Rowbuck Inn

Location: East side
Period: 17th century

The
Rowbuck
Inn

---

83 Bucks. County Archive. DAWf 18/60. Earlier draft of Michael Hipwell's will.

First reference: 1642[84]

Commentary: This was leased to William Sheppard in 1642. That is is only appearance ever. It was on the Wolverton side and it might possibly have been the same building that appeared later in the century as The Queen's Head. We don't know that, but a change of name is more likely than the idea of an inn appearing out of nowhere and then disappearing.

Royal Engineer

Location:1 Stratford Road, Wolverton
Period: 19th to 20th centuries
First reference: 1841[85]

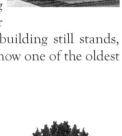

Commentary: The Royal Engineer was born out of a costly mistake by the owners of the Radcliffe Arms (qv) where they rushed to build and built in the wrong location. The Royal Engineer opened two years later as partial compensation for their folly. The original building still stands, although it has been a restaurant for many years and is now one of the oldest surviving buildings in Wolverton.
See Radcliffe Arms

Royal Oak

Location: Unknown
Period: 18th century
First reference: 1753[86]

Commentary: The name appears in licensing records in the Stony Stratford parish in 1753. The licensee was Diana Williamson. The name does not occur again in Stony Stratford. It should not be confused with the Royal Oaks on Horsefair and Silver Street as these were licensed later in the century in the Calverton parish.

New Royal Oak

Location: Horsefair Green
Period: 18th to 20th centuries
First reference: 1776[87]

Commentary: This house was first licensed in 1776 and continued uninterrupted in business until the

---

84   MS. Radcliffe dep. deed 3
85 MS. Radcliffe, dep. c. 54. Bodleian.
86 Register of Licensed Victuallers, Bucks. 1753-1828.
87 Register of Licensed Victuallers, Bucks. 1753-1828.

1970s. Since that time it has been a private residence.
See Old Royal Oak and further discussion Chapter 7.

Old Royal Oak

Location: Silver Street
Period: 18th to 19th century
First reference: 1780[88]
Commentary: This Royal Oak, a small cottage with a brewhouse next door to the longer lasting New Royal Oak was first licensed under that name in 1780. It closed in the 1830s. It is peculiar to find two inns carrying the same name side-by-side; it is even more disconcerting to discover that the first to be licensed under this name became the New Royal Oak while the one that arrived four years later assumed the name the Old Royal Oak. A full discussion and possible explanation can be found on pages 113-118.
See New Royal Oak

Queen Victoria

Location: Vicarage Road, Bradwell
First reference: 1841[89]
Commentary: This house appears in the 1841 Census with Thomas Byfield as publican. It probably opened up between 1837 and 1840. It may have preceded its rival across the street, the Prince Albert by a year or two. The house has operated continuously since its foundation.

Saint Peter's Keys

Location: Unknown
Period: 15th century
First reference: 1470[90]
Commentary: This house is cited by Markham who suggested it was an ecclesiastical lodging house for priests. I have not discovered or seen this reference. He also suggests that it may have been a forerunner of the Cross Keys. I have some reservations about these interpretations. Inns were certainly run by priories and churches in the Middle Ages but they were not exclusive and were open to all travellers to bring in income. A specialised house in the 15th century was probably well before its time. Secondly, if an inn was run by the church one would be more inclined to look for it near

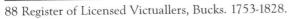

88 Register of Licensed Victuallers, Bucks. 1753-1828.
89 1841 Census.
90 F.E. Hyde & S.F. Markham. A History of Stony Stratford. 1948, p. 191.

to the church itself rather than way up the High Street, and if there is an association to be made because of the name, perhaps one should consider The Key.
See Cross Keys, Key.

Saracen's Head

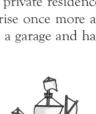

Location: On the west side of the Watling Street, at the start of Old Stratford facing north.
Period: 18th to 19th century
First reference: 1734[91]
Commentary: Not much is known about this inn. The former Saracen's Head was converted into a boys' school in the 1830s under the name of Belvedere House. New owners renamed the school Trinity House, which closed in 1894. It was a private residence for about 30 years before becoming a commercial enterprise once more as the Green Parrot Hotel and Cafe. In the 1950s it became a garage and has remained so since.

Ship

Location: Possibly at 32 High Street
Period: 18th century
First reference: 1754[92]
Commentary: This was probably the location of the old White Horse, which changed its name in 1754 and then reverted to the White Horse in 1767. It is not to be confused with the present White Horse.
See White Horse (East side)

Shoulder of Mutton

Location: Calverton
Period: 18th century to present
First reference: 1779[93]
Commentary: The Shoulder of Mutton is still operating in Calverton. Up to its name change in 1779 it was called the Green Dragon.
See also Swan (Calverton, Green Dragon (Calverton).

91 1734. Act for the Repair of the Highways.
92 Register of Licensed Victuallers, Bucks. 1753-1828.
93 Register of Licensed Victuallers, Bucks. 1753-1828.

Silent Woman

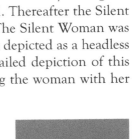

Location: unknown
Period: 18th century
First reference: 1753[94]

Commentary: The licensee, when we first hear about this inn was Elizabeth Edwards, widow, clearly a woman with a sense of humour. The widow continued until 1757 when the licence was taken by Mary Edwards, most likely a daughter or daughter-in-law. She last took out a licence in 1761. Thereafter the Silent Woman sign is never again seen in Stony Stratford. The Silent Woman was not an unknown sign in England and was sometimes depicted as a headless woman, carrying her head under her arm. One detailed depiction of this sign was found at Pershore in Worcesterhire showing the woman with her lips sealed by a padlock.

Sow and Pig

Location: Unknown
Period: 18th century
First reference: 1753 [95]

Commentary: The Sow and Pig was for about 20 years the alehouse of Thomas Judge. This is all that is known. It can be noted that Thomas Judge lost the Sow and Pig licence for one year in 1768 and in that year was the licensee of the Green Dragon at Calverton - later the Shoulder of Mutton. One interpretation that can be placed on this is that the Sow and Pig was refused a licence one year for various infractions, possibly disturbances of the peace, and it was restored the following year after things had settled down.

Sun

Location: Next door to the present Plough Inn.
Period: 18th century
First reference: 1753[96]

Commentary: From 1753 it was licensed to the Barnbrook family, Edward Barnbrook and presumably his widow Mary until 1766. In 1766 it reopened as the Plough and although The Plough moved to the building next door in 1937 has operated continuously since that date. The Sun, and the Plough, was

94 Register of Licensed Victuallers, Bucks. 1753-1828.
95 Register of Licensed Victuallers, Bucks. 1753-1828.
96 Register of Licensed Victuallers, Bucks. 1753-1828.

always registered in the Wolverton parish until the Wolverton UDC was created in 1922. Markham suggested that the name may have changed at one time to the Angel but I have been unable to find any evidence of this.
See Plough

Sun and Moon

Location: Market Square
Period: 17th Century
First reference: 1660[97]
Commentary: This appears to be an earlier name for the Crooked Billet which was on this site until it was demolished in 1937. If so, it would have been more of an alehouse than an inn. The earliest reference to the Crooked Billet is 1694 and the last reference to the Sun and Moon was 1672, so at some time during that interval the Crooked Billet name was introduced.
See Crooked Billet

Swan

Location: 92-94 High Street
Period: Medieval to 18th century
First reference: 1470
Commentary: See the Three Swans
See Three Swans

Swan (Calverton)

Location: Shoulder of Mutton
Period: 18th cetury
First reference: 1753[98]
Commentary: This appears to be an earlier name for the Shoulder of Mutton although one cannot be absolutely certain without corroborating evidence. It was however the only Calverton licence for some years and it could have been at another location. It carried this name from 1753 until 1767 when it changed hands, and changed to the Green Dragon.
See also Green Dragon (Calverton), Shoulder of Mutton.

Swan (Old Stratford)

Location: Old Stratford Crossroads
Period: 19th century to present

---

97 Notes from Mike Brown, author of ABC: A Brewer's Compendium
98 Register of Licensed Victuallers, Bucks. 1753-1828.

First reference: 1830[99]

Commentary: The Swan was a relatively small house which at one time had other buildings between it and the corner of the Cosgrove Road. It does have the distinction of being the sole survivor of Old Stratford's four inns.

Swan with Two Necks

Location: High Street, west side
Period: 17th to 18th century
First reference: 1609[100]

Commentary: The Swan with two Necks makes its first appearance in Michael Hipwell's famous will of 1609. It is also documented in the 18th century in licensing records from 1753 until its closure in 1790. It is also mentioned in Mary Wilmots's will, proved in 1803. From the available evidence it was almost certainly on the west side of the High Street and is not to be confused with the Three Swans on the other side. The Swan with Two Necks (originally "two nicks") was a sign of the Vintner's Guild, signifying their right to keep swans on the River Thames and the marks on their beaks to denote their property. At one time the sale of wine was restricted to members of the Guild, and men such as Michael Hipwell would have happily used that sign to demonstrate their bona fides in the trade. See Appendix 5.

Talbot

Location: 81-83 High Street
Period: 18th century
First reference: 1680[101]

Commentary: The Talbot had a recorded life of just over a century. On record it makes its first appearance in 1680 in the Overseer's Papers. It is in the licensing records under Richard Whitmay from 1753 to 1761. It closed down for good after the death of Richard Whitmay, whose burial was recorded in the St Giles parish register on 21st April 1762.

Like most buildings in Stony Stratford that may have survived from earlier times, the Talbot was substantially rebuilt in the 18th and 19th centuries, although some medieval timbers survive in the roof. The name Talbot itself

99 Pigot & Co. Buckinghamshire Trade Directory.
100 Michael Hipwell's Will.
101 Overseers Papers, St. Giles, 1680.

213

is certainly an old medieval name. It was a name for a white hunting dog and this may have been the origin of the surname of Sir John Talbot who became the first earl of Shrewsbury. Talbot was a very famous warrior in the 15th century and inns may have been named in his honour. Either way the name has medieval origins and it is possible that the Talbot in Stony Stratford is much older than its recorded history suggests.

The presence or absence of any written records, as we have already discovered, not a great deal of help. Most affairs were conducted without much paperwork and even in the 18th century in Wolverton you can find substantial farmers who were illiterate. When we do find records it is usually for some purpose incidental to the activities of an inn. It would certainly make sense for an in to be established in that loation, central to the town and on the High Street in medieval times and in the 16th and 17th centuries. So the Talbot may have had a longer life than appears at first glance but certainly no life as an inn after the third quarter of the 18th century. The building itself survives and is now separated into two, numbers 81-83 High Street. There was probably a central entranceway at one time, although this has now been filled in.

Three Horse Loaves

Location: Fictitious, Stony Stratford
First reference: 1600[102]
Commentary: This fictional name appears in act V, scene iii of a play called Sir John Oldcastle, Part I. It has been thought by some to refer to the Horseshoe Inn, but as a made up name it could refer to any of them.
See the full discussion in Appendix 4.

Three Pigeons

Location: Unknown
Period: 18th century
First reference: 1713[103]
Commentary: This is mentioned by name on a deed for a property transaction in Lillingstone Lovell. From this source alone we know that it existed between 1713 and 1735.

---

102 Anthony Munday et al. Sir John Oldcastle, Part 1, Act V scene iii.
103 Deed.

Three Swans

Location: 92-92 High Street
Period: Medieval to 18th century
First Reference: 1687
Commentary: This was the old medieval inn known
as the Swan. Its foundation date is unknown but it may
be early. At some time in the 17th century the name
was changed to the Three Swans and since there is a datestone on the site
inscribed "WE 1687" This may give us reason to believe that the Swan may
have been rebuilt at this time. A name change could have coincided with
rebuilding.

At 10 o'clock on the morning of Monday 25th November 1782, the auctioneer
John Day opened the sale of all of the property of the aged and ailing Mrs.
Ann Whittaker. She and her husband had been tenants of the Three Swans
since 1759. William Whittaker had died in 1763 and for almost 20 years she
had gamely run the business of one of Stony Stratford's larger inns. This
marked the end of an era. For reasons that are not altogether clear there was
no other tenant willing to purchase Mrs. Whittaker's inventory and take on
the business. Everything went under the hammer.

The auction prospectus was as follows:

A GENERAL SALE

To be sold by auction by John Day, on the premises, without
reserve, on Monday the 25th of this instant November 1782 and
the following days,

The neat household – furniture, plate, linen, china, wines,
liquors, and beer, &c. belonging to Mrs. Ann Whittaker, at the
much esteemed old inn, the Three Swans in Stony Stratford in
the county of Bucks – (Mrs. Whittaker's long ill state of health
obliging her to retire from all business.) The sale comprises
about 30 Bedheads, with various genteel furniture; fine goose
coat and other feather beds, cranky and other mattrasses; cotton
counterpanes, quilts and blankets; 50 pair of sheets; table linen
in proportion; bureaus; chests of drawers; pier, dressing and
other glasses; chairs &c. &c. in mahogany, walnut tree &c. (very
neat); a great quantity of kitchen-furniture in good condition,
brewery and cellars the same; wines, liquors, beer &c. inviting.
A great quantity of hay to be sold, and the keep of the grounds
until lady day next.

Sale to begin each morning at Ten o'clock.

N.B. All persons having any demand on Mrs, Whittaker, are desired to send in the same to the Three Swans, on or before the sale is ended.

On the third day's sale will be sold, the useful plate (about 150 ounces) in lots. Also several lots of useful plated ware in good condition.

The sale took three days so there was a large inventory. The amount of money the sale realised was unreported.

The actual property was still owned by the Radcliffe Trust and there being no interest in leasing it as an inn the house was then converted to a private residence, while the pasture and meadows were leased to farmers.

The foundation of the inn was almost certainly medieval and the first documented evidence appears in a schedule of the properties of Bradwell Priory, drawn up in 1526 for Cardinal Wolsey who had dissolved the Priory and appropriated its revenue to his new Oxford College two year earlier. This schedule describes the "Brotherhed House" and a plot of land bordered by the Brotherhood House and the Swan Inn to the south. This would locate the Swan Inn at what is now 92 High Street.

There is no further documentary evidence for almost two centuries when it appears in records as The Three Swans.

There may have been written leases, or it may have been leased on a customary basis without signed documents. Although many documents from the de Wolverton and Longueville families survive from as early as the 13th century, not a single one makes reference to an inn lease.

So it is only at the beginning of the 18th century when Sir Edward Longueville put the manor up for sale that written evidence is preserved for us. The first document was essentially a prospectus for sale detailing the leases and the tenants. This is dated 1710 and is in the papers belonging to the Duke of Newcastle. The document contains this paragraph

The Three Swans Inn has been lett time out of mind with the Ground that belongs to it, in the same manner. Part of Greenly field is newly laid to it, and is well worthy the Money, it's lett for 21 years by lease, the tenant has held it for years without Lease. The yearly value of the property was estimated at £19 4s 6d, which by itself means little to us today, but in comparison with the Horseshoe at £30 10s 0d and the Bull at £27 5s 0d. And the Red lyon at £9 12s 6d, places it in the middle rank of the inns of the day.

And there is a clue here to its antiquity and the absence of earlier documentary evidence. It has been let "time out of mind and without lease".

Once Dr. Radcliffe took over in 1713, the management of the estate was tightened up and everyone was put on a lease, but under the same terms as before. It emerges under documents drawn up a few years later that the property included an orchard, gardens, Lammas Close and Leyes meadow, totalling 12 acres. The Greenleys pasture, recently acquired, added a further 24 acres. The annual rental for all this was £67 14s 0d.

The Three Swans was caught up in the great fire of 1742 and rebuilt. It may also have been rebuilt in 1687. Mr Paul Woodfield, while undertaking an architectural assessment, discovered a charred stone wall on the site with the inscription "W.E. 1687". He interprets this as a rebuilding date and it is quite possible that this was the moment it changed its name.

Paul Woodfield has noted that the High Street widens here and suggests that this was probably the centre of the town and that there may have been a market place here. If so, this would have been a location for one of the premier inns of Stony Stratford. Certainly Browne Willis, who knew the old inn before it was burned down in the great fire of 1742, believed this of the inn and it was his opinion that it may have been the inn where Edward of York was staying when he was arrested by his uncle Richard of Gloucester in 1483. That remains controversial but the 1526 reference would imply that it was well established, and discoveries of walls which define the ancient burgage plot lend weight to the assumption that its foundation was medieval. *See Swan.*

Three Tuns

Location: Unknown
Period: 18th Century
First reference: 1753[104]

Commentary: The   Three   Tuns   makes   a   brief appearance in recorded history. When licensing records begin in 1753 John Franklin was the licensee. He was the licensee of record in 1754 and his name is on the register in 1755. The inn name does not show up in any year after that.

There are two possibilities. The inn closed down and went out of business permanently, either because John Franklin retired or died without heirs. The inn may have been taken over by someone else who changed the name. If that was the case there is The Black Cock which opened in 1757 under

---

104 Register of Licensed Victuallers, Bucks. 1753-1828.

the licensee Thomas Cattle. This lasted only until 1762. Unfortunately the clerk who drafted the register for years from 1758 to 1773 did not bother to record the inn sign, so all we can do is infer from the licensee's name some continuity. Suffice to say that we have a Three Tuns of record for the years 1753-1756. Its location is unknown and will probably remain so.
See Black Cock.

Valiant Trooper

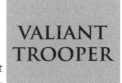

Location: Unknown, west side of High Street
Period: 18th century
First reference: 1753[105]
Commentary: The Valiant Trooper was on the west side. It was most likely on the High Street. It appears as a name in 1753 under the name of James Mullender (sometimes spelt Mulliner). After the death of William Frayne in 1762 he took over his business, The Swan with Two Necks, and the Valiant Trooper disappeared from Stony Stratford. The Trooper made a brief reappearance in the last year of Ann Mulliner's life but that may have been a mistake, or it may have been a slip of memory on her part when in old age she gave a name to the registrar of licences. She died shortly after and that was that. James Mulliner was the licensee until 1772, when, probably after his decease, he was succeeded by his widow, Ann, who ran the business until her death in 1789. After this the name (and the Swan with two Necks) disappears from history. As there are no new licensees appearing after this last date we must conclude that the business died with her. It is also possible that James Mulliner took over the vintner's business from William Frayne and continued at his own premises, formerly the Valiant Trooper.

The Watling Street had a lot of troop movement along the road in the 18th century and it may have been an attempt to capture this trade that led James Mulliner to so name his house. It was most likely an alehouse.
See also the Swan with Two Necks.

Victoria Hotel

Location: 73 High Street
Period: early 20th century
First reference: 1911[106]
Commentary: This opened as a temperance hotel in 1911 and had a career that fell slightly short of 20 years. The proprietors, Watts and Becks, were also pastry

105 Register of Licensed Victuallers, Bucks. 1753-1828.
106 Kelly's Directory.

cooks and this part of the business continued after the hotel side closed down. The was later sold to W H Haseldine under which name it flourished for most of the second half of the 20th century.

Victoria Hotel, Wolverton

Location: 42 Church Street, Wolverton.
Period: 19th century to present
First reference: 1864[107]

Commentary: The Victoria Hotel in its heyday grew to become the largest hotel in Wolverton. It is much diminished today but it still commands the corner of Church street and Radcliffe Street. The very large corner lot, and several others, were taken for development after Church Street was created in 1860. The new hotel was probably completed around 1864.

Waggon and Horses

Location: unknown
Period: 18th century
First reference: 1754[108]

Commentary: In 1754 the licensee was John Davis. In 1756 he was licensed to the Black Horse and the Waggon and Horses disappears from record. One could conclude that this was the same premises under a different name. The last time he took out a licence was in September 1763. Markham suggests that the Waggon and Horses may have been a former name of the Red Lyon Alehouse.
See also Black Horse, Red Lyon (South)

Welch Harp

Location: Unknown
Period: 18th century
First reference: 1754[109]

Commentary: From the licensing records we learn that it was first licensed to Mary Redfern in 1754 and to Amy Redfern (possibly her daughter) in 1764 and 1765. After that date it either goes out of business or is taken over by someone else who changed the name. It was probably an alehouse.

---

107 Post Office Directory 1864.
108 Register of Licensed Victuallers, Bucks. 1753-1828.
109 Register of Licensed Victuallers, Bucks. 1753-1828.

White Hart

Location: Unknown
Period: 17th century
First reference: 1625[110]
Commentary: See discussion below.

White Hart

Location: 8 Market Square
Period: 19th century
First reference: 1820
Commentary: There is an entry in the Victoria County History which offers a 1625 date for the White Hart and there is a reference in 1670 to a White Hart in the Stony Stratford Overseer's Papers. It first appears in the licensing records in 1758 when the licensee was Samuel Langley. In 1761 this was George Dodson who held the licence until 1772. After this both George Dodson and the White Hart disappear from record and the name is not used again until 1820 when the licensee was Robert Ketton. Thereafter it was the White Hart until the end of the century when it was taken over by the Stony Stratford Working Men's Club. From a historian's point of view this is the only period to which we can attribute the name White Hart to these premises with any certainty.

Undoubtedly there were houses under the name White Hart before this date, but they may not necessarily have been at this location. This is not to say that the house itself was not there in the 17th century. Clearly it was, but it may not have been in use as an inn called the White Hart.

There are connections that can be made, but without any certainty and inspired only by a hunch. For example the Cross Keys, which we know to be a much older establishment, only starts to appear in the licensing records in 1773, the year after the White Hart disappears from the record. Could it be then that the former White Hart was at the site of the Cross Keys and that its name was changed after Richard Longman took over? Possibly, but we may never know.

See Cross Keys

White Horse (East side)

Location: East side
Period: 18th century

110 Victoria County History, Buckinghamshire.

First reference: 1753[111]

Commentary: The White Horse is an old name in Stony Stratford's records; however, the presently named White Horse at Number 49-51 may not be the same White Horse as earlier inns of that name

In 1753 one William Ashpool was registered as the licensee of the White Horse. In 1754 the same man is the licensee of The Ship and the White Horse disappears from record. Ashpool (Ashpole) continues as the licensee of the Ship until 1759 and then the White Horse re-appears under the stewardship of Samuel Gayton. He held that licence until 1772. In this case there is corroborative evidence. The Constables Book for the parish on the east side records Samuel Gayton as the landlord of the White Horse in 1770. It has been supposed that this was the White Horse on the west side but it is then difficult to explain why the constables of the eastern parish would be interested in an inn on the Calverton side. Indeed all the other inns where billeting and stabling were recorded are all known to be east side inns - the Drum and Anchor, Horseshoe, Cock, Bull, Red Lyon - so one must conclude that this White Horse was an inn on the east side of the High Street. It is not mentioned again after 1772 so it either went out of business or changed its name.

White Horse

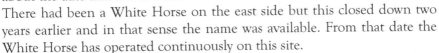

Location: 49-51 High Street
Period: 18th Century to present
First reference: 1773[112]
Commentary: Although the name of the White Horse is an old one in Stony Stratford, this may not have a history under this name prior to 1773, which is about the date that it was built.

There had been a White Horse on the east side but this closed down two years earlier and in that sense the name was available. From that date the White Horse has operated continuously on this site.

It does seem highly probable that there was an inn at this site going back to antiquity. Its location next to the church would suggest as much but as often seems to be the car in Stony Stratford inn names are fluid and there is not as much continuity as one might suppose. The White Horse on the west side makes its first recorded appearance under that name in 1773. The landlord was Edward Proctor in 1773 and he was succeeded by Thomas Ward in 1798. Since 1773 however, the White Horse has been continuously licensed and

111 Register of Licensed Victuallers, Bucks. 1753-1828.
112 Register of Licensed Victuallers, Bucks. 1753-1828

remains in business today.

See also White Horse (east side), the Ship and a full discussion on pages ??

White Lion

Location: Market Square, possibly Number 2
Period: 18th Century
First reference: 1765[113]
Commentary: The White Lion first appears in licensing
records in 1765 under Thomas Honeybone, a year after
The Plough ceased trading. There is also an advertisement
for the sale of the White Lion in 1777 saying it is the
Market Place, so it is possible to infer that it was formerly the Plough. He
was last licensed in 1772 and then his widow, whom he married as Hannah
Bowman in 1756, took over. She decided to go out of business and the
premises were advertised for let on December 1 1777, "to be entered upon
immediately". The last licensee was Edward Knight in 1783 and it is likely
that after that the house and yard was used for other purposes. There was a
brewhouse which may have later been used by the George, which backs on
to the former Plough yard.

See Plough (Market Square)

White Lyon

Location: Unknown, Old Stratford
Period: 17th century
First reference: 1647[114]
Commentary: This White Lyon was purchased by
William Harlye in 1726 and from the deeds we learn that
it had been sold by Sir Robert Bannetre of Passenham to
John Wodall in 1647. There are no clues pointing to its actual location.

White Swan

Location   32-34 High Street
Period: 19th - 20th century
First reference: 1823
Commentary: There are some reasons to believe that
this may be the site of an older inn, possibly the White
Horse in the 18th century. If that is so it was unused as
an inn for about 50 years. It opened as The Swan and
then 1877 when it was taken over by Thomas Amos, a butcher, it was re-

113 Register of Licensed Victuallers, Bucks. 1753-1828.
114 1647 Deeds.Markham op.cit. p. 190.

named the White Swan. It was briefly known as the Stratford Arms in the 1990s.

The main building was rebuilt in 1915 in a retro half-timbered style.
See White Horse

The Windmill

Location: 117 High Street
Period: 18th - 19th century
First reference: 1753[115]

Commentary: The house acquired its first licence on September 1773. Thereafter it continued in business at that address until 1850. For one brief period it was licensed as the Ducks and Drakes by the new tenant John Marshall but the old name was restored in the following year's licence application and we must assume that Mr Marshal met with a great outcry from his regular customers.

It continued in business as a licensed public house until the mid 19th century when it became a tailor's shop and house for the better part of 80 years.

In 1858 the house was sold as part of an extensive estate as:

A very convenient PRIVATE DWELLING HOUSE and PREMISES, formerly known as the "Windmill Inn," likewise situate in Stony Stratford West, containing large kitchen, two parlours, four sleeping rooms, and the attic, yard, commodious outbuildings, garden, and a well of good water, now let to Mr. Arnold, at a rent of £16 per annum.

Then it had a spell as a cafe. It is presently a restaurant.
See also Ducks and Drakes

Working Men's Clubs

Stony Stratford Working Men's Club

Location: Various
Period: 19th to 21st century.

Commentary: The first Working Men's Club was established on the High Street. In 1895 it moved to the former White Hart on the Square and stayed until 1948 when the club moved to the London Road. This last place closed down in 2009.

---

115 Register of Licensed Victuallers, Bucks. 1753-1828.

Stony Stratford Conservative Club

Location: High Street
Period: 20th century to present
Commentary: Although not a Working men's Club,
the Conservative Club on Stony Stratford's High Street,
performs a similar function and is still open after over a century.

Wolverton Workmen's Social Club

Location: 49 Stratford Road, Wolverton
Period: 19th century to present
First reference: 1895
Commentary: The Workmen's Social Club first
opened in 1872 in a house on Church Street. When
Cambridge Street and Windsor Street were built in
the 1890s the Club acquired a lot on the Stratford Road for a purose built
facility. In Wolverton it is known as the "Bottom Club."

Wolverton Central Working Mens Club

Location: 6 Western Road, Wolverton
Period: 20th century to present
First reference: 1907
Commentary: This club opened as Western Road
was being built at the turn of the 20th century. It is
popularly known as the Top Club.

Stantonbury Social Working Men's Club

Location: St James Street, New Bradwell
Period: 19th century to present.
Commentary: The Stantonbury Club is in the heart
of New Bradwell and remains open today.

New Bradwell Working Men's Club

Location: Newport Road, New Bradwell.
Pweiod: 20th century.
Commentary: New Bradwell's second club opened
in a purpose-built building on the Newport Road. It is
now closed and used as a dance school.

Part Three
Appendices

Appendix 1 Where were they?

A lot of names have come down to us through various records. The location of many of them will probably remain a mystery. Many of the different names may be the same place under different ownership.

The tables below list names of inns and public houses from the first period they appear on record. In some instances the location can be accurately stated, in other cases it is approximate. The last known address is given where buildings have been demolished.

Table 1: Inns and Taverns to 1600

Inn name	Location
Cock	Cock Hotel, 72-4 High Street
Fleur de Lys	unknown
Grilkes Herber	North entrance to Stony Stratford
Horseshoe	St Paul's School/Fegan's Homes
Key	approximate site of White Horse
Red Lyon	St Paul's School/Fegan's Homes
Rose and Crown	26-28 High St.
Swan	92-4 High Street
Swan with Two Necks	High St., West side

Table 2: Inns, Taverns and Alehouses 1600-1699

Inn Name	Location
Angel	Wolverton side, south end
Bell	High St., Wolverton side
Black Boy	High St., Wolverton side
Blue Anchor	possibly 106 High St.
Bull	Bull Hotel, 64-66 High Street
Crooked Billet	Market Square, north side
Crown	9 Market Square
Crown	High St., Wolverton side
George	George Hotel
Golden Lion	Unknown
Kings Head	11 Market Square
Old Boar	unknown
Peacock	unknown
Rowbuck	High St., Wolverton side

White Hart	unknown

Table 3: Inns, Taverns and Alehouses 1700-1819

Inn Name	Location
Angel	11 High Street
Angel/Barley Mow	185 High St.
Barley Mow	10 Market Square
Bell	16 Market Square
Black Cock	Unknown
Black Horse	Unknown
Boot	Unknown
Castle	131 Hugh Street
Coach and Horses	106 High Street
Cross Keys	95-97 High Street
Dog and Monkey	Plough corner
Drum and Anchor	124 High Street
Ducks and Drakes	117 high Street
Fighting Cocks	14 Market Square
Gate	possibly 12 High Street
Globe	69-71 High Street
Green Dragon	5 or 6 Market Square
Green Man	unknown
Hare and Hounds	High St., Wolverton side, south end
Horse and Jockey	Unknown
Marlborough Head	unknown
Nag's Head	Wolverton Side
Plough	London Road
Plough	2 Market Square
Queen's Head	High St., Wolverton side, south end
Red Cow	possibly 34 Silver St.
Red Lion	High St., Wolverton side, south end
Rising Sun	131 High St.
Royal Oak	Unknown
New Royal Oak	34 Silver St.
Old Royal Oak	22 Horsefair Green
Ship	possibly 32 High St
Silent Woman	unknown
Sow and Pig	unknown
Sun	Plough Corner

Sun and Moon	Market Square, north side
Talbot	81-83 High Street
Three Pigeons	unknown
Three Swans	92-4 High St.
Three Tuns	unknown
Valiant Trooper	Unlnown
Waggon and Horses	possibly 12 High Street
Welch Harp	unknown
White Horse	possibly 32 High St
White Horse	49-51 High St.
White Lion	2 Market Square
Windmill	117 High St.

Table 4: Public House and Hotels 1820-Present

Name	Location
Case is Altered	83 Wolverton Road
Different Drummer	92-4 High St.
Dog and Gun	Wolverton Road
Duke of Edinburgh	Wolverton Road
Duke of Wellington	Wolverton Road
Engineer	Wolverton Road
Foresters Arms	Wolverton Road
Fox and Hounds	87 High Street
William Marlow Beer Shop	Horn Lane
Prince of Wales	68 Wolverton Road
Red Lion	Mill Lane
Victoria Temperance Hotel	73 High St.
White Hart	8 Market Square
White Swan	32 High St.

Table 5: Known Locations.

Name	Historical Names	Location
Angel		11 High Street
Barley Mow (Old)		10 Market Square
Barley Mow (New)	Angel, Grilkes Herber	185 Hugh Street
Bell		11 Market Square
Black Horse (OS)		NW end O Stratford
Coach and Horses	Drum & Anchor, Blue Anchor	106 High Street
Bull	Bull's Head, Black Bull	62-64 High street
Case is Altered		83 Wolverton Road
Cock		72-74 High Street
Craufurd Arms		59 Stratford Rd., Wolverton
Crooked Billet	Sun and Moon	Market Square
Cross Keys		109 High St
Crown		9 Market Square
Duke of Wellington	Dog and Gun, Duke of Edinburgh	61 Wolverton Road
Falcon		Crossroads, OS
Fighting Cocks		14 Market Square
Foresters Arms	Engineer	3 Wolverton Road
Fox and Hounds		87 High Street
Galleon	Locomotive	Old Wolverton
George		41 High Street
Green Dragon		5-6 Market Square
Horseshoe		St Pauls/Fegans
North Western		11 Stratford Rd., Wolverton
Plough (Market Sq)	White Lion	2 Market Square
Plough	Sun, Angel	London Road
Prince of Wales		83 Wolverton Road

Name	Historical Names	Location
Red Lion (Mill Lane)		Mill Lane
Red Lyon		St Pauls/Fegans
Rising Sun	Lyon, Castle	131 High Street
Radcliffe Arms		Wolverton Park
Royal Engineer		1 Stratford Rd., Wolverton
Royal Oak		22 Horsefair Green
Old Royal Oak		34 Silver Street
Saracen's Head		Trinity House (OS)
Shoulder of Mutton	Swan, Green Dragon	Calverton
Swan (OS)		Cross Roads (OS)
Talbot		81-83 High Street
Three Swans	Swan	92-4 High Street
Victoria Hotel		42 Church St., Wolverton
Victoria Hotel		73 High Street
White Hart		8 Market Square
White Horse		49-51 High Street
White Swan	Swan, Stratford Arms	32 High Street
Windmill	Ducks & Drakes	117 High Street
Key	Functioning	
	Building survives,	
	Redeveloped	

Appendix 2 Continuity

Stony Stratford, from its foundation at the end of the 12th century, grew rapidly and there was no other reason for its growth than the inn trade. It is quite probable that there has been an inn on the site of the *Cock* since those early days. It may have been called something else or it may not even have had a unique name. We simply don't know. It is also likely that there was an inn on the site of the *Bull*, but it was not recorded as the *Bull*. In 1619 it was recorded as the *Bulls Head* and most likely known as the *Bull*, a name it retains today. It may have had another name in the previous century under another tenant. The *Swan* and the *Horseshoe* are both medieval foundations and Sir Frank Markham has also suggested that the *Red Lyon*, next door to the *Horseshoe*, may also be early 16th century, although it was almost certainly not called the *Red Lyon* - that name only came into general use after King James ascended the throne in 1603.

On the west side, the *George* may pre-date the existing building and the *White Horse* also, next to the church, seems to be an obvious place for a medieval inn. The next obvious medieval inn is quite a way to the north The *Cross Keys*, so one suspects that there may have been inns in the section that was burned down in 1736. In each of these cases there may have been continuity of usage, but there was no continuity of name.

In some cases the continuity is illusory. We know from the famous deed of 1317 that there was a place called "Grilkes Herber" and we have been able to deduce its approximate location from other documents. Its location, quite far out of Stony Stratford on its habitable edge only makes sense if there was a toll bar there, and indeed we do know that a strip of land was acquired by the Wolverton family precisely so that they could control both sides of the street. Markets were occasional but they were good business and the host jurisdiction usually charged an entry fee on market days.

Grilkes or Grik's Herber may originally have been a toll booth which expanded to an inn. We have no idea how long it continued but once the medieval practice of charging entrance to markets fell away (instead they taxed the stall holders) it is possible that the inn so far out of town died too. It is 350 years after the first record that we find another inn at this location, in this case the *Angel*.

When licensing records come to us as an annual record from 1753 it become very apparent that inns do not always keep the same name. In fact relatively few do. The *Bull,* together with the *Cock,* the *George* and the *Crown* are the only examples of name which has been held from at least the 17th century. The majority have been, at one time or another, subject to fashion. For this reason we have to be very wary of seeing an entry for one inn name and encountering the name a century later and assuming it to be the same place.

The *White Horse* at its present address in the High Street makes an appearance in the licensing records in 1773, after it was newly built. It has held a licence every year since then and we can be very confident about the historical record since that date. Yet only a year or two before that the Constable's Book makes a record of a White Horse on the "east side of Stony Stratford." Without that record, and with the dates so close together, it would be tempting to conclude that the White Horse as we now know it had a longer history. The name certainly does, but not at this location.

In 1753 William Ashpool (Ashpole) is the licensee for the *White Horse.* The following year, and until 1758, he is the licensee of the *Ship* and the name *White Horse* is nowhere to be found. We might reasonably assume that he changed the name after 1753 and later retired and went out of business. He may have used the sign of the *White Horse* prior to 1753. It also becomes clear from the 1756 accounts, where for once the licences are broken down between east side and west side, that the *Ship* (and by inference the former *White Horse,* was on the East side of the High Street. He was succeeded by Samuel Gayton in 1761 who reinstated the older name, the *White Horse.* It was he who was recorded in the Constable's Book.

The use of the name *White Horse* in Stony Stratford can be traced to 1540; however the location must therefore be marked as unknown.

We encounter similar difficulties with the *White Hart,* known with some certainty to have been on the Square next door to the *Crown* from 1820. It first appears in the licensing records in 1753 and continues for 20 years. The name is then no longer used until 1820. This 1820 establishment was the *White Hart* on the Square that later became the Working Mens Club but although we are certain of this history of the house we cannot the assume that earlier references to the *White Hart* are records for this house. There is a *White Hart* recorded in 1625 and another in 1670. In neither instance can we establish the location with any certainty.

In this context we can note that the *Cross Keys* is given its first licence under that name in 1773. The building is much older than that and given the configuration of the buildings was quite likely to have been an inn. Yet there is nothing else to connect to the property. There are no earlier mentions nor are there any names that are dropped in the previous year or two to be resuscitated at the *Cross Keys*

In summary then historical continuity cannot be inferred. Inns, taverns and public houses came and went in earlier centuries just as they do today. There were periods of expansion and periods where numbers went into decline. In some cases inn signs carry a "brand" name that is worth preserving, but more often it seems, publicans were more willing to change the name than keep up with tradition. One striking example is when John Marshall takes over the *Windmill* in 1789. He changed the name to the *Ducks and Drakes*. The following year, presumably after popular protest, the name was restored to The *Windmill*. If we only had the reference to 1789 we might assume that there was once an inn called the *Ducks and Drakes* with more years to its name than this brief spotlight. As it is we can see here how whimsical and impermanent some of these names were. Marshall apparently made a practice of changing names. When he briefly went to manage the *Drum and Anchor* he changed the name to the *Coach and Horses*. This time the name stuck, even though Marshall was only there for a year.

Where we do have numbers, such as in 1577 and 1753, it would appear that the number of licences in Stony Stratford at any one time was between 27 and 29. We have uncovered over 80 and with it evidence of deliberate name changes. The use of the same name over centuries seems more rare than common and therefore early references to a *Red Lion*, a *White Horse* or a *White Hart* cannot be connected with a later use of that name.

Appendix 3 Origins of the Cock

Around the 14th century the Cok or Coccus family was strong in the town and it is thought that the Cock Hotel may have its origins with the family name.

Or, if there is an association, the family name may have its origins in the Cock Inn. It is true that there are men and women with this name who appear in 13th and 14th century deeds. They variously bear the name Cocus, Coccus, Cok, le Cok and le Cooc. Could there be a connection? Is this a basis to date the Cock Inn earlier than the 16th century?

There are two things to say first: spelling was by no means as precise as it became in the age of print, and at the time that some names were written down surnames were only just beginning to emerge, and even there you could not find the hereditary consistency you might find today. William the Miller, for example, might have a son named John, who was later known as John of Cosgrove because he was born there.

It was really only in the 14th century that English words began to appear on official documents. Hitherto they had been mostly Latin with a mixture of French. We can put two interpretations on these surnames: they could either mean Cook or Cock. I have only included those parts which relate to those named Cocus or le Cok.

There is a group of surviving deeds from the lordship of William, son of Hamon, and can only be dated between 1214 and 1247 (the period of William's lordship) since the deeds themselves carry no dates. These documents were written in a mixture of Latin, French and English on parchment and have survived remarkably well for 800 years. Some of them make direct reference to a family with the surname of Cock or Cook. There is of course a vast difference between the meaning of the two words and both are possible, as I shall explain. The name is written as Cocus, Coccus, Cok, le Cok and le Cooc. There is no consistency. The first uses of Cocus or Coccus are attempts to Latinise the name; later, French intrudes.

In one deed Lord William son of Hamon grants a half virgate of land (about 15 acres) to *Robert son of Hugh Cocus of Wolverton*, for a rent of 18d. Per annum. This was land that Hugh Cocus already held and it is presumably upon his death that the hereditary right is granted to his son Robert.[116]

Another transaction, not involving this family tells us that one of this family had some land on the Watling Street. This involves "6 half acres of land in Wolverton abutting on Watling Street between the land of Dom William son of Hamo and the land of Adam Coc.[117] Other deeds from the same period produce Richard Cocus as a witness on several and a reference to a property occupied by John Cocus.

This is all highly circumstantial but we can make two observations about these individuals. Surnames were very rare at this date and to have a surname at all implied some importance, and only the most prominent members of Wolverton's small community would be called to witness a deed.

As implied above it is almost impossible to translate the name. We could take the theory that the family took its name from their inn at the sign of the Cock, or we might offer the suggestion that Hugh was known as Hugh the Cook.

From this very slender evidence we can make the following inferences. The Cocus family was important enough in the 13th century for their land transactions to be documented. Some part of their land abutted Watling Street. That's about all we can say with certainty. There is a clear relationship between Hugh and Robert, but not between those two and Adam, Richard and John.

Henry Cok,[118] witnessing the deed below and another of the same period, was possibly a serving priest at a chapel that pre-dated St Mary Magdalen, although there is no way of corroborating this. This does support the idea that the family were well connected in the district.

Another set of deeds survive from the early 14th century. The Latinised version of the name has gone, and if it is the same family, it is now Cok or le Cok or some variant.

> Nicholas Cok, son and heir of William Cok of Stonistratford releases to Robert de Hyntes of the same his claim on one acre of the meadow due Est of Wolverton above Heeforlong which is called Fourtyrodes. Of this, Robert has 2 parts by release from Nicholas and a third part Robert had by release from Agnes,

---

116 Ms. Radcliffe dep. deed, 50.
117 Ms. Radcliffe dep. deed, 47.
118 Ms. Radcliffe dep. deed, 242.

widow of William Cok as dower.[119]

Richard de Houghton of Stonistratford grants and confirms to Biclas de Ardena and Dionysia his wife, 8 acres land in Wolverton; 2 acres are together at Depedene next land of Andrew le Cooc (and) of Geoffrey Hasteng; 2 acres abutt against Richard's headland next (unreadable); 1 acre called le Heydacre against which the aforesaid 2 acres abutt.[120]

This set of documents confirms that the Cok family had land in Stony Stratford. This is also a period when Stony Stratford was beginning to emerge as a place separate from Wolverton; hence William Cok is identified as "of Stony Stratford." Although this deed refers to an acre in the east of Wolverton, the Coks clearly have their roots on the west side of the manor.

Isable le Cok, widow of Thomas le Megre of Wolverton releases to Henry son of Anketil of Stoni Stratford junior all claims in 2 1/2 acres in Le Est field of Wolverton, which she obtained from her husnband as in the deed of feoffment of 5 Edward II.[121]

John Auncell of Wolvertone grants and confirms to Thomas Oxe of the same and Agnes his wife 1 messuage with curtilage in Wolvertone and 2 selions adjoining next those of John le Cok. The messuage is between that of the grantors and that of John le Cok in le Est ende of Wolverton.[122]

There is an Alric the Cook who was granted Steeple Claydon by William I, then assessed at 20 hides, equivalent to Wolverton. There was also a Gilbert the Cook who held land from William in Northamptonshire. These were men of status, not men who stirred the broth in cauldrons, but men who organised and oversaw the kitchens. So the name Cook, often written as Cok, is one of the older surnames and not necessarily ascribed to humble kitchen workers.

This is not to say that the name was passed on from generation to generation. Sometimes they were - Butler and Chamberlain are good examples of this, but the practice was not universal. It is really not

119 Ms. Radcliffe dep. deed, 78. 1304.
120 Ms. Radcliffe dep. deed, 130. c. 1320.
121 Ms. Radcliffe dep. deed, 481. 24th Dec. 1331.
122 Ms. Radcliffe dep. deed, 90. 1331

until the 13th century that some surnames begin to take root and not until the 14th century that they were required.

It is quite possible that the name originated locally. Hugh Cocus, or even his father, may have been the cook, that is the man who supervised the kitchens for the Baron of Wolverton. In return for this service he was granted some land to support himself and his family. The Coks or Cooks may have sprung from these origins.

The suggestion that the name derives from the Cock Inn is plausible but equally difficult to substantiate. There is a man called Bules and le Bole (Bull) around in the 13th century and there is no evidence one way or another that he took his surname from the Bull Inn - if indeed it existed. It may be that the Cok family, with land abutting Watling Street, were in a position to exploit their location by building an inn or tavern and since they were a family of some status it is possible that their prosperity came from such income. It may well be that they called their inn the Cock and took their name from that, although I would be more convinced if the name were de Cok rather than le Cok.

The problem with both words is that they were both rendered in Middle English in the same way. Cock is latinised as coccus in most documents. Equally Cook is rendered in popular latin as cocus. So there is really no way for us to distinguish between the two after seven or eight centuries.

Another observation to make is that Cook is a very common surname and that Cock is extremely rare. There were only 729 people with the surname Cock in the last census - an imperceptible number. Not that this proves anything much but even if there were only this one Stony Stratford family bearing the name in 1300, one would expect many more after 30 generations. But there again, names do die out, or they get changed or modified. For example, the family who became the first earls of Southampton, changed their name from Writh to the rather more complex Wriothesley. Neither name today has survived as a surname.

The conclusion is that there is some linguistic evidence to make the connection between the Cock Inn and the family Cok, but no solid documentary evidence. We have two facts: there has been a Cock Inn in Stony Stratford for several centuries and there was a family named

Cock or Cook living in the area in the 13th and 14th centuries. They may or may not have owned a hostelry, but it could have easily been called the Horseshoe or the Three Swans as The Cock. The apparent similarity of the names is not evidence of association.

Documentary evidence of the existence of the Cock Inn start to make their appearance in Chancery documents from 1500 to 1515, according to William Page in the VCH. I have not looked at these documents, but they would probably relate to taxes, which Henry VII was addicted to raising by any means.

The next piece of early documentary evidence is frankly controversial, and seems to stem from a footnote in George Lipscomb's History of Buckinghamshire, published in 1847.

He wrote: "Mr. Serjeant Piggott willed in 1529, that the Town of Stoney Stratford should have his Inn there, called The Cock, towards the sustenation and reparation of the Bridges." (p.367) This information is re-presented and expanded upon by Sir Frank Markham in his History of Stony Stratford, but without any caveats. William Page, however, in the Victoria County History, does point out that there is no mention of The Cock or any bequest in Thomas Piggott's actual will, and concludes that there may have been a separate deed, now perhaps lost.

All of these conclusions may be correct, but these historians have arrived at these conclusions by inference rather than by evidence. Thomas Piggott did marry into the Edy family, who owned The Malletts and a fair amount of land abutting the Watling Street. It is a fair assumption that this included The Cock Inn, but their ownership is not documented.

Once again we have some scraps of factual evidence that may or may not be related and a lot of inferences that have been drawn from this to create a picture, which may or may not be reasonably accurate. Such are the pitfalls of history.

Archaeology will probably help us, when and if the work can be done. Dendrochronological analysis on timbers in the building can give us an earlier date, and deeper excavations across Stony Stratford may unearth some medieval foundations.

For now we can theorise that, as one of the original three burgess plots in what was to become Stony Stratford, the site of the Cock may have been an early medieval inn. It may or may not have been given the sign of the Cock. Certainly, at the end of the 16th century it was known as the Cock and has held that name ever since.

Appendix 4 The Three Horse Loaves

Around 1600 a play appeared on the Elizabethan stage called Sir John Oldcastle. It was once thought to have been written by William Shakespeare and indeed there was a printed edition in 1619 which put Shakespeare's name on the title page. Modern scholarship does not now believe that Shakespeare was the author of this play although some have said that Oldcastle (a real historical figure) was used by Shakespeare to create the character of Sir John Falstaff in the Henry IV plays. The Oldcastle play was a collaborative effort between Michael Drayton, Anthony Munday, Robert Wilson, Robert Hathaway, and it shows. The play is episodic and disjointed. Many of the scenes are set in or near inns.

The lines that caught the attention of those interested in Stony Stratford come from *Act V Scene II: A high road near St Albans*

[Enter Hostler.]

HOSTLER. What, gaffer Club? welcome to saint Albans. How does all our friends in Lancashire?

CLUB. Well, God have mercy, John; how does Tom; where's he?

HOSTLER. O, Tom is gone from hence; he's at the three horse-loves at Stony-stratford. How does old Dick Dunne?

The Hostler in the play say that Tom has gone to the three horse-loves. (In the printed version it is loues, but "v" was conventionally printed as a "u" in 1600. The actual printed line is this:

"Hees at the three horse-loues at Stony-stratford"

This would strike the modern reader as confusing, but in a later edition (1685) the phrase is spelled as " Three horse-loaves" and this version is used in Rowe's 1709 edition. The intention, if not the meaning of the Elizabethan text is to refer to a horse loaf. What that may mean is usefully explained by Dr. Samuel Johnson in 1778 in his Supplement to the Edition of Shakespeare's Plays jointly edited with Edmund Malone. He offers this footnote:

It appears from the earl of Northumberland's Household Book, that horses were not so usually fed with corn loose in the manger, in the present manner, as with their provender moulded into loaves.

From this explanation we at least know what a horse-loaf was - presumably the feed was mixed with some water into a pan so that it made a block that could be pitchforked into the hay manger - a horse loaf. It may also have been a practical method of ensuring some equal rationing at feeding time, and at an inn with a lot of horses to feed offered some cost economies.

It is still a strange name to apply to an inn and perhaps it was intended as a joke, witty enough to the public at the time but to us today completely obscure.

In a 19th century edition of the play the phrase is rendered as "Three horse loades" and it must have been such an edition that led Dr. George Lipsomb to put this phrase in his book in 1847 and for Oliver Ratcliffe to transcribe his words for his book *The Newport Hundreds*. Lipscomb suggests in parentheses that "Loades" might mean "shoes." Sir Frank Markham also picks up the same reference. Whether he arrived at this independently or took his cue from Lipscomb I do not know, but he also repeats the "Three Horse-loades" and associates this name with the *Horseshoe Inn*.

It may indeed be a reference to the historical *Horseshoe*. The writers, or one or more of them, had travelled and certainly knew of Stony Stratford but where this was intended as a joke against the *Horseshoe* or another inn in the town that rationed horses to three horse loaves, we may never know.

Appendix 5 The Swan with Two Necks

In his 1948 book, co-authored with Dr Francis Hyde, *A History of Stony Stratford*, Sir Frank Markham identified the *Swan*, the *Swan with Two Necks* and the *Three Swans* as variant names for the same institution. It seemed to be a fair assumption to make in 1948, and he was partly right, but there are some documents which he may not have been aware of in 1948, which show that the *Swan with Two Necks* was a different establishment

The Swan, located on the High Street at what is now Nos. 92-94 was almost certainly a medieval foundation, although it does not appear in documentary records until 1526, or possibly in an unnamed document mentioned by Markham, 1470. In the late 17th century and 18th century until its final closure in 1782 it was called the *Three Swans*. Browne Willis, who knew it as the *Three Swans*, was also able to identify it as the medieval *Swan*. However, we need to note that it was always a part of the Wolverton Manor and remained so until the end of the 18th century, when, as noted by Sir Frank Markham (p 189 "The Swan with Three Necks belonged to the Radcliffe Trustees from 1713 to 1802, and was then sold to Mr Harrison.) Therefore it was always rented to tenants. It was never owned by anybody other than the Lord of the Manor. This point is actually crucial, and I will come to it in a minute.

The will of Michael Hipwell, probated in 1609 after his death contains a reference to his house the "Swan with Two Necks" which he bequeathed to his wife. The *Swan*, if it had ever been in Michael Hipwell's hands, was not his to bequeath to anyone. It was rented property. He could have happily bequeathed all the furniture and contents of the house but not the buildings themselves. They were always the property of the Longuevilles and later the Radcliffe Trust. The *Swan With Two Necks*, which was probably Stony Stratford's wine shop for many years, was a separate building and nothing at all to do with the *Swan* or *Three Swans*.

The *Three Swans* finally ceased to trade in 1782. The sale of all the contents, the furniture, the linen, the plate and so on, took three days. Mrs. Ann Whittaker, a widow and the last licensee, then retired. The buildings and the land were not for sale, and to belabour the point had never been sold until the Radcliffe Trust sold it in 1802.

The *Swan with Two Necks* meanwhile, survived to 1790 and appeared annually in the licensing records from 1753 just like, and contemporaneous with, the *Three Swans*. It had been operated for several years by Ann Mulliner (sometimes written Mullender), herself a widow, and previously by her husband James.

But then we come to Mary Wilmot's will proved in 1803 which bequeaths her property the *Swan with Two Necks*, establishes the link with the last tenant, Ann Mulliner, places it on the west side in corroboration of the licensing records.

> I Mary Willmot of Stony Stratford in the County of Bucks widow do make this codicil which I hereby direct shall be taken as and for a part of my last will and testament and which is herewith annexed I give and devise all that my messuage tenement or Inn called the Swan with Two Necks with the barns stables and outbuildings thereunto adjoining and belonging with their appurtenances situate and being on the west side of Stony Stratford aforesaid and tenure or occupation of Ann Mulliner or her under tenants to be equally divided between all the children of the said Joseph Scrivener of Potterspury aforesaid and Richard Scrivener of Pouxley and their heirs for all to share and share alike to take as joint tenants and not as tenants in common and thereby satisfy and confirm my said will in every other part thereof.
>
> In the year of our Lord one thousand seven hundred and eighty-six.

Now its precise location remains unknown; however there may be deeds that record the Scriveners as owners in the 19th century. If we can discover these we may be able to pinpoint the location of the *Swan with Two Necks*.

The name "Swan with Two Necks " was essentially the sign of the Vintners Company and referred to the practice of marking swan's beaks with two nicks or notches. This distinguished Swans on the Thames as belonging to the vintners and distinguished them from royal swans. It has nothing at all to do with necks,

Swans were kept in plentiful supply at one time as a source of food and quite early the royal prerogative was asserted over swans, which still prevails today. In the 15th century the King agreed that the Vintners Company and the Dyers Company could keep a number of birds on the Thames for their own use. To distinguish the Royal Swans from the Vintners' and Dyers' Swans a system of marking was developed. The Vintners chose to mark the bills of their swans with two notches or nicks. Subsequently they adopted a sign of a swan with two nicks at the entrance to Vintners Hall in London. In time the Swan with Two Nicks became corrupted to The Swan with Two Necks.

Like most guilds the Vintners Company strove hard to regulate and control the trade and they could usually ensure that only their members across the country could deal in wine. So it must have come to pass that an inn holder became a member of the Vintners Company and as a consequence may have had a monopoly on the retailing of wines in Stony Stratford. Therefore an inn sign advertising a swan with two nicks would be a way of asserting his status as a member of the Company.

Naturally when Michael Hipwell became a member of this distinguished guild he lost no time in hanging such a sign over his establishment. It could have had any other name before that. In 1577 Michael Hipwell was listed on the west side of Stony Stratford as a "taverner and inn holder" Being called a taverner would suggest some association with selling wine and therefore with the vintners.

Appendix 6 Sources

Primary Sources

A lot of valuable documents, primarily deeds, were handed over to Dr. John Radcliffe upon his purchase of the Wolverton Manor in 1713. Many dated back to the 13th century. These together with 18th and 19th century documents were deposited by the Radcliffe Trust in the Bodleian library at Oxford. Two deposits were made: one in 1928 and a second group in 1949-1950.

Various state papers make reference to Stony Stratford, and in some cases to inns. These are held in the National Archive at Kew.

The Buckinghamshire Archive holds several useful documents, particularly the register of innholders for 1577 and the annual register of licencees from 1753 to 1828. These records end in that year because the Licensing Act of 1828 no longer required the Clerk of the Peace to retain records.

Scraps of information can be found in wills. The most useful have been those of Michael Hipwell (1609), Joseph Malpas (1796) and Mary Wilmot (1802).

Title deeds, where they are available, offer some clues from the 18th century onwards.

Trade Directories for Stony Stratford start in 1830 with the Buckinghamshire Directory of Pigot & Co.

Brewery records, such as those maintained by Phipps and NBC, are useful sources from the 19th century onwards.

Secondary Sources

Sir Frank Markham's appendix to *A History of Stony Stratford*, jointly authored with Professor F.E. Hyde, has provided a foundation for our work.

Oliver Ratcliffe. *The Newport Hundreds*, published in 1900 makes a stab at compiling a list of Stony Stratford inns.

Mike Brown. *ABC: A Brewer's Compendium*. Brewery History Society, 2007. Mike Brown has kindly shared the notes he made on Stony Stratford pubs, which has been most useful in making this compilation.

Paul Woodfield, Stony Stratford's Architectural Historian, has written a number of reports over many years for private and public sector clients. We have drawn upon this information where it is applicable.

Precise references to pertinent documents and other books are annotated in the text.

Other Books of Interest

The Lost Streets of Wolverton
Bryan Dunleavy
ISBN 978-1-909054-00-4
This book reconstructs the original railway town of the 1840s, now almost completely vanished under redevelopment.
Published 2012

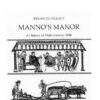

Manno's Manor
ISBN 978-1-909054-05-9
The history of Wolverton is a long one. After 1066 Manno le Breton established the centre of his barony here to administer his estates in Buckinghamshire, Northamptonshire and Leicestershire. Just over a century later the baron granted land to create Stony Stratford, which became an important stopping place on the Watling Street. In the late 18th century the canal arrived, which laid the foundations for the railway town and subsequently Milton Keynes. This book describes the history of the manor from the earliest times to 1838, when the railway arrived.
Published 2013

First Impressions: Contemporary Accounts of Victorian Wolverton
ISBN 978-1-909054-06-6
Wolverton was the first railway town of its kind in 1838 and held national attention in the 1840s. For the 175th anniversary, Bryan Dunleavy, compiled accounts of Wolverton from newspapers, journals, letters, board minutes and reports, travel writing to show what the early Victorians thought of the New Wolverton.
Published 2013

Lightning Source UK Ltd.
Milton Keynes UK
UKOW07f0645030715

254556UK00009B/33/P

9 781909 054080